BIOVIOLENCE

Aylan, Isis, Begum, Grenfell, Trump. Harambe, Guantanamo, Syria, Brexit, Johnson. COVID, migrants, trolling, George Floyd, Trump!

Gazing over the fractured, contested territories of the current global situation, Watkin finds that all these diverse happenings have one element in common. They occur when biopolitical states, in trying to manage and protect the life rights of their citizens, habitually end up committing acts of coercion or disregard against the very people they have promised to protect. When states tasked with making us live find themselves letting us die, then they are practitioners of a particular kind of force that Watkin calls bioviolence.

This book explores and exposes the many aspects of contemporary biopower and bioviolence: neglect, exclusion, surveillance, regulation, encampment, trolling, fake news, terrorism and war. As it does so, it demonstrates that the very term 'violence' is a discursive construct, an effect of language, made real by our behaviours, embodied by our institutions and disseminated by our technologies. In short, bioviolence is how the contemporary powers that be make us do what they want.

Resolutely interdisciplinary, this book is suitable for all scholars, students and general readers in the fields of IR, political theory, philosophy, humanities, sociology and journalism.

William Watkin is Professor of Contemporary Philosophy and Literature at Brunel University, London. He is the author of numerous books including *In the Process of Poetry: The New York School and the Avant-Garde*, *On Mourning*, *The Literary Agamben* and *Agamben and Indifference*. His most recent work *Badiou and Indifferent Being* is the first of two volumes looking at Badiou's Being and Event project. The second, *Badiou and Communicable Worlds*, came out in 2020. He is currently working on a study of a philosophy of indifference called, simply, *Indifference*, and a follow-up to *Bioviolence* called *Anti-Social Media: How Big Tech Makes Us Do What It Wants*.

BIOVIOLENCE

How the Powers That Be Make Us Do What They Want

William Watkin

Routledge
Taylor & Francis Group

LONDON AND NEW YORK

First published 2021
by Routledge
2 Park Square, Milton Park, Abingdon, Oxon OX14 4RN

and by Routledge
605 Third Avenue, New York, NY 10158

Routledge is an imprint of the Taylor & Francis Group, an informa business

© 2021 William Watkin

British Library Cataloguing-in-Publication Data
A catalogue record for this book is available from the British Library

Library of Congress Cataloging-in-Publication Data
Names: Watkin, William, 1970- author.
Title: Bioviolence: how the powers that be make us do what they want/
William Watkin.
Description: Abingdon, Oxon; New York, NY: Routledge, 2021. |
Includes bibliographical references and index.
Identifiers: LCCN 2020053307 (print) | LCCN 2020053308 (ebook) |
ISBN 9780367438173 (hardback) | ISBN 9780367438180 (paperback) |
ISBN 9781003006015 (ebook)
Subjects: LCSH: Biopolitics. | Violence–Social aspects. | Power (Social
sciences)–Political aspects. | Social control. | State, The.
Classification: LCC JA80 .W37 2021 (print) | LCC JA80 (ebook) |
DDC 320.01–dc23
LC record available at https://lccn.loc.gov/2020053307
LC ebook record available at https://lccn.loc.gov/2020053308

ISBN: 9780367438173 (hbk)
ISBN: 9780367438180 (pbk)
ISBN: 9781003006015 (ebk)

Typeset in Bembo
by Deanta Global Publishing Services, Chennai, India

CONTENTS

PREFACE

Long Hard Read: The Grenfell Tower Murders

It was warm the night Behailu Kebede's fridge exploded. People had their windows open, curtains stirring in the air up and down the edifice of the tower, like strings of flags. The eternal London thunder of traffic, sirens, thumping base and lubricious voices floated into those flats, borne by a listless breeze coming in from the far distant Atlantic, easing its way across the Oxfordshire plain, before tumbling down the shallow lee sides of the nearby Chiltern Hills.

bang

Mr. Kebebe was rudely awoken from his fitful sleep. Something had gone off like a firecracker nearby, from the room next door it sounded like. Behailu jumped from his bed and rushed into the small kitchen where he saw the flames coming from the white goods. His first thought was to wake his neighbour Maryam, but she had already heard the commotion and met him in the hallway between their two flats. Behailu, clearly agitated, told Maryam there was a fire. She went with him into flat 16 to see if it was cause for concern. It was 12:50 am precisely.

The flames coming out of Behailu's old fridge weren't very big, but it was enough to alarm the pregnant Maryam. A hasty call was made to the police, then she exited the building in such a panic she left the mobile phone she used to make the call behind. Behailu, meanwhile, lingered long enough in the building to wake all his neighbours on the fourth floor. One of them, Alison Moses, remembers meeting firemen on the stairwell, as she left, descending from higher storeys. They told Alison that the 13th floor was full of smoke which confused her. It was quite a jump from the 4th to the 13th floor, maybe around a hundred feet. From what Behailu had told her, it seemed impossible that such a small appliance fire could have travelled that far, that quickly. Confusion at this news began to percolate down the stairwell, as the unchecked fire boiled up the outside walls.

> I went back to my mother's kitchen:
> peas were soaking on the stove
> and a lettuce was unfurling on
> the counter.
>
> *(Bernard, "Kitchen," p.15)*[1]

It was later discovered that flames had managed to exit flat 16, Kebede's home, through his kitchen's open window. Sneaky as they are, these tongues of fire had then finagled themselves between the tower block walls and their new cladding. The cladding had been attached to the exterior of the building during a recent refurbishment, by all accounts, not very professionally. The seals between the cladding and the new windows, for example, were often broken, letting in drafts. Many residents had taken to plugging up the gaps with bits of material. Flammable stuff, for the most part. A classic inner-city hack in lieu of a centrally sanctioned solution. Even worse, between each panel of cladding should have been a seal to stop the spread of fire but the seals failed or were never installed. This permitted the cavity between the walls and the cladding to act as a kind of chimney, speedily drawing up the flames from floor 4 to floor 13, where all that smoke was that the firemen had spotted. Then, rapidly, up the entire flank of the 221-foot, 23-storey West London tower block, home to around 350 people. As these flames met with one of those ill-fitted windows, dodgy frame stuffed with old newspaper and suchlike, you can imagine how easy it was for the fire to penetrate into the flats themselves. Within a remarkably brief time, the conflagration was out of control and engulfed the whole block, raining down smouldering fragments of that flammable cladding onto the moneyed streets and gathering, well-heeled crowd below.

And so it was that Grenfell Tower was lost.

> snap, crackle
> amen
>
> *(Bernard, "Arrival," p.1)*

That Cladding:

> Going in when the firefighters left
> was like standing on a black beach
> with the sea suspended in the walls
>
> *(Bernard, "Hiss," p.25)*

You only have to read the testimony of the firefighters to appreciate how rare this kind of conflagration tends to be. Not that tower block fires are rare, far from it, meaning the drill for containing them is well-established: stay put. When emergency calls started to come in from other flats however, on the 10th floor, on the 8th, the operators were turning to each other in shock and disbelief.

"It's impossible," they kept saying. Tower block fires just don't behave like that. Something had gone very wrong. That something was, of course, the flimsy cladding.

During the refurb of Grenfell Tower in 2016, the cladding chosen, added to the exterior of the building as part of the £10 million refit, was flammable. The application of the cladding was intended primarily to beautify the tower, built back in 1975 as one of the many regulation grey and brown pebble-dashed columns that still punctuate the London skyline, forming part of the texture of its unlovely but inimitable built environment. The cladding didn't start the fire, cheap appliances, a workaday component of London's generation-rent, were the cause of that. Rather, it contributed an unpredictable factor, a new risk, that caught the fire service off guard. Because of this environmental abnormality thanks to that cladding, once the fire took hold, residents were advised to stay in their flats, against their natural instincts to flee, in accordance with standard regulation. This policy has been aggressively questioned by the first report of the official enquiry published in the autumn of 2019 and is now set to change (More-Bick 2019, pp.595–634). Yet according to one chief fire officer at least, in 99% of all cases, staying put in your flat is the best thing to do (Wankhade 2019; Halliday 2017). Flats are designed to be stand-alone fire-resistant boxes, surrounded by the fire-resistant tower block itself. As long as the fire isn't in your kitchen, being in your flat ought to be the safest option by far. So that in 99% of cases staying put is best. Grenfell however was that dreaded 1%, the statistical abnormality. It remains, however, a politically charged policy, not least because the cladding manufactures are reported to have put aside a £30 million pound budget to fight any claims that their cladding is to blame when the enquiry, in its second iteration, decides to deal with that aspect of the tragedy (Booth 2019).

At this stage I think it is safe to say that accepting the systemic issues within the woefully underfunded fire service, a hangover of Boris Johnson's tenure as mayor, and admitting no doubt that the senior management of the service made grave errors, all the same it was due to the cladding's combustible nature and ill-fitted application that the fire service professionals gave the wrong advice. The burnable centre of the cladding, plus the gaps between the cladding and the wall acting as a flue, caused the flames to shoot rapidly up the sides of the building with a celerity many described as unexpected and unprecedented (although it had happened in blocks similarly clad more than once before). The fire's spread and speed was perhaps impossible in a perfect world but, as we all know, people in low-cost London accommodation live in a world located a long, exasperating, perpetually delayed and woefully overcrowded tube-ride from perfection.

The people versus the powers that be

remember we were brought here from the clear waters of our dreams
that we might be named, numbered and forgotten

(Bernard, "Arrival," p.1)

During the fire 72 people died, including a number of young people and children. The flats were mostly occupied by the poorer members of Kensington and Chelsea Borough, one of the wealthiest places in the world. Many were immigrants or the children of immigrants. A large proportion of working-class folk certainly, but also youthful hipster types just starting out in life. A young Italian couple, artists drawn to the world-class London art scene, made their last phone call to their families far away, before being burnt alive in their Grenfell flat. Perhaps this demographic mix explained a common response on hearing the news that it could have happened to any of us 10 million Londoners. Remember that flat we rented where the fridge gave off sparks and the windows were sealed shut? Or that landlord who stole our deposit and never fixed the dodgy boiler that made us feel woozy? There but for the grace of God and good governance go we all, or have gone, as we tried to make our way through the confounding yet remarkable defiles of this vibrant global city. A sense of community and of lucky escape, of togetherness and yet separation, we are the ones that got away with it was, I feel, the immediate emotional response of millions of Londoners when they heard on the morning of 13 June of what had happened at Grenfell Tower, W11.

Yet of those 10 million Londoners sharing the pain of their fellow Grenfellers, at least one resident of the capital appeared to feel no affinity with them. Immediately after the fire, the then prime minister, Theresa May, was as lumbering in her response as she famously is in her gait. It is clear looking back that she did not grasp how personally felt the Grenfell Tower fire was across the capital. For her it was just another flying turd in the perpetual shit-storm of her beleaguered premiership. Her reluctance to go to the scene of the disaster because of the palpable anger against her and her government was immediately read by many as a sign of culpability. Her inaction did nothing but confirm a general feeling among the survivors that the government didn't care about them because they were not rich or powerful. A sensation many had been experiencing, actually, for years as they tried unsuccessfully through various residents' group to get issues such as fire safety addressed by the owners and managers of their block.

That Grenfell Tower was owned by The London Borough of Kensington and Chelsea, a perpetually Tory-run council, only made matters worse for May. Although in reality while Kensington and Chelsea owned the building, as is the way of neoliberal Britain, they didn't manage it. Rather, it was overseen by the Kensington and Chelsea Management Organisation, a large, anonymous company in charge of over 9,000 residences across the borough. Both organisations appear to have been somewhat absent and unsympathetic landlords, it being generally felt amongst the occupants of the block that neither agency really cared about their welfare if it meant spending money. It was probably because of the general intimation among the 350 residents that their concerns were habitually ignored, that the 2016 refurbishment I mentioned left a bad taste in the mouths of many of them who thought that £10 million could have been better spent on their safeguarding. Their suspicions echoing with the general unease in austerity Britain that the Tory government were cutting corners, on social care for example, and, it transpires, the fire service, while protecting the wealthy through tax benefits. Whatever your political feelings as regards the post-2008 collapse of the Tory policy of austerity, there is no denying now that the residents' organisations were right about the misallocation of the refurbishment funds. The management company not only failed to spend money on making them safer in their homes, in fact it squandered vast sums on beautifying the now-ruined building, and in doing so, according to many, made the tower a death trap.

Prime Minister May knew nothing of this at the time it would seem, and so she made the grave error of seeming to side with the council and the developers through choosing what she might have thought was a neutral response of distance and inaction, a wait-and-see policy she generally made her own and which, eventually in terms of Brexit, was to prove her undoing. We Brits adore caution but, in certain circumstances, to be seen to be doing nothing is more offensive than hurrying to the scene and doing the wrong thing. If inaction becomes politicised in a policy of belt-tightening austerity, then doing nothing suddenly makes you appear culpable. Our PM in absentia came to be seen as a kind of national absentee landlord; director of an elected, impervious, unfeeling management company called the government.

You criminals!

> the officer said—oh, it's very common for culprits to go missing—I said my son isn't a culprit
>
> *(Bernard, "+," p.13)*

Thinking about those absentee landlords, all the way up from the flats to our nation at a time of need, I'm struck by the comments of Zainu Deen, father of Zainab Deen who perished in the fire along with her young son.

> You go to bed in the house that keeps you safe, don't you?
>
> *(O'Hagan, Chapter 1)*

Zainu's simple wisdom appears to speak to the moral duty of every housing corporation, management agency and landlord. I don't have to tell you that it is a moral duty flouted every day across the UK as this has, of late, become something of a national scandal. As a sovereign state, you cannot prevent disasters, but not only can you ameliorate the risk of their occurring, in our age of managerial politics, that pretty much sums up the governance of firefighting as both a metaphor and, in the case of Grenfell, a reality. And if that risk management fails, at the very least our leaders should be judged by how they respond in a crisis of their making. The problem was that May's government was already tainted with blame before the fridge in flat 16 even began to go on the blink. It was, after all, their aggressive austerity measures that many attributed to cutting corners at Grenfell. Not that the refurb had anything directly to do with government policy. Instead, the Tory council was seen as a synecdoche for the Tory government, lining their pockets yet again at the expense of the less well off, blame leaping from council to government like flames leaping from floor to floor of the tower.

These incendiary feelings were further stoked by the failure of adequate response in the days and then months that followed. The rehousing of the 250 plus residents made homeless by the fire was generally thought a fiasco. Although the borough is full of unoccupied property, the council struggled to find the resources to rehouse often traumatised survivors, many of whom were relocated in temporary accommodation far from their friends and community at a time of acute emotional need for just such support structures. Well over a year later, many residents had still not been permanently rehoused. This inaction did not go unnoticed among the wider population, to their credit. At the 2018 Brits music awards, grime artist Stormzy used his performance to publicly ask the question on the minds of so many of us.

> "Theresa May, where's the money for Grenfell?"
> "You criminals, and you got the cheek to call us savages
> You should do some jail time, you should pay some damages
> We should burn your house down and see if you can manage this."
> *(Stormzy 2018)*

It was an interesting example of turning the tables from a community assumed to be criminal—immigrants, the underclass and, let's be honest, non-white people—pointing out that the neglect of our leaders is itself the real criminal act. There is also a vengeful, punitive aspect to these bars I think. Stormzy is, on the surface, suggesting we should burn down number 10 to see how May would cope, a regicidal implication. More widely I feel he is suggesting the poor should burn the houses of all the rich, shoot at the clocks and start a riot. The Grenfell Tower riots. I find Stormzy's use of the term 'manage' particularly loaded with meaning, not least when it is rhymed with 'damage', reviving the ancient homonymic magic of the poetic for a new generation. It was mismanagement after all that led to the deaths of the Grenfell 72. It is management rather than leadership that appears to mark the failure of modern politics. It is politics as management that is at the heart of the neoliberal neglect of the poor in Great Britain and, almost universally, around the Western world. If Theresa May watched the Brits that night, she may have had difficulty sleeping in her now slightly more precarious bed, which alone is surely some kind of political victory?

The murder of neglect

When I could no longer see a window to jump from
I remembered the boy.

(Bernard, "Window," p.19)

Considering the mismanagement of Grenfell before and after the fire, it is not surprising that the anger of the residents over-spilled into harsh words and acts, which Stromzy was simply channelling into political art. Some even charged into the offices of the local council. Speaking to the media with eloquence and moral authority, survivors explained their battle to have their concerns heard by the developers and council about fire safety. They had a clear sense that their lives were seen as worth less than the financial benefits of development and the cost burdens of improving safety. Around the country many spoke out about the belief that the victims of Grenfell were victims not of fire, but of neglect, exclusion and poverty. Addressing the perceived greed and dismissiveness of the planners and council members alike, it was not uncommon to hear the accusation 'Murderers!' Understandable in the circumstances, emotions were running high, but perhaps excessive? Andrew O'Hagan's book *The Tower* suggests these feelings were stoked by the liberal media, that the Borough Council had been made into scapegoats, even that the expensive cladding might not have been lethal if the fire agencies had given better advice (O'Hagan, Chapter V). On this matter I strongly disagree with him. Blame must surely rest at the doors of the well-appointed council chambers. All the same, murder, would I go that far?

Murder after all is something of a shocking word speaking of an ancient taboo, the taking of one human life by another human being, whose very existence in the lexicon reminds us however that this is a taboo that we regularly flout. There is, isn't there, a tension or paradox attendant on the term 'murder'? Why, after all, have laws that forbid it, if it were not for the fact that without rules, regulations, conventions, laws and punishments, Cain will kill Abel? This intimation has, indeed, been the basis of much modern political theory, especially pertaining to the issue of violence. The inevitability of murder not only identifies the need for a judiciary and a sovereign, it also reminds us that life is unfathomably precious. When someone dies, that loss is absolutely irredeemable. Zainu Deen's lost daughter and her son may live on in our minds when we read O'Hagan's moving celebration of their lives in *The Tower*, but there is a great lie at the heart of all elegy is there not? It is, to me, the most despicable of all our ancient art forms. Truth is, nothing you can say will approach the impossible: someone who once was, is now no more. Certainly not pretty words and well-meaning sentiment.

Yet the ancient interdiction on life-taking reminds us that the precious is precarious precisely because it is held to be of value. It is only murder, you see, if that person *is* valued. It is only murder if in killing them you flout the law. It is only murder, perhaps, if their death is fully mourned. It is only murder, in fact, if calling it such is in some way sanctioned by power, political or, in the case of Grenfell, a low-key, quite polite and unmistakably British, people's power. Murder, therefore, is a construct, a way of talking about a violent act designed to result in certain actions thanks to the said act or no actions if, for example, the life lost is deemed worthless, base and irredeemable. This is our first lesson, I think, in understanding that violence is not simply doing physical or psychological harm to someone else, but is just as much the discursive effects and intentions that surround, promote, permit or forbid said action.

Murder has, since at least the 18th century, been a term not only applied to the act of unlawful killing, but also causing someone's death accidentally or through omission. Not doing all you could to save someone or neglecting a duty which led to their death can, in some circumstances, be taken to be murder. It is this murder of neglect that residents accused Kensington and Chelsea Council and their management company of committing. So let's assess this accusation, as if in a court of law, and look at the evidence. It is certainly true that one cannot deny that the concerns and circumstances of the Grenfell residents were the result of neglect. The etymology of the word comes from the ancient Latin "to fail to choose" by the way. Neglect, therefore, is the failure of selection, of separation of one person from all the rest or of one person as worthy of your regard. It speaks, I feel, of treating others as worthless because they are part of an indifferentiated mass: the unchosen, the non-preterit the zombie-like horde. To neglect another person is to fail to select them in their difference, which is also, paradoxically, their universal value, because we are all valuable by virtue of being unique or so we are repeatedly told by the impossibly cheerful spokespeople of Silicon Valley and big tech.

More specifically, as a legal term, it marks a failure of duty of care that is primarily used in inquests rather than criminal court cases. There is, at the present time, no crime of the murder of omission or neglect on the English statute books, for example. Perhaps understandably considering the politics of not-doing that defines our political culture and limited social expectations. Neoliberal Britain is a political economy of neglect, of a shrinking state, blighted by a decades-long superstitious fear of intervention in free markets such as the lucrative London property and money launderette.

Neglect and the murder of omission are both defined by a Theresa May-esque inaction. Yet although neglect is in some sense criminal, one cannot, surely, consider it as a mode of violence worthy of the terrible name murder? Violence, if it has a definition, is the application of force against another to cause them harm. An intentional hurting of others where you cross the threshold between you and your victim and, in some way, strike them. In that neglect in its ancient roots, and modern legal definition, is primarily not doing something, of refusing to cross that sacred threshold, not reaching out to another person, but of turning one's back, walking away and keeping your hands in your pockets, can the neglect of the Grenfell residents really be seen as a form of aggression directed against them? Isn't it going too far to suggest the 72 dead were murdered by

cost-cutting and profiteering, if indeed you accept, as I do, that this was the primary cause of the Grenfell Fire disaster?

The survivors don't think so. Stormzy doesn't think so. Mercury Prize win-
ner Dave doesn't think so (Dave 2019). I don't think so. And if he were alive
today, I am pretty certain that French philosopher and political theorist Michel
Foucault would not think so either.

> Where to put the burning house, the child made ash, the brick in the back
> of the neck, the shit in the letter box and piss up the side of it?

> I file it under *fire, corpus, body, house*

> *(Bernard, "Ark," p.3)*

Note

1 All citations from Bernard are taken from Jay Bernard's Grenfell-inflected poem
sequence about the 1981 New Cross fires, *Surge* (2019).

INTRODUCTION

Michel Foucault, biopolitics and the abolition of violence

The abolition of violence

Michel Foucault is famous for the invention of many concepts, but what is not often mentioned is that on 17 March 1976, he effectively abolished one—the concept of violence. It happened almost by accident, during the now-famous final lecture of the course he was offering at the Collège de France on the topics of knowledge and war. The previous ten lectures were all scintillating, but it was the eleventh that was to prove to be world-shattering, for it was during this last talk of his academic year that Foucault was to inadvertently prove that violence, political violence anyway, was, in a sense, no longer tenable. A curious outcome for a man who had made his name through a fascination with modes of coercion and control that more than bordered on sadomasochism.

Foucault had been appointed to the Collège de France in 1970, after much behind-the-scenes lobbying and favours called in. It was, in many ways, a dream appointment that asked of the scholar merely that he gave one lecture a week to an audience made up of literally anyone who flâneured by. Foucault was energised, initially, by the arrangement, but by 1976, the attractions of the role had begun to diminish in direct proportion, it would seem, to the growing success he was enjoying, or rather not enjoying. The pressure to perform had become a source of stress, an anxiety that was not alleviated by the set-up of the famous auditorium, which was both too intimate, you had to walk through the audience to get to the podium which many found unnerving, and too distancing, with Foucault unhappy with simply holding court to crowds of avid listeners, yearning instead for the more dialogic nature of a seminar.

Let us assume that for all intents and purposes, 17 March 1976 was a typical day at the lectern. Foucault arrives on time and yet in haste at the imposing façade of the Collège and makes his way inside to the main auditorium. There are students everywhere, and he has to almost force his way into the room. Moving through the cavernous chamber to the podium at the far end, he steps over recumbent bodies, his papers clasped to this chest. He is dressed in a smart jacket and his trademark turtleneck sweater. Foucault's bald pate seems to glow; his teeth are slightly too much for his mouth. My is he handsome, bathed in that extra aura of celebrity that follows him wherever he goes, like an expensive cologne.

An altogether different miasma of patchouli oil, tobacco and other more recherché substances lightly perfume the otherwise fusty air. The desk at the front is so full of microphones that Foucault has to push them to one side to find space for his notes. He does this tetchily, his tutting recorded for posterity. There are no preliminary niceties. Instead, he switches on a lamp which seems to do little to dispel the 400-year-old gloom that pervades the place. Admittedly, dotted around are stucco lamp holders, but these appear designed to almost accentuate the gloaming of reverential learning, rather than to flood it with the enlightening rays of new knowledge. The great thinker sets to it, a racehorse in an otherwise empty field, because he is the field, because with each sentence he creates the field. That's why so many people are here, to see him in full tilt, clearing all intimidating obstructions, taking his very life into his hands as he careens ever forward.

Foucault declaims loudly through the old-fangled Bakelite mic, his voice reverberating from the speakers that hang incongruously around the ancient hall as tropical fruits adorning the pollarded bowers of the nearby Bois de Boulogne would be deemed to be. He talks briskly but clear. If he took the time to look up from the lectern and try to establish some kind of rapport with his audience, he might note, with grim satisfaction, that the 300-seat theatre is occupied by at least 500 souls. He might then remember the second lecture theatre somewhere in the building where his voice is being remotely transmitted at the same time and imagine that this one is as equally packed with bodies, which indeed it is. But he doesn't look up. Partly out of concentration, mainly due to dismay at the numbers and their terrifying passivity at the feet of the unwilling, yet naturally selected, master.

At precisely 7:15 p.m. he stops. He has been speaking for just over an hour. Students rush to his desk not, as you might expect, to ask questions, but to switch off their tape recorders which they then hug to themselves as they leave, like so many precious offspring. Foucault oversees their departure, impassive. All it would take is one question, he reflects, one query and the conversation could begin. But week after week, year after year, that inquisition hardly ever convenes. This lack of interaction, no doubt fostered by the place, the stultifying French system and Foucault's own aloofness, was a source of sadness to the great man. He once reflected:

> As there is no feedback channel, the lecture becomes a sort of theatrical performance. I relate to the people who are there as though I were an actor

or an acrobat. And when I have finished speaking, there's this feeling of total solitude.

(Cited in Ewald and Fontana 2008, p. xiv)

The loneliness of the long-distance runner, who has left his fellow competitors far behind. The isolation of an actor, in a perpetual one-hander, yearning for something other than the solipsism of soliloquy. The high-wire act of true thinking, where there is only room for one genius on the rope.

Who knows, perhaps the students mistook his melancholy for displeasure as he gathered up his things and strode from the room that momentous evening. What is certain is that by 1976, the post at the Collège was proving to be something akin to a hindrance of success. In short, Foucault was too far ahead of his time, his ideas too high above the heads of his ardent followers. All things considered then, it was unlikely that on that mid-March day, he had the time or inclination to reflect on the impact of what he had just proclaimed, his first coherent formulisation of what is now called biopolitics, certainly, but also the invention of an all-but-impossible chimera, a world of coercion without harm, force or injury that we are calling bioviolence on his belated behalf.

You've never heard of biopolitics?

When I began my career in philosophy back at Sussex University in 1991, the concept of biopolitics was never mentioned, even though the MA in Critical Theory I was taking was probably the most cutting edge in the world and deeply in debt to the work of Foucault. One reason for this is the deleterious effects the Collège de France gig had on Foucault's publication record. His last 'published' work in his lifetime was *The History of Sexuality Volume 1*, which exploded onto the world-scene the same year as the lecture inadvertently abolishing violence by inventing biopolitics. After that, until his premature death in 1987 at the age of 57, no other major publication under Foucault's name came out. All his energies, disastrously depleted towards the end by the onset of the AIDS virus, went into those damn lectures. Lectures which, when they finally began to appear in print, transformed our conceptualisation of what his biographer James Miller calls "perhaps the single most famous intellectual in the world" (Miller 1993, p.13). Even then, biopolitics was not the first big concept to emerge from the publication of the lectures, that was probably what Foucault called governmentality (Burchell, Gordon and Miller 1991).

The initial invisibility of biopolitics is certainly not due to lack of availability. The final pages of *The History of Sexuality* concern themselves with a pretty complete sketch of biopolitics, literally riddled with brilliantly memorable quotations on the topic. It was the book that everyone read, when I was a student, being mercifully short and gratifyingly sexy, but no one ever mentioned the bit on biopolitics as I recall. Even the publication in French of *Society Must Be Defended* (Foucault 2003), the unparalleled lecture series capped by the speech on biopolitics, didn't suddenly make biopolitics more widely intelligible, to use a Foucauldian word. Perhaps because that lecture series is primarily a consideration of war and violence, concepts very dear to Foucault's heart, but which typify more the other modes of power that biopolitics slowly regulated out of pole position, namely, sovereign and disciplinary power.

When Foucault picks up the thread the following year in the exhilarating series of lectures now called *Security, Territory, Population* (Foucault 2007), a triumvirate of concepts so prescient of the issues of our globalised age that it is almost uncanny to think the lectures were delivered in the late 1970s, it is with the promise of a full course on biopower. But this intention fizzles out after the third lecture, and instead, Foucault turns his attention to the aforementioned governmentality, a great and important topic, but not quite as great and important as biopower has proven to be. Then, another year later, when he gives the course called *The Birth of Biopolitics* (Foucault 2008), rather than rap on biopolitics, the entire course is another preternaturally prophetic demolition of our much-vaunted liberalism. It is an amazing course, but it doesn't exactly do what it says on the tin. After that, the biopolitical trail goes cold until its importance is excavated by one Giorgio Agamben in 1995, with the publication of his controversial and game-changing portrait of modernity, politics and life: *Homo Sacer: Sovereign Power and Bare Life*. Agamben's study is incendiary, lighting the fuse on what has become a dramatic conflagration of ideas from all spheres of intellectual life that we thinkers now call biopolitics, as casually as we might say feminism or Marxism. We caught up with Foucault in the end then, but only thanks to another unparalleled field-defining racehorse, Agamben, and only after an unforgiveable hiatus of some two decades.

If intellectuals such as myself neglected biopolitics overlong, we have more than made up for being so remiss in recent times. Idle one morning, I did a search for books published in the last ten years that had biopolitics in the title. Amazon returned over 600 entries, like an overexcited puppy. When, intrigued, I did another excavation on Google Scholar for articles on biopolitics in the past decade, Google, in all its nominative hyperbole, suggested an improbable 60,000 articles. And that is not including all the concepts associated with biopolitics like biopower, regulation, thanatopolitics, bare life, the homo sacer, immunisation, sovereignty, security, surveillance and, of course, cyborgs. Indeed, if ever you were looking for another name to replace the problematic Age of Terror, you might call ours the Age of Biopolitics.

"But what exactly is biopolitics?" I hear you mutter just in earshot. Permit me to explain.

The definition of biopolitics

Foucault argues that during the period of the 18th into the 19th century, power itself changed. Old forms of power were overhauled, although not eradicated, by new contraptions of force and coercion. Primarily, sovereign power was replaced by governmental administration, the system we still labour under to a large degree to this day. This shift is inscribed in the most compelling of all discursive texts, punishment. States moved from torture to capital punishment to imprisonment, not thanks to an increasing development of civilisation and liberalisation, as we would like to convince ourselves, but because the traditional tools of domination were inadequate, faced with the dramatic change in material conditions, for the distribution and deposition of force. Large national states, which emerged across Europe after the treaty of Westphalia in 1648, were increasingly host to vast, unwieldy and often uppity populations. The old intimacies of threat, "obey or I may kill you," became ineffective once a citizenry and a people became a population.

The result of these momentous changes was that power suffered a series of anamorphic mutations, reminiscent of Holbein's *The Ambassadors* tumbled with a couple of Francis Bacons. First, the sovereign was pushed away from their people, searching for a vantage point from which to survey them, now that the castle on the hill was insufficient to scope a disparate, even diasporic, crowd of millions. Then they were compacted into one of the people. No longer semi-divine, sovereigns were increasingly rather drab, grey-suited, middle-class bureaucrats. Finally, the powers that be were stretched to their very limit by being required to oversee and administer populations made up of millions, distributed across large territories or, in the case of colonial powers like Great Britain, spanning the entire globe. "Do what I say or I will kill you" no longer works when questions like "You will kill all of us?" or more pointedly "Who are you again?" come to the lips of those uppity masses.

Power at this juncture had no choice but to change, because its ancient threat of violence was no longer effective or acceptable as a method of control and coercion. At this moment, Foucault famously observes, "One might say that the ancient right to *take* life or *let* live was replaced by a power to *foster* life or *disallow* it to the point of death" (Foucault 1978, p.138). This, for Foucault, became the defining question of power in the 19th century, namely, "its hold over life. What I mean is the acquisition of power over man insofar as man is a living being" (Foucault 1978, p.138). A hold over life is how the powers that be make us do what they want, now that directly threatening us is a busted flush.

And there we have it: biopolitics is the administration of biopower from around the 18th century to our present day. Often replacing, sometimes displacing, sovereignty with governance and ruling with administration, modern states began to renounce pre-emptive, vengeful, punitive, mortal, cruel, excessive and random violence towards their own people, in favour of the governance of their populations by other more placatory means. Central to this alteration is an ontological shift in the nature of the subject of power. Their rights no longer pertain to their being a people, or a citizen, or indeed a subject of a particular sovereign state, but to the one right we all share in common: the simple right to life.

In some sense this right to life, which we associate with Thomas Paine's revolutionary *Rights of Man*, the American constitution, the French Revolution and more recently the invention of the UN and other global regulatory institutions after the Second World War, is not a great movement of civilisation towards a more universal and respectful means of ruling, but a gross simplification of the definition of the political subject, in preparation for a meticulous ramification and complication of the same subject, into a wide array of regulatory procedures. In answer to the question, "How do I rule over millions of subjects when they know I can't kill them all, as is my natural and God-given predilection, or for that matter throw them in jail?" the answer is, treat them all as one, then divide them into different, overlapping and occasionally opposing groups. The old cliché divide and conquer is however somewhat inappropriate within a biopolitical context. The full extent of the procedure of dominance is: cohere, then divide and now rule, through regulation. May not trip off the tongue so well, but being inarticulate and nit-picking is one of the central methods of biopower, which thrives on an invisibility it promotes through its technical tediousness and pedantic bean-counting.

When the life of a subject is no longer political only when it is available for a punitive action because it broke a law, the essence of the precursor to biopower which Foucauldians call governmentality, but constitutes the very core of the political subject, then the conception of political action that has been in place since Aristotle, that man is a living animal with the additional capacity for political existence, is gone forever, replaced by a conception of the subject as "an animal whose politics places his existence as a living being in question" (Foucault 1978, p.143). And that question is not should you let me live or not, but rather, considering that I have a right to live, how are you as a state going to achieve that and what will it cost me? The only way to rule due to the same right of life possessed by all your subjects is, first, to protect that life, second, to enhance it, and finally third, to prolong life. In return, the state will ask permission to enter into the one zone of human existence that, according to Foucault and others, power had not had untrammelled access to before, namely, your domestic, biological and private life. This is why biopower is not just governance by law with the threat of punishment, but rather, as I said, something a good deal more intimate: direct regulation of your personal life on a daily, perhaps hourly, basis. How much booze you quaff, how to medicate your depression, what kind of cladding is fit for your building, that sort of thing.

This, in short, is the biopolitical deal, our new bio-social contract. It is declared from the rooftops, endlessly, that my life is a sanctity, as valuable as anyone else's. I ask what a state will do to honour that remarkable life that they now part-own. They answer we will protect, enhance and extend your life, but in return you need to give us the keys to your house, your body and your data. And you will stop doing harm to yourself, not because I am threatening you, but by virtue of the fact that I am regulating your very being to such a degree that harm is something you cannot easily indulge in, harm to yourself and harm to the rest of us. This brings us to the risky contention I made apropos Foucault and the end of violence.

The problem of the end of violence

Aggressive force was a great thing for the perpetuation of sovereign power, but is lousy as a mode of protecting, enhancing and prolonging biopower because violence, simply put, is the enemy of life. In addition, if you are going to sign over your life to someone and invite them into your home, your genes and give them access to your Facebook account, you are unlikely to do that if they appear homicidal. It would seem therefore that whatever else biopolitics is, it is primarily the ability to rule in a nonviolent, nonthreatening and, for the most part, non-punitive manner, unless you are one of those abnormal populations that tend towards recidivism and malcontent. So that while some celebrate Foucault's 1976 lecture for the invention of biopower, what most, if not all, have missed is its true importance I think, the announcement of the total negation of violence as a political means to an end. Not the end of violence per se, but the end of 'violence' as a political tool embedded into the science of governance and control, and the commencement of a new kind of 'bioviolence' in its stead.

Foucault's more fully developed formulation of the biopolitical credo shows this with enhanced clarity I think. Sovereign power, according to Foucault, took life and made death. Biopower consists instead of making live and letting die. What one can see here is a theory of the entire investment of the energies of ruling. In the first, sovereign model, the state is active in the process of killing, and laissez-faire in the business of living. Live as you will, it basically says, I am only present in your lives at the moment of your transgression or your death. In the second, biopolitical regulatory vision rather, the energy of the state is that of active creation of life. The state's power resides in how it constructs our vision of what life as a right should be: protected, fostered and extendable. It is, in contrast, neglectful when it comes to coercive intervention of the mortal kind. The biopolitical state kills you mostly only when it actively neglects to look after you, a violence of neglect that is our first indicator of a possible bioviolence to replace the sovereign violence that biopolitics makes impossible thanks to Foucault. Even if the state is America, it is arguable that the death penalty is really only the mortal endpoint of the assault of the neglect of the poor, the mentally ill, the addicted, the abused, and of course, young black males.

Yet even taking this on board, bioviolence per se seems unlikely given Foucault's own comments on the issue which seem intolerant of *any* kind of biopolitical coercive force. About midway through the 1976 lecture, having outlined the basics of biopower, he almost seems to stop himself in his tracks and throw out a question that is most un-Foucauldian, given his fascination with modes of violent coercion especially manifested in the provocatively gory details of torture that launch his famous *Discipline and Punish*. Speaking of his newly minted biopower, he wonders:

> How can a power such as this kill, if it is true that its basic function is
> to improve life, to prolong its duration, to improve its chances, to avoid

accidents, and to compensate for failings? How, under these circumstances, is it possible for a political power to kill, to call for deaths, to demand deaths, to give the order to kill, and to expose not only its enemies but its own citizens to the risk of death? Given that this power's objective is essentially to make live, how can it let die?

(Foucault 2003, p.254)

How indeed? Well one answer is if the power of the biopolitical state is granted to governments by us, by allowing a state the privilege of managing our very well-being, in our homes, in the middle of the night, while we are asleep, then if it fails in its duty, it must be held accountable. By the same gesture, if a state values one set of citizens a bit more than another, rather than directly victimise that group say through punitive laws or expulsion, they indirectly make victims of them through the withholding of resource, the relaxation of regulation or simply turning a deaf ear to their complaints. And in doing so they commit instances of the violence of neglect simply, as the term suggests, by doing nothing. I am thinking here, of course, of Grenfell, but also of innumerable other examples of the violence of neglect both at home and at large around the globe.

The power to make live or let die

According to Foucault's theory of biopolitics, modern governments no longer rule by the ancient right over life and death, but rather gain our permission to rule based on a new right to make live or let die, as he famously termed it. If a liberal state's role is to protect the lives of its citizens, he suggests, and to enhance and prolong them, then any state that fails in this duty is committing an act of violence. He speaks of it as the aggression of exclusion and neglect. We might call it the cruelty of letting die those you are duty-bound to protect.

Letting die, regrettably, is a common component of all forms of regulatory governance. Take the issue of drugs in the NHS. Drug funding is based on the statistical efficacy of a drug across a population overseen by the regulatory agency NICE in response to the funding restrictions imposed on the NHS by government. You fall ill, grievously ill. If you happen to be one of the 1% who benefit from an expensive, experimental treatment, rather than the 99% who respond to a cheaper more reliable version, then you will not be prescribed that drug on the NHS because available funds are diverted towards the majority. The drug can still be bought, but it is too expensive for you. Without the drug your health deteriorates. You have been victim of the let-die tendency of governance based on statistical norms across populations spliced with funding limitations, political realities and the influential power of big Pharma. Rather than make live, the duty of the NHS, you are let die.

Foucault rarely pulls his punches on such matters, knowing that the whole discourse of governmental regulation is defined by neutral impassivity often enhanced by scientific rigour that is so well-suited to the denial of culpability or vindictiveness. When, he says, a regulatory or governmental agency which exists to protect and enhance your life instead opts to neglect this duty due to statistics or money, then he calls this neglect of life on the part of the state or regulatory agencies a form of murder. You can apply this logic very easily to the regulation and application of the flammable cladding used on Grenfell. The cladding was not illegal, but it had been banned in other countries. It had also been the cause of several fatal conflagrations around the world and in the UK, in each case sending flames shooting up the outside of the towers in a lethal signature all too readable in the images broadcast of the Grenfell Tower disaster. When an even cheaper version of the cladding was chosen again this was not illegal either, but it was neglectful. Safety concerns were ignored in favour of profit margins. The risk of death was balanced against financial risk, a classic mode of regulatory bioviolence.

It is not just that regulation failed Grenfell. One could even go so far as to say the existence of regulatory agencies and norms made possible the use of the life-threatening cladding because, as the industry was seen to be extensively regulated, blame and responsibility could be farmed-out to those agencies if something went awry, while developers could focus their attention on profit rather than more costly belt-and-braces improvements that were safer. The subcontracting of blame to another party is a typical component of modern regulation. This is surely one reason, for example, why Kensington and Chelsea Council subcontracted the management of the block to a separate agency. It produces a distanciation of inaction that makes it harder for you to be blamed or to feel blame. Subcontracting is the technical-professional equivalent to war by drone.

If subcontraction is one means of regulatory distanciation, the dreaded independent enquiry is another effective weapon in the apparent pacifism of the biostate. Following the Grenfell disaster, the inevitable enquiry was set up. Just the activity of enquiry suggests a regulatory, investigative, expert-driven and implacable process that masks, of course, a governing power's reluctance to take responsibility for their own actions. The enquiry was split into two, it being felt that it would take too long otherwise and therefore delay redress for the victims and, more importantly, psychological closure. And yet the decision was then made to report on the culpability of the local council and the cladding manufacturer after the first investigation into the fire services was conducted. This simple decision was, presumably, justified according to all kinds of norms, but it had the specific effect of kicking the issue of the council and the cladding, the most contentious element of the accusation of the murder of neglect, into the long grass. Instead, we were presented with a lengthy document detailing the failings of the fire services. While this concentrated some fire on the senior management of the service who had been, admittedly, unsympathetic and rebarbative in their response to any suggestion that they may have got it wrong on the night, quite a lot of print was reserved for fire service professionals themselves. What the report was effectively doing was further distancing the disaster from the powers that be. Meanwhile, it has been reported that the cladding company have a war chest of up to £30 million to defend their product during the enquiry, while the prime minister in charge at the time, due to the febrile nature of contemporary British politics, is a distant memory and so beyond blame. Regulation therefore, so apparently impassive, can indeed be an active agent in the negligence of the death of our citizenry. Indeed the rhetoric and ideology of dispassionate professionalism, as we shall see later when applied to capital punishment, is one of biopower's most common modes of invisible and inoffensive coercion, the independent enquiry being one of its most effective weapons.

Foucault's reasoning in all of this is devastatingly simple and so very effective as a form of political critique and resistance. If the modern state extends its power over its citizens by the promise of valuing their lives, through protection against violence, longevity due to health care and risk assessment-based legislation, and if it regulates and surveys its citizens with the argument that it is for their own protection, then it has entered into a social contract with them. The state basically argues, "I will take from you rights, cash, privacy, and power, in return for the promise of protection of your life, and enhancement of your living." This is certainly the promise of social housing in Britain's capital. If you allow London to continue to be one of the most neoliberal and unequal cities in the world, then in return we will allow you uncommon freedoms to work, play and live here. And if, for whatever reason, it doesn't work out for you, then we will make sure that there is enough cheap housing that you can continue to be a Londoner until you turn things around or choose to commute in from Wales.

Building dwelling thinking

Affordable housing isn't just a social policy however. It speaks more deeply of the basic human right to shelter. In a famous essay called "Building Dwelling Thinking," philosopher Martin Heidegger traces the origin of the German word *Bauen*, to dwell, back to etymological roots entangled with the word *bin*, to be (Heidegger 1971, p.147). He asks that we listen carefully to the word *Bauen*, to dwell, through such attentiveness hear three things. That building is really dwelling. That dwelling is how mortals exist on the earth. And that this leads to a sense of building as dwelling that cultivates growth and erects buildings. He has invented, in effect, an ontology of architecture, a philosophy of town planning. Building, he argues, relates to dwelling which in turn relates to the universal question of how we mortal beings exist on this earth. We don't dwell because we have built, he suggests, but we build *because* we dwell: "human being consists in dwelling and, indeed, dwelling in the sense of the stay of mortals on the earth" (Heidegger 1971, p.149).

What Heidegger means by this, I think, is that a building almost organically emerges from a question of human being, specifically how are we, as mere temporary residents, going to live on this earth? Isn't this the existential question of our global lives at the present time? We must therefore ask which buildings are appropriate to what is, in effect, always going to be a short-term lease.

#GenerationRent is not just a millennial catchphrase, it is an ontological condi-tion, made all the more pressing in this age of the Anthropocene and Extinction Rebellion. Heidegger's language is infamously opaque, but what is clear is that if the German phenomenologist had been on the steering committee of the man-agement company in charge of the Grenfell refurb, for all his many faults, it is unlikely he would have opted for cheap cladding.

Housing is dwelling, dwelling is being, being is mortal and so, by definition, housing policy is directly in charge of a basic life right, the right to be and so dwell and build on this earth we all share, and which none of us, in our mortal-ity, can ever be said, existentially at least, to own. There is such a strong link here between ethics of planning and architecture in "Building Dwelling Thinking" and Foucauldian bioviolence. When you build a house, you make life. And when you cut corners with cheap, combustible materials, however legal, you are let-ting die.

If the state's job is to make your life safe and worth living right up until your dying breath, then when it lets you die, here through short-term profit and the disregard of the voices of the poor, then it has, by definition, killed you, accord-ing to Foucault. Not through direct action, as used to be the case centuries ago when despots and torturers ruled the land, but through indirect inaction, Theresa May style. Letting someone die, when you have a moral, legal and even ontological responsibility to keep them alive, is already a form of manslaughter. To build, Heidegger says, is to make a dwelling suitable for human beings as such. Hearkening, for a moment, to the voices of some of the most influential thinkers of the last century, rather than the right-wing press and the Twitterati, is it all that outlandish actually to suggest that Grenfell was murder?

Proving Grenfell was murder: notes on method

Many would still, truculently, answer yes, and it is to you sceptics that I now speak, trying to vainly burst my filter bubble. You want proof don't you? Good, I am a philosopher, proof is what I do, although don't expect the proof of fact as much as of deduction. A year after Grenfell, while commentators spoke of the neglect of the victims and the survivors, few would agree, it seems, that the 72 dead were murdered, perhaps viewing this as overly emotive, too extreme. I'll give you that. Yet on Foucault's terms the violence of exclusion and neglect on the part of a state whose power is based on the promise of protection and enhancement of the life of its citizens resulted in precisely that: the murder of neglect. He doesn't mean this in the heat of the moment, losing his rationality due to extremes of emotion. If any-thing, Foucault's cold-blooded reflections on all kinds of state-sanctioned cruelty are so dispassionate that they border on sociopathic. Rather, he is simply taking the argument of bio-governance—give me your rights and I will look after your life—to its logical end point—but if I fail in my duty of care then I will be held responsible for your death. It is one of handfuls of basic operators that constitute all logical thought; the "if … then" construction of implicative relationality if you need to know. It is not assertoric, opinionated, trolly or doxa. Rather, it is indulging in rational deductive thought based on a historical fact taken to its indubitable conclusion by one of the world's most influential thinkers. I am not pitching you journalistic op-ed any more—this is philosophical reasoning, the oldest art and science known to humanity, based on journalistic commitment to facts and details gleaned from a variety of sources, left and right. This philosophical journalism, as I tend to call it, is effectively the methodology of the rest of our study.

Even taking the extreme Foucauldian position and granting Heidegger his due, by accepting this to be the case, what purpose is served by calling Grenfell murder rather than an unfortunate accident? Naturally one outcome is prosecution but that is the least likely outcome of philosophical reasoning. No one is going to be prosecuted for murder, or even manslaughter it would seem, thanks to the truth-preserving qualities of the "if … then" operator. Why then does it matter that we call it murder rather than manslaughter? One reason is that murder implies intent. Did the developers and council intend to kill the residents? Not exactly, but that isn't how the logic of bio-governance, the right to rule based on the stewardship of your day-to-day life, works. The intent of the modern state is, Foucault explains, to 'make live.' The active disregard of that intent is, logically if paradoxically, the intent of 'no intention to protect.' This then is murder, proven by another of those basic logical operators without which we would not have computers, social media platforms and the stock market, without which we would not have science, namely, the fundamental law of non-contradiction or the excluded middle.

Calling it murder also makes the political point more powerful when those that ought to listen have switched off. The wealthy of London town, and the cronyism that serves and supports them, live aggressively at the expense of the ability of poor people to be able to live normal, safe lives. Everyone knows this. The less well-off are increasingly forced into substandard rented accommodation that, due to lack of real enforced regulation, is often dangerous or made to live in tower blocks which then have to be beautified by cladding to enhance the views of the palaces that overlook them for the folk who live inside who are in some way embarrassed or just disgusted by having to be proximate to such poverty. Leading to the lethal, cheaper cladding option, to maximise profit using a product that is entirely cosmetic, so why waste money on the heftier and more costly alternatives?

The money that should have been spent on vouchsafing the lives of the residents of Grenfell was instead spent adding value to the property and to the area. This is just a fact. Money that could have been used to 'make live' was instead squandered on 'make money,' and the result was 72 people we left to die, who were 'let die.' This is the very quintessence of definition of the murder of neglect.

Power: the right to kill that is not murder

Grenfell Tower had an immense impact on British culture. It ought to have been a turning point in how the poor are housed in this country. Yet evidence shows that already lessons learnt are being ignored, those who are culpable are being protected, ex-residents are not being looked after and meanwhile over a hundred tinder boxes, containing tens of thousands of ordinary souls, are just waiting for the next spark to set them off. Yes, accusations of murder were initially emotions boiling over, but on sober reflection, with just a little bit of help from some of the world's most respected thinkers, it would appear that those emotional accusers had a point. The murder of neglect is an invisible crime, most of the time. Grenfell brought it out into the open. A 23-storey tower burning through the night, people leaping from the windows and debris raining down, in one of the richest places on earth, are all but impossible to ignore. But what of all those other tower blocks around the land dressed with equity-enhancing but life-threatening cladding in places where TV reporters don't tend to make their nests? Each is just one more crime scene waiting to happen. Moribund, tardy non-responsiveness is a typical and brutally effective way of perpetuating a violence of neglect. British bureaucratic neoliberalism forced into the ossification of a society still dominated by class and lack of social mobility, being the perfect breeding ground for a politics of inaction and subcontraction through which the violence of neglect can readily thrive. Bioviolence, on this reading, is almost a paradox, which is why Foucault struggled to see it in his own work; it is the violence of doing nothing, of not striking someone, of failing to pull the trigger. At times it can even be mistaken for the ideology of pacifist nonviolence, an intentional doing nothing when one is duty-bound by one's own bio-social contract to intervene and help.

Heidegger, writing in 1951 from a Germany of ruins, asks: "What is the state of dwelling in our precarious age?" (Heidegger 1971, p.161). He is literally addressing the housing shortage of post-war Germany so his comments are prescient for a nation such as my own, which finds it impossible to adequately house its people after seven near-unprecedented decades of peace. Heidegger, as an avid national socialist, emerged from the war a disgraced and to some degree an unrepentant figure, yet he still has more of value to say about housing than our current prefab governors when, for example, he pinpoints that the housing shortage is not just lack of houses, rather,

> the real plight of dwelling lies in this, that mortals ever search anew for the nature of dwelling, that they *must ever learn to dwell*. What if man's homelessness consisted in this, that man does not even think of the *real* plight of dwelling as *the* plight?
>
> *(Heidegger 1971, p.161)*

One year on from Grenfell, some residents remained unhoused, many tower blocks were still potential death traps and the streets of our cities became increasingly littered with recumbent forms cocooned in sleeping bags or splayed on cardboard. Isn't it time we woke up to the plight of dwelling? A plight Grenfell made so visible on the West London skyline until the authorities yet again clad the blackened, dead monolith, sticking up like a rotten tooth in capitalism's rictus smile, this time with tarpaulin to stop the building from becoming a lasting memorial or, god help us, a symbol. Or maybe it was just those mansion dwellers again, desperate for a nice view from the en suite of their third guest room. It is a plight that Heidegger names *the* plight in 1951: how are we to dwell together as mortals on this earth under the sky before our divinities? Which divinities are those, you might ask? There remains but one in truth, the universal, divine right to life which means, also, to dwell, to be housed.

For all his complex terms, ontological portentousness and dodgy Nazi-lite language of homeland and destiny, isn't Heidegger asking, in the end, the same question as Zainu Deen who lost both his daughter and grandson that warm June night in Grenfell Tower? How can we go to bed in a house that keeps us safe? On a local level, and on a global level, Grenfell shows we are very far from answering that simple demand. The very fundamentals of making live then, and surely dwelling is one of those, are letting die far too many and this, by my reading, is a mode of murder.

Yet I cannot, in clear conscience, rest there. In truth the point about the Grenfell murders is a wider one than apportioning blame and looking for punitive redress. Murder, we can now see, is a constructed concept based on the relative lawfulness of taking another person's life. There would be no such crime as murder if it were not the case that taking someone else's life is not always taken to be murder, meaning that there are ways and means of killing that escape the institutions of punishment. The easiest legal loophole here is, as ever, power. Those in power are, quite simply, able to take or cost the lives of those who are not, with a much reduced risk of being held responsible for their mortal actions. In fact one could go further and define power as a right to kill that is not murder. To this we must add the proviso that the 'right to kill' extends in governmental states such as our own democracies to cover the right to let die, because the deal we have done with power is no longer obeisance under threat of death, but compliance in response to the promise of life, a protected life, an enjoyable life and a long one. Who a government lets die is, thanks to our complicity with the powers that be, who we all allow to perish also. They are the ones we care less about, the ones whose value while alive is of a lesser degree than our own and of those around us.

In calling Grenfell murder, therefore, what you are effectively doing is trying to enhance the life value of the dispossessed of our society, to remind the government of the day that they have a duty to make these people live as well, irrespective of the inconvenience, cost and political fallout. That we have to shout murder at the top of our voices over and over to make the world accept that residents of social housing are human beings is regrettable. As is the fact that it is only in death that the 72 lives lost in Grenfell are now taken seriously through a process of national grieving. It is almost as if we can only recognise the right to make live of the poorest among us when the regulations have failed them and they have been left to die.

As there does not appear to be any chance that political change will emerge from Grenfell, with national anger dissipating under the daily tedium of that most effective of all biopolitical inactivities, the enquiry, then I think our only hope for a revolution in neglect is to make demands on the language of violence and neglect, to call a thing like Grenfell murder and mean it and prove it, so that the lives of those who remain, whose existence has now been made precarious in their homes due to a regulation of neglect, can be developed by the issue of the cladding in a related way to the development of the real estate. What if the accusation of a murder could so increase the life value of the victims of Grenfell that the crisis of the housing of the poor in this country became impossible to ignore? Is it possible, through words alone, to literally change the value of people's lives such that they are no longer neglected because of their amassing of political biocapital? Not only is it possible, it has happened, recently, and you were probably part of the social movement that brought to pass this remarkable, affective metempsychosis.

PART ONE
Regulatory bioviolence

1

AYLAN KURDI AND THE INDEX OF RESPONSIBILITY

Your Twitter feed *pings*. Your Facebook page drips two drops into a pool. A WhatsApp group fires an arrow into a target. Instagram tumbles pebbles onto a pristine rocky beach. You scroll through, queuing for groceries, meeting a colleague for coffee, standing at the school gates, boarding a plane to Barcelona, killing a few dead moments to see what is trending. Without thinking much about it, inattention being a chronic feature of most online activity, you click and are hailed by an image everyone seems to be sharing, immediately interpolating you into a massive, multi-participant conversation, which we shall call an MMC, although at the time you thought you were just innocently browsing.

The picture shows a doll lying face down in water. Tiny little thing. Amazingly well-crafted, but you instinctively know it is a mannequin. It has to be. It can't be real. Probably they photoshopped it? Actually, looks more likely to be some kind of puppet. These were the days just before deep faking. A policeman is standing over the dummy with what appears to be a clipboard, taking notes. He doesn't rush in to save the infant who must be drowning. There is no need. It's just a doll after all.

Rather than scrolling on or clicking away, the power of the picture holds your gaze momentarily. The shop assistant starts to get impatient. Your colleague has to tap you on the shoulder. Your daughter calls out "Mum!" three times to get your attention. You almost fail to board. The toy is pointed head first down the incline of a beach. Awkward position all told. The face has sunk into the sand a little. That feels unnatural. The doll has been fetched up on the nether zone between sea and sand that recalls to you those wonderful words at the end of Wordsworth's "Ode on Immortality," which you otherwise hated at school:

> Though inland far we be,
> Our souls have sight of that immortal sea

Which brought us hither,
Can in a moment travel thither,
And see the children sport upon the shore,
And hear the mighty waters rolling evermore.

(Wordsworth in Wu 2012, p.553)

Such a wee object, the head oversized as they tend to be in these theatrical contraptions. The back of the cranium is bulbous and pronounced with that close-cropped haircut. How pleasing it would be to cup that head in your hand, ruffle its bristles before guiding the little dissembler across the stage. Once, as a child, you went to see the story of Pinocchio enacted with just such a marionette on a houseboat moored on the Thames. You found it both scary and sad. All Pinocchio wanted was to be a real boy, but in the end it would have been better for him to remain a wooden facsimile, better for everyone really, or at least that's how it seemed to you at the time, on that crowded little theatrical boat. The theatre is not there anymore, the boat having slipped its moorings and been lost to the vast ocean of the past.

Someone is tutting behind you in the queue. You notice that its t-shirt has ridden up where the waves caught it. Your co-worker looks a little concerned at your distraction. The mid-length trousers rest on calves whose curves echo that of the head and that camber of the beach. Nice touch that. She is starting to pull you across the playground to where a displeased teacher is waiting. This photo is more than just some meme; it has the complexity of art somehow imbued in it. You give them the wrong boarding pass and delay departure. Lifeless arms rest by the side, each hand with knuckles down, fingers curled, palms like shells expecting their pearls, awaiting animation at the hands of some powerful sorcerer.

Having dispensed with your worldly commitments in all their variety and intensity, later the same day you find a private moment and return to the original post. The image of the boy on the beach has been bothering you all afternoon. You scroll down with your left index finger looking for the name of the artist, it must be a work of fabrication, and see there is another image just below. It shows the same man as he makes his way up the curve of a beach. The sea behind looks unwelcoming. He is clumsy-looking, this man, bent over, dressed in what is more likely a military uniform, on top of which he sports the ubiquitous Hi-Viz vest. What he carries in his arms appears to be a sleeping child, also dressed in cheerful colours. The man moves carefully up the shifting surface so as not to wake his son, who he is taking to bed you would imagine. The boy is so light that the policeman, the brother, the father or the human does not carry him so much as guide him, weightless, through the air.

Other details now detain you. The boy's shoes are tiny. They close with Velcro. You know because looking at the image again now, you can see one of the straps sticking up. My son wore the same shoes when he was that age. The boy looks like my son did, when he was that age. Same hair, same gorgeous olive skin. I recognise the creases in the fat of his palms as the same creases my son used to have. The boy, whose name is Aylan, is three years old, and he will always be three. He will not wake up or increase in size. He will no longer be a brother or a son. His shoe-strap will never be folded back into place by his mother, to stop him from falling.

Like some melodramatic Sunday night drama you come to realise the full horror of a nagging doubt that has pursued you through the day. The photos are real. The beach an actual place. The child, the child, a real dead child. Overwhelmed by shock, anger, sorrow and other emotions you perhaps couldn't append a name to, your response is instinctive, yet mediated. You hastily thumb in some words of anguish and empathy, accuse yourself and your echo chamber of complicity of some vague order, rail against the intractably brutal current state of things, and click, retweet, share, send, post. It is a moment of protest, and you are far from alone in your digital remonstration; millions, you later discover, felt precisely the same way, did precisely the same thing. Without realising it at the time, you had joined one of the largest mass protests the web has ever known but, looking back on that day, can you stipulate precisely what you were remonstrating about? That young boys shouldn't drown at sea and be washed up on beaches? Obviously something more specific and, well, political than that, but what precisely? This has become, for me at least, one of the great questions of recent times. What do you slacktivists want, precisely, do you even know yourself?

Meanwhile, in a land far, far away, a Twitter feed *pings*. A Facebook page drips two drops into a pool. A WhatsApp group fires an arrow into a target. Instagram tumbles pebbles onto a pristine rocky beach. Someone you don't even know, scrolls through, queuing for groceries, meeting a colleague for coffee, standing at the school gates, boarding a plane to Manila, killing a few dead moments to see what is trending. Without thinking much about it, inattention being a chronic feature of most online activities, this anonymous person clicks and is hailed by an image everyone seems to be sharing, immediately interpolating them into a massive, multi-participant conversation, which we shall call an MMC, although at the time they thought they were just innocently browsing. And so it goes on, not hundreds, nor thousands, but millions of times.

The new auratic potential of memes

The photos of the drowned Aylan Kurdi were taken by journalist Nilufer Demir on a beach near the Turkish city of Bodrum. The first of them in particular became a famous meme, that we all shared, that left us beside ourselves in rage and yes, grief, for a small boy who died needlessly because we are selfish. How to approach it and revisit it a handful of years later is not an easy matter, ethically, I find. The celebrated Chinese artist Ai Weiwei, for example, caused some dismay when he posed as the boy on the same beach a few months later. It was seen as an insensitive and self-serving appropriation of someone else's tragedy. In an interview soon after, he equated his own problems with the Chinese authorities with the death of Aylan, a parallel that has since come to be seen as self-absorbed and crude, for all his struggles in China (Ridley 2016). Although Weiwei's response was obviously thoroughly considered and, irrespective of the critical hostility, certainly a work of art, it seemed inappropriate, outmoded, superfluous to some degree. What Weiwei came up against with his ill-conceived appropriation of Demir's work is the problem of grieving and the ethics of relation in a post-digital age. In trying to establish a connection between his own plight and that of a drowned boy, the parallel appeared to look to augment his own suffering and in so doing to drain some of the power and affect from the original image which his appropriates.

If Weiwei's work suffered from being too mannered, the more spontaneous way in which the world at large responded to the image, it was tweeted up to 53,000 times a minute at the height of the Twitterstorm, reaching 20 million people in only 12 hours, is equally problematic. In contrast to the heft of art, Weiwei's form and reputation were seen as likely to overwhelm the delicacy of the image of a dead child, the insouciance of social media responses could have been deemed superficial in relation to the imagery being shared. If it were not for the fact that the MMC, as I termed it, composes its own heft, the accumulated weight of small acts of outrage and upset, that alone or in small clumps, might seem ineffectual but like 20 million pebbles set loose, can form a whole beach, or 20 million drops poured, inundate an entire raft.

The problem with Weiwei's art, aside from his overweening self-absorption, is that it is out of step with mass, digitised participatory culture. Although shared online of course, it seemed woefully digitally illiterate. His work of mourning is out of time, old school, 20th century. A singular and unique work of art, made by a single artist-genius, given what Walter Benjamin famously terms the auratic potential of the work in his much-cited essay "The Work of Art in the Age of Mechanical Reproduction," no longer seems to be in touch with its times (Benjamin 2010, pp.228–59). Benjamin, of course, could never have predicted that the innovations in image reproduction of his time, the 1930s, were precursors to our current age, not of mechanical reproduction, but, more accurately, digital repurposing. In becoming active participants in the technology of iteration and distribution—we are all publishers now, just as we are all writers, editors, critics, even texts—with the Kurdi images, it was almost as if we had somehow decided to attempt to recapture the religious aura of the work of art.

For Benjamin, aura was suspended around a unique art work thanks to the presence of some preternatural being, called up by the searing will of the artist, located in a specific space one had to travel to. In contrast, the Kurdi images benefitted rather from the sacred atmosphere composed of the real source of all religious power, the ritualistic participation of the worshipper in the cult of death and immortality that, in the elegy and the ode, respectively, formed the basis of Western art forms and culture. It was not, in truth, the content or even the intention of the 20 million participations that made the Aylan Kurdi phenomenon important and unique. All our responses, good, bad, indifferent, were mere component parts, digital tesseracts, in one immense mosaic-like transformation of the life value of this little boy, through an act of mass mourning in the form of digitally facilitated sharing that is unprecedented in the history of humanity. Using different genres, materiality, and indeed an entirely novel kind of literacy, the Aylan Kurdi meme became the contemporary equivalent of our bewoaded and intoxicated ancestors, dancing around a bonfire, lost in the repetitive cadences of hallucinogenic incantations, or of Greek folk on the side of a hill, keeping the lost beloved alive with oaten flute and musical cadence slow. Sharing the Aylan meme was a gesture of auratic restitution gifted with the same magic as the ode and elegy to apostrophise, and hence give a body to, abstract eternal truths and the tragedy of lost forms. In short, the problem of the loss of aesthetic aura inaugurated by mechanical means of reproduction was only a temporary hiatus in modern conceptions of the value of art, tied into the ideology of individualism, until digital reproduction was able to take art back to its ritualistic, communal, reiterative roots as a means of giving material form to spirits through instances of mass participation. All through the simple, communalising act of click.

The resurrection of Aylan Kurdi

Aylan Kurdi was the youngest son of Syrian refugees Abdullah and Rehan Kurdi. Having fled Syria they had been living in Turkey for some time before returning to their home town of Kabani. When Kabani fell to ISIS they fled for a second time and returned to Turkey with the intention of joining relatives in Canada. However, for reasons that now lie lost in the mists of time, their application for Canadian entry was refused and, in desperation, they paid several thousand dollars for passage on an inflatable boat to the Greek island of Kos. The boat was small, and there were twice as many people crammed into it than it was designed to carry. If there were life jackets, they were ineffective, as was the outboard which failed sometime during the planned half-hour crossing. The boat flipped in choppy seas and Aylan, his brother and several other passengers including some other children, drowned. Their bodies were washed up on a beach on the second of September 2015, not far from the Turkish city of Bodrum, from whence they had departed in the early hours. Like Ulysses' mythical periplus on the self-same seas, they had taken a circular journey to nowhere.

The photos taken of Aylan by Demir were celebrated as some of the most powerful of 2015, causing global outrage as to the fate of refugees trying to cross the Mediterranean Sea to escape war, poverty and oppression in their home countries. The first picture I mentioned was one of the most seen, shared and discussed of 2015, transforming Aylan from yet another anonymous refugee into a nexus of emotion and rage, and finally an agent for political change. Who, in the end, was responsible for his death and was it, in its way, another form of murder by neglect? How did it come to pass that the most vulnerable amongst us, the Aylan Kurdis of the world, were left to drown and be washed up on beaches? These became urgent questions within the online communities who participated in a politicised act of mass-communication through the process of sharing and commenting, inventing a new kind of digitised global mourning we have yet to really process.

As the story gathered momentum journalists spoke to other passengers on the tiny craft as well as Aylan's distraught father and family and, perhaps inevitably, conflicting versions of events emerged. Some accounts linked Abullah Kurdi with the smugglers, suggesting he was at the helm of the raft and hence responsible for it shipping too much water. Perhaps because the responses to the images of Aylan were so unprecedented in scale, counter-narratives emerged around the morality of the sharing of images of this nature in a pretence of liberal outrage. Wasn't the truth that pictures such as those of Aylan Kurdi were little more than snuff for a digitised age, a kind of emotional mourn-porn where we were using our outrage at the fate of refugees as an excuse for sharing pornographic images of dead bodies to hide what is really voyeurism, prurience, a depoliticised sense of political activism without having to do anything more than press share?

As these debates developed and the photo was not only shared, but discussed, contested and even, in the case of Ai Weiwei and others, emulated, it was as if that little boy had risen from the dead and taken on an afterlife beyond anything he could have aspired to had he lived. The satirical magazine *Charlie Hebdo* even projected Aylan into the future, grotesquely imagining him as a grown man, sexually molesting a German woman, memeing on contemporary cases of sexual harassment in Cologne ascribed to local immigrants, a story which itself has been subsequently contested as a right-wing moral panic. Aylan had died a child, and was resurrected as a meme, in a process that is peculiarly of our age, but which was predicted, perhaps, by an essay published when Web 2.0 was a niche term for a few techies in the know.

From grievable to responsible lives

A decade before the Aylan Kurdi case, feminist theorist and political thinker Judith Butler published an influential book called *Precarious Life* where she argued that how you die determines the value of your life. Or, more specifically, value is fixed by how you are mourned when you die. "The question that preoccupies me in the light of recent global violence is," she says, "Who counts as human? Whose lives count as lives? And finally, *What makes for a grievable life?*" (Butler 2004, p.20). Grievability, as Butler calls it, is an accurate enough means of assessing the true value of your life on the national or global stage. While most see grief as private, Butler instead thinks of it as a public, indeed political act. "I think it furnishes a sense of political community of a complex order" (Butler 2004, p.22), made up, she suggests, of indexing human relations through their sudden interruption due to loss of life, and also acting as kind of reminder of our corporeal vulnerability that we share in common as part and parcel of our assumption of universal human rights to life.

If, she argues, we are all equally vulnerable physically, when someone dies, the degree to which they are grieved indicates to what degree this universal vulnerability is placed in a hierarchy of precarity during life and response to loss of that life. Precarious lives appear to be, on the global political stage, less grievable. Not because the relatives of victims of precarity care less, Grenfell is testament to that, but rather because the social connectivity of precarious lives is diminished so they have fewer 'relations' of another order, we shall say relations of and to power, and so the impact of their loss is relationally diminished. Put simply, anonymous children in Idlib make less of a specific impact when they die, than the death of Assad would have, although if one of those children were to be photographed in death and this image go viral, as was the case with Aylan Kurdi, suddenly this single death is much more grievable and so, politically, of greater significance.

Butler's theories of grievability and precarity as a measure of human worth undercut the bogus myth that all humans are born equal, with equal rights to life. If you are born into precarious circumstances, she explains, your life is worth less, evidenced by the fact that you are more likely to die, and, if you do, are less likely to be grieved in the specific sense of your death making an ethical and social impact politically or globally. This is a pleasingly disruptive argument to make. Modern biopolitical states are founded, after all, on the idea that each citizen's life is of equal value. When this is proven not to be the case, the argument goes, this isn't because a state starts to disregard you, but because uncontrollable circumstances, statistical norms, vagaries of populations, resource limitations and war mean you were unfortunate enough to fall into the category of the disregarded, because to disregard you, to let you die, is regrettably necessary to enhance the chances of life for the large majority. Butler seems to think that this disparity of life right is tied to a related question of life value that is often not perceived until lives have been squandered.

The argument has had legs but Butler is in fact wrong to define mourning as some kind of universal test of life value. For example, she suggests that spontaneous outpourings of grief where you are 'beside yourself' establish an ethical moment where you see yourself as dispossessed and ontologically displaced in an old-school Hegelian manner. This essentialisation of mourning from a modern, Western perspective is just not borne out by the evidence, which shows excessively emotional grieving is socially constructed and so not a universal test of who we are as humans (Watkin 2004, pp.23–52). All the same, her book has made widespread the useful idea that life-precarity is an important ontological value that has direct political consequences. The response of the world to your vulnerability, say to famine if you live in the Yemen, and to your death, if you are one of the thousands of migrants every year that drown trying to cross the Mediterranean, still remains a very good indicator of the political value of your existence compared, say, to the death of one US soldier in Afghanistan or Iraq.

This being the case, instead of grieving, which Butler Westernises and essentialises, let's talk instead of simple responding. And rather than focusing on responses after a life has been lost, can I suggest we move the debate towards responses while subjects are alive but under threat of harm and death? Responses of states to the life rights of the precarious, the vulnerable; let that be our register of human worth. Responses of citizens when they see those rights devalued; let that be an ambivalent yet significant indicator of our ethics and politics. Instead of *grievability* as the definer of life value, we should speak in terms of *responsibility*, not just as a duty of a state towards those who need protection, but also the response of state and citizens alike to the clear precarity of those whose right to life is in some way threatened. I am speaking of responsibility in two senses, duty and reaction, as a test of the assumed universal human right to life, and a sad admission that this right is not universally applied with the same rigour and interest to all the peoples of this earth. Responsibility does not have to be grievability as Butler insists, but we ought not dispense with mourning altogether for it can take the loss of life to make degrees of responsibility visible, as we saw with Grenfell and Aylan Kurdi. Although in the case of Kurdi, the constructible nature of our 'spontaneous' grieving took on a unique and peculiar character that I think yet again outstrips Butler's limited sense of the process.

To share is to care: the real politics of clicktivism

Aylan died. We all know that. He drowned. He was three. His brother Gaylip also died. He was five. But Aylan is by far the more widely known of the two. Inseparable in life, they became divided in death not just in the obvious sense, but also as regards how they were mourned. Aylan, the youngest, overtook Gaylip, in the eyes of the world. All because of that photo, and social media of course. As I said, the image of his corpse was seen by 20 million people in less than one day. Gaylip's body, instead, was lost at sea. No image of him was available. He was, let us be brutally frank, grieved less, was worth less, to the world, by the simple measure that he received no attention, while his brother was the subject to 20+ million attentive acts, in addition to countless millions of other kinds of responses which we call sharing. This is where treating the index of human worth in terms of responsibility rather than grievability is particularly significant for, in the 21st century, in the age of Web 2.0 and clicktivism in particular, responsibility is often determined by a digitally mediated, public response. It is not how Aylan was grieved in the hearts of each of those 20 million subjects that determines his worth; this is a very 20th-century, emotionalist, way of viewing things. It was that he was grieved 20 million times through the politically connected act of digital sharing that was the measure of his life-worth in death. Which is how we mourn in the new century.

Some may grieve more strongly than others. Some responses were appropriate, others, like Ai Weiwei, were perhaps not, but the content of the response is rather irrelevant in the age in which we find ourselves. We live by the political slogans 'Response is Responsibility' and 'To Share Is to Care,' even if to care is very much a constructed affective response, not a deeply felt one such as one might find celebrated in Wordsworthian spontaneous outpourings, for example. Those 20 million shares were, in truth, approaching a kind of content neutrality. None of those sharers made the content; they simply used it to make a connection. Although the content of the image was certainly key to its meme-worthiness, the process of sharing tends to erode content-power in favour of action. How you feel is that you share, and all emotions are worth equal weight, the weight of a finger, pressing a button marked *share*, *like*, *retweet* and so on. What I am arguing is that regardless of the content of an image and the strength of your emotional response, the basic functional limitations of the plat-form remain the same, and the quality of your *like* or *share* is neutralised in favour of the quantity of such responses as an indicator of worth. Not least because after all, Facebook, for example, is the world's largest ever co-authored text, and as such is a text that no one can actually read, in its entirety or even a significant portion. Our digital literacy therefore is no longer concerned with reading, that arbiter of quality, and is instead tied up with other activities which we might call curating, the activity of selective collecting through a process of looking and sharing.

Yet if all our responses were content-neutralised and indifferently the same in terms of their negligible heft, the push of a finger on a virtualised button, their accumulated mass created a global population of grievers that politicians felt it was their duty to respond to. It has to be said that the response of a politician, even if it is on Twitter, is of a very different order than mass responsibility, as the tweets of Trump have shown us. It is pretty clear that it was the death of Kurdi that convinced Angela Merkel to briefly lift the embargo on immigrants to Germany, leading to a mass migration from the borders of Hungary to cities such as Hamburg and Munich, where refugees arriving by train were cheered from the platforms as they disembarked, something very much against the grain of perceived public opinion at the time. And definitely the death of Kurdi was the prompt for British Prime Minister David Cameron's craven caving in of his hard-line policy against immigrants. Having called them 'the swarm' in a speech in 2015, causing something of a national outrage, and refusing to agree to the UK's rather low quota for refugees, he changed track in September of the same year and allowed a small trickle of immigrants to cross our hallowed borders, in a belated attempt to show that he had some modicum of humanity, a decency crumb soon flicked from the high tables of British party politics.

These political responses were short-lived, the attention span of the meme-iverse is notoriously brief and fickle, but they certainly changed the lives of significant numbers of migrants. That said, they also had deeper ramifications for European politics as a whole. Instead of improving the situational stand-off between Fortress Europe and migrants crossing the dangerous waters between Libya and Italy, since the death of Aylan Kurdi, it is arguable that the situation has deteriorated further. Kurdi could be said to have contributed to this, although by this we very much mean the constructed 'Kurdi effect,' not the poor, lost soul himself. Merkel's apparent generosity appears to have contributed to a loss of popularity, especially in the more reputedly racist and nationalistic eastern portions of her country, that plunged her into domestic political crises and led to the shocking rise of far-right politics. Cameron's prevarication between good cop and bad on the issue of migration was part of a general crap shoot he decided to play with British society, leading to a referendum on exiting the European Union (EU), which has changed the political future of Great Britain for generations to come.

Since Kurdi's death, far-right populism, fuelled by the febrile digital debates on migration, of which the Kurdi meme was undeniably an aspect, led to the Five Star Movement, in conjunction with the extreme right-wing Lega Nord, seizing power in Italy and refusing to allow their navy to rescue further Aylan Kurdis. On this reading one can see that the increased life value of one little boy turned his death into a political football that, as it bounced across Europe, caused windows to smash and citadels to topple. All of which suggests that our much-vaunted internet slacktivism does have tangible political impact, but not of the order that we, as a so-called community of mourners of Kurdi's death, intended.

This is reminiscent of what we will come to see as a Foucauldian politics of large and small numbers, as well as a politics of categorisation, in particular that ür-category upon which all our political fates hang, the category of the human. Born into the human species, Aylan's life value however remained well below the norm, because he was also born into Syrian civil strife. Taken by his parents on a flimsy boat in restless seas, the precarity of his existence, as Butler calls it, was dramatically increased in proportion to their calculation of risk, risk of going back to Syria, risk of staying in Turkey, dangers of unsafe passage to the EU. When Aylan died he joined a mass of unnamed migrants who drown every year in their thousands, trying to cross the Mediterranean Sea to penetrate Fortress Europe. In 2015 an IOM poll said that 3,695 died trying to do just that. Nameless because some are without papers; nameless because as a community we did not choose to respond to their deaths. One project funded by Dutch NGO UNITED is simply a list of names, consisting of over 35,000 migrants who have died since the mid-1990s (UNITED 2018).

Only one of them is called Aylan Kurdi, the only one of the 35,000 I would imagine you could actually name. This stark fact demonstrates if nothing else the power of the meme-ification of Aylan, dead on a Turkish beach, that somehow touched a chord and went viral in an unprecedented fashion. From being less than human when he died, about to enter the mass of the anonymous drowned, suddenly his categorisation as a human exploded exponentially so that he became one of *the* humans of the year. As a child victim he seemed to speak to the complexities of what it means to be called human in this age of mass migration and mass participatory social media platforms. As I said, a politics of small numbers and large, of intimacy and excessiveness, of trying to identify the one piece of relevant data in an unyielding sea of information that threatens to inundate us all at any moment.

Butler has given us a head start on how to understand our reaction to Aylan's death; we are calling it a politics of responsibility from which the index of the life value of certain humans can be ascertained, against a backdrop of the fiction that all our lives are of equal value and weight. Could the forces that resurrected Aylan be the same ones that contributed to his death in the first place? And could his status as one of the most precious of all members of the human species during 2015 be nothing more than a by-product of a mode of coercion that is tied directly to the idea of a human species as sacred?

We ended the introduction considering how the movement to call the Grenfell deaths the murder of neglect was an essential moment in changing the value of the 72 lives lost, with an aim of enhancing the life value of the many thousands of low-earners living in tower blocks around the nation, clad in the same dangerously flammable material. Aylan Kurdi was as much a victim of neglect as the residents of Grenfell Tower, none of whom, I imagine, you know by name. Gaylip Kurdi was subject to the same neglect. In this sense they are all victims of murder by neglect, of letting die those who we should have made live. But what we took from Butler was that neglect is tied to an index of life value. Those with low life value live precarious lives; they are more likely to be let die, when push, as it always does statistically, comes to shove. And when they die their deaths will usually mean less, be grieved less perhaps, but more accurately they will garner fewer responses, result in less political or social or digital capital. Yet Aylan Kurdi's death elicited millions of responses in less than a day, became a meme, a work of art, a single name phenomenon, an agent for political change. One image of one boy on a Turkish beach transformed an anonymous victim of immigration, one of thousands, into a global, cultural and political phenomenon. From this we learn something new about life value or the basic human right to life enshrined in the political imperative on the part of the state to make live its citizens as much as it possibly can, to the point of letting die others, to maximise the life chance and life rights of the majority. The state is concerned with the "making live" of the majority, at the exclusion of an abnormal minority, a numericality of checks and balances, an invisible, coercive system looking to maintain equilibrium against the unpredictability of populations and the vagaries of milieu. In contrast, the meme-ification and resurrection of Aylan Kurdi dealt with extreme numbers, a system of regulatory control that, through a process of a Massive Multi-participant Conversation (MMC), the powers that be lost control of. Could this be the locale of future resistance to the incursions of biopower into our private, biological lives?

Clicktivism, resistance and the digital draft

As we move forward into precisely how biopower operates through bioviolence, a basic fact will stick in the craw of any activists out there who wanted to make things better through their smartphone. The day we invited power as such into our lives, both in terms of our private, domestic set-up and literally as caretakers of our biological well-being, it appeared to be game over as regards political resistance. Not only is the extent of power now all-pervasive, what is left for power to colonise except perhaps our troubled dreams, it resembles somewhat a jihadi wearing a suicide vest. If you move to disarm her, you can be successful only at the cost of your own life. For if power is concerned with the making live, the letting die being unfortunate collateral damage, then challenging power means going against the principle of life itself—a principle we shall see, in the chapters which follow, power controls absolutely because it invented the idea of life itself.

I can see why, therefore, so many of us are addicted to net clicktivism, how so many are willing keyboard warriors. As the response to Kurdi's death shows, social media as a mass participatory event can have astonishing results which resist the make live–let die injunction of biopower. As we saw, over 20 million shares of the Aylan meme had the effect of raising the life index of Aylan from no one to, perhaps at one point, one of the most important humans on the planet. Even though this was a post-mortem response, we also observed, and we will see again later, that becoming a meme can result in a kind of immortality. You may scoff and say a digitised eternal life is not a life to speak of but if, according to Yuval Noah Harari (2015) and Ray Kurzweil (2005) we move towards digital singularity and genetic engineering on a mass scale, Aylan may yet be celebrated as one of the most important precursors of a net immortality that many tech visionaries are already touting round the venture capitalists of Silicon Valley.

If clicktivists made Aylan live, it was against the better wishes of the regulatory powers that be. Why, after all, did Aylan die? It is harder to accuse states of the violence of neglect with the Kurdi boys in that they were not under a state's care, in contrast to the residents of Grenfell. But, as we shall see going forward, one of the most effective ways a state has to make life is to compose a body politic, say the three quarters of a billion citizens of the EU, so as to let die others through the violence of exclusion from the body, which is, in essence, the impetus behind the lamentable Fortress Europe mentality. When we as a community responded to Aylan's death, we named him and attached 20 million quanta of value to his name, forcing political leaders to speak Aylan's name, accept culpability and change policy on the excluded immigrant populations accordingly. Interestingly it is built into the language and functionality of Web 2.0 to counteract the violence of neglect and exclusion. The idea of sharing, after all, is one of attention and inclusion, as if the Twitterati have the combined power to say to states, you must support these children and include them. Such that the regulatory powers of the state can, it seems, be counteracted by the deregulated nature of online activism. It is as if online we, the public, can take over the make live injunction and use it as imperative against the biopower of our states.

The potential, disruptive power of the net has been commented on many times of course, most notably due to its impact on the Arab Spring movement of the early 2010s. Yet in his corrosive study *The Net Delusion*, journalist Evgeny Morozov (2011) is rather scathing as regards the wider effectiveness of what he calls net slacktivism noting more than one expert, for example, arguing that Twitter and Facebook had zero impact on the Iranian protests of 2009. It is a suspicion of ineffectiveness he shares in common with Judith Butler whose excellent book *Frames of War* tackles the relation of precarity to modern meme warfare. In the introduction she speaks of the means by which war negates the human by transforming human animals into weapons or instruments of war. The rape of women, the use of children as human shields, even beheading are all means of making humans into beings which live but which have no actual, human value to us and so they become profoundly precarious as an ontological condition. In this context, Butler says, those like Demir who use cameras become agents of war, however unwittingly. The framing of images, their censorship and their dissemination all become weapons. By the same gesture our mass participation in this visual culture 'recruits' us into the war. When we view images of violence online we may be passive receivers, but we are also part participants in that violence.

Butler believes that "without the assault on the senses, it would be impossible for a state to wage war ... As we watch a video or see an image, what kind of solicitation is at work?" (Butler 2010, p.xvii). She is speaking here about specific images of war atrocities, but her argument is easily applied to the Aylan Kurdi meme for Aylan was, after all, a victim of the war in Syria. If you were one of the 20 million who shared this image it is beholden upon you to ask yourself what kind of solicitation you have set up by misframing the image through the simple click of a button? More than this, if you have unknowingly become an instrument of a state at war, which state are you complicitly serving by your actions? For example, in forcing Merkel to change her immigration policy, you were complicit in the rise of the European far-right. In protesting against the refusal to allow the Kurdis into Europe, you were part-culpable in allowing movements like Italy's Cinque Stella and the UK's UKIP party to violently reshape democratic politics around vindictive anti-immigration policies. In sharing Demir's image you may have been a participant in other modes of unwitting empowerment while at the same time appropriating the journalist's initial intentions, weakening or strengthening them in ways we still don't fully appreciate.

Having looked at both sides of the divide, it is perhaps an overstatement to pitch the deregulation of the net against the regulatory powers of the biopolitical state. Perhaps closer to the mark is that meme–activism in this case simply shifted the locale of regulation or rather made us realise that biopolitics is not just about changing the kind of power and coercion a state indulges in, but also what a state actually is. Those 20 million shares constituted, we now realise, 20 million bits of information that the big tech platforms now hold on us as regards a wide and potent array of our beliefs and reactions. Sharing the meme of Aylan was a political act, always valuable data to accrue, an ethical stance, important for influencing voters and consumers, and an emotional response, a mass act of mourning novel in itself, that also gave Facebook and Twitter direct access to how we feel when confronted with certain imagery. If the biopolitical state can have dominion over us through an invitation into our lives, the biopolitical covenant would never be complete unless we accepted that our private sphere was no longer our home, but rather our handheld device. An observation that allows us to say that Shoshana Zubov's brilliant theory or surveillance capitalism is incomplete unless we respond by delving into the philosophical consonance between the economy and its origins in the Greek term *oikonomia*, meaning our domestic economy, our private sphere, our homes (Zubov 2019). A surveillance economy, after all, is not one that monetises your private sphere, but rather encourages you to monetise it, through sharing your data, and relocates the private sphere from a fixed mode of dwelling, thinking one last time about Heidegger, to a tool you can carry around with you. As a child I was captivated by an episode of cult kids' TV programme Bagpuss in which a toad sang a folk song about silly old uncle Feedle, who build his house with the insides out, with disastrous and peculiar effect. That is what the net has urged us to do. We have turned the domestic *oikonomia* inside out, so that private dwelling becomes public portability. In so doing, every act of slacktivism is an emotional release of guilt and a political act of resistance for us, but another quantam of data-currency for the digitised biodatastate of the future.

We pressed a button: responsibility and the meaning of life

The Aylan Kurdi meme was a unique moment in human history. Never before had we spontaneously curated a mass participatory movement of that kind that had both political and emotional impact. It is of course important in relation to Butler that this was a mass act of grieving and everything about it supports her theses regarding precarity and what she calls the digital draft. Contemporary digitised mass mourning also formed an uncanny alliance with the most ancient form of mourning, the elegy. That said, it is not the emotional sadness that is important here, but rather the manner by which the elegy, like the ancient ode, was a means of conveying a material and lasting presence to someone who otherwise was absent from your regard. In these ancient forms it was the repetitious rhythm of the prosody that gave material form to the immaterial. Contemporary meme culture is primarily image-driven however and so this iterative function, the very essence of the idea of the meme taken from Richard Dawkins' original definition as the replicator principle applied to culture rather than DNA (Dawkins 1989, pp.189–201), is taken up by the participatory act of sharing. Repeated, curtailed and controlled acts of spontaneous yet mediated 'sharing' become the means by which the ethics of contemporary responsibility is constructed, both in terms of our irresolute responsiveness, clicking share, for example, when you see the image of a drowned child for the first time, and also as regards the ethics of responsibility. Yet if we are to suggest that responsibility of the Twitterati can act as a necessary corrective to the irresponsible stance of states as regards the precarity of child migrants, then I think we can be justifiably be accused, after Morozov and others, of naïve digital utopianism. Because in the end Merkel and Cameron were not being responsible, they were being responsive, their actions not dictated by ethics or political vision but, like the rest of us, meme culture's uncanny ability to entice us to press the button marked *share*. Remember when you are tempted to do so, that the button may say *share*, but what it means to the state in its war on terror is *fire*, and what it says to the big tech firms which own your platform is *sell*.

The great moral question of the last century was how to be a human when faced with the horrors of history, holocaust and Armageddon. It was, truth be told, a rather self-regarding and solipsistic pursuit. In our century the question is much more: how do you make a human? At some point this will be literally true, digitally and genetically, at the moment it is rather true at the discursive level. Social media is a mass participatory social experiment where we dehumanise ourselves through the occupation of mediated avatars and then systematically add in elements that may or may not eventually accrue into something akin to a human being. Indeed, the very modalities of each platform and their variety create a kind of sociology of the human, albeit one written by a bunch of introverted sociopaths, of which I am one. The great economic innovation of social media, to my mind, is not so much surveillance capitalism as anthropo–capitalism because what each platform has basically done is identify a single human behaviour, enhance it digitally, respond to its affordances, until it can make money. Google is all about hunter gatherers, we search we buy! Facebook about friendship and family. Twitter is gossip and bullying. Instagram, social display and persuasion.

In the case of Aylan Kurdi, the offence of his death, captured by an image, itself a technology that will soon be faked into skeuomorphised nostalgia, spurred us to ask the great questions: what is a 'human,' what does it mean to be a human, how can we be taken for human beings when we let this happen? These were our 20th-century, existential protestations. Yet what we then did about that was use social media to remake Aylan into a life, a human life, a child's life, a precarious life, a valuable life. What this revealed to me at least is that in our age, the great question is not so much what does it mean to have human *being*, but what does it mean to have human *life*, and how can we build a human out of our constructions of biopoliticised life? After all, it was not what Kurdi's death meant that made it a significant event; it is the meaning of what we did about his loss of life that carried the most significance. And what did we do? We pressed a button.

2

THE CONSTRUCTION OF LIFE

Specie-fication, race war and *immunitas*

The origin of 'species'

It should not be underestimated how significant the impact of the development of the human species is, as a concept. Nor should you assume that we humans have always conceived of ourselves as a species. The specie-fication of the human, the process of our coming to accept ourselves as a species rather than a people or a citizenry, runs alongside the process of classification of species thanks to the genetic process of *speciation* that commences with Linnaeus in the 18th century. Speciation, after all, is the law of life on this planet at the present time. This mode of classification, from Linnaeus on, is the subject of Foucault's first great success, in fact, the improbable bestseller *The Order of Things* (Foucault 1970). What Foucault demonstrates there is how scientific classification is a historical, discursive process designed to regulate life through its being captured by definition, as much as it is to expand our knowledge of it as a pre-existing phenomenon. Foucault traces the first emergence of the idea of the species back to 1689, and from that point on, he sees the movement of the collective noun of humans from 'mankind' to 'species' as a primary alteration in what we tend to call the political, or here ontological and biological, *imaginary* of the human; the means by which a social group comes to imagine a cohesive, narrativised and symbolic whole for themselves based on the ideas, beliefs and institutions they have created. As the term imaginary suggests, this is a creative construct out of existing realities.

In terms of our imaginary activity of self-identifying as a 'species,' a number of benefits are accrued to the human being. First, their primary designation is in terms of their vitality and biology, such that it becomes intelligible, over time, indeed by the end of the 18th century thanks to Paine and others, to think of rights appended to a human animal simply because they are alive. Human rights are, after all, species rights not strictly life rights. What this movement requires is not just an indifferent and neutral designation of humans as beings which live, consider how in general we treat beings which live, but rather it allows human beings to be entered into a classificatory hierarchy, much aided by Darwin's own tendencies to apply an eschatological value to his idea of survival of the fittest through his infamous degeneracy-inviting comments about the indigenous peoples in Tierra del Fuego in his *Descent of Man*, for example (Darwin 2004).

The shift that occurs here is first of all an inclusivity. Your rights are no longer determined by where you were born and what guild you belong to, as often was the case during the period of what Foucault and others now call sovereign power, but rather in terms of being, baldly, a human animal. Life alone however is not enough to guarantee rights as I said. Rather life, human life, has to be classified such that it is not only differentiated from other similar and dissimilar animals, say primates and mayflies, but that it is established as fundamentally different. The specie-fication of the human then is not just rights attendant on human life but also attendant on human beings imagined as the living beings par excellence, the animal of animals or rather, in a movement that has been part of Western dreams about ourselves since at least Aristotle, animals with an extra x. In some ways the human as species also problematises our sense of self; dreams can often be disturbing of our reality. Historically it was never clear if humans were just animals, as they were usually presented as animals who can also speak or laugh or lead qualified, political lives. Now, with the development of the human as species with rights, we have to justify those rights agglomerated to life, rather than other more tangibly human and political data such as being Roman or being born a king.

The right to life as a human right which defines what it means to be human is central to Foucauldian biopolitical theory. As he says: "With the emergence of mankind as a species, within the field of a definition of all living species, we can say that man appears in the first form of his integration within biology" (Foucault 2007, p.75). This momentous shift leads to biohistory or the entry of life into the institutions of history, politics and thus power. It marks the construction of life, the inscription of life, the discourse of life and the imagining of life. It is, in effect, the invention of 'life.' A subject is no longer defined as an object of legal regard but rather a 'living species in a living world.' All other rights fall away at this juncture and the remaining central right is the right to life, from which all other rights, laws and norms emanate like rays from a never-to-be-dimmed sun called vitality. A process of jurisprudence that is, however, itself a kind of imaginary, as actual legal rights to life were not enshrined in international law until the 1950s, well over a century after the discourse of *The Rights of Man* began to be a regulatory, political dispositif or discourse-driven institution of power.

The right to life is seen by many as the crowning glory of the enlightenment and indeed liberal Anglo-Saxon culture. Britain, for example, was the first country to ban torture from punishment in the 19th century. Even today, people talk about human rights with reverence as if they really exist, like they caught a glimpse of them, as if they are, by virtue of being simply alive, special and protected. Of course it means nothing of the sort. Perhaps it helps to think of speciefication as a special mode of regard therefore. Foucault is perhaps most famous for this reading of the Panopticon jail design of British philosopher Jeremy Bentham (Foucault 1977, pp.195–228). The Panopticon is an architecture of state surveillance of inmates wherein every cell is visible from a central viewing point, meaning one guard can see the activities of all the prisoners at all time, but inmates can never see if the guard is at their post observing them. It is widely used as a metaphor for our contemporary surveillance states.

The right to life, by contrast, uses a different kind of optics. Rather than being able to take in all subjects with one glance, a problem when the citizenry becomes a massive, dispersed and diverse population, it rather brings into focus the human being as a living locus of rights by allowing them to see themselves in terms of their rights. This makes the concept of rights eminently portable; pleasingly self-reflexive and self-constructed. It is, in this sense, the smartphone of political categories because your rights are tied in to your essence as a self-conscious, ambulatory being. Think of it, if you will, not as the Panopticon of governmental power but the Sui- or Self-opticon of biopolitical power, selfie for short, with all your privacy rights given over to a benevolent third party in order that they may know how best to serve you, based on your general needs as a living human being and the specific data they already, unbeknownst to you, hold about you.

These are, indeed, the Aylan optics we came across in the previous chapter. You see something online and you share it with other subjects. The net facilitates not only your godlike eye in the sky ability to broadcast and receive any kind of image at any moment, it also permits you to publish your vision so that others can see it. On the surface the optical networking seems liberating and democratic, if everything is published then everyone can see everything, the very opposite of the Panopticon. Except, each time you show something to someone, you show something about yourself to an logarithm which is very Bentham in that is it a guard which sees all but which you cannot see, the logarithms being protected by powerful intellectual property laws and created by inhuman artificial intelligence (AI).

Yet Bentham's punitive means, being markedly sovereign, are ill-suited to our biopolitical age. For example, Bentham argues, because the inmates couldn't see you, they assumed you might be watching and so behaved well even when the guard was absent. In contrast, the ethos and economics of the net is such that it wants you to forget it is watching you, and yet it always is, perpetually gathering your personal data. The net doesn't want you to feel watched and self-conscious, it much prefers you instead to behave as you would at home, to be yourself online as much as possible, because that is where it makes its money, selling your natural behaviour to companies who want to sell it back to you in the guise of products and selling the fake sense of yourself as you behave online back to you as the digitally facilitated and enhanced 'best you' ethos. The Aylan Kurdi event, therefore, is archetypal in performing and publishing a collective hive ontology that at the same time expresses the biopolitical optics of life rights that develop out of specie-fication. In seeing Aylan as valuable through the sharing of his image in death, slacktivists and keyboard warriors were making a point about their own life rights, that they are universal and indifferent to nationality, political status or race. It is Aylan's species that they are calling attention to surely, that he is one of us, and so should be protected as one of our own, as if he were our own child lost at sea. The paradox of the activity of sharing however is that this life right is an event, a one-off, a first time kind of thing, that is not reproducible. There have been many more Aylan Kurdis but there have been no more #AylanKurdis.

This encapsulates the problematics of biopolitical specie-fication being suspended, as it is, between a discourse of universal bio-indifference, we are all alive the same, and specific anthropo-difference, and yet we are a special species. To be seen as universally special is the Aylan optic, an optics that you have to succumb to, like all modes of coercion and power, and yet also opt into, by choosing to share. It raises the question: what were you were looking at, when you shared those images, a small boy who should not have drowned, or an image of yourself, as someone who cares enough to depress a virtual button?

Evolution, degeneracy and indifference of power

We already saw that the political possession of the human in terms of their biological classification served to generalise human beings in terms of bio-rights rather than citizens' rights. It was this biological deposition of the human being into a scientific classificatory schema that made it possible, towards the end of the 19th century, for the various pseudo-sciences to emerge, leading seemingly ineluctably to the creation of the bogus classificatory differentiations of human life along the lines of human races. These fake sciences then formed the basis of the discourse of degeneracy as the dark concomitant of evolution which fuelled, in particular but not exclusively, the rise of Nazism with its credo 'Nazism is just applied biology.' Biopolitical philosopher Roberto Esposito explains the precise logic of the science of degeneracy in his remarkable work *Bios: Biopolitics and Philosophy*:

> To say that the degenerate is abnormal means pushing him toward a zone of indistinction that isn't completely included in the category of the human. Or perhaps better, it means enlarging the latter category so as to include its own negation: the non-man in the man and therefore the man-animal [*uomo-bestia*] … Degeneration is the animal element that reemerges in man in the form of an existence that isn't properly animal or human, but exactly their point of intersection.
>
> *(Esposito 2008, p.119)*

We will return to the construct of the *uomo-bestia*, or humanimal in my translation, in later chapters; for now, instead, we need to understand the energies and drivers behind the efficacy of degeneracy as a justification of genocide, energies which come from the common root of both disturbing terms in the Greek word *genos*, meaning common descent.

The rise of evolutionary theory meant that the term *genos* was extended to such a point that it threatened to collapse the very idea of commonality of descent. If we all could be shown to descend from the same source, then the human animal certainly did enter into a zone of indistinction: how can I separate myself out as a species, let alone a favoured species? Commonality of descent became indifferentiated and indistinct, presenting politics with a dangerous problem. As Hobbes in particular stressed in the celebrated 13th chapter of his *Leviathan* (Hobbes 1996), indifferentiation of potency is the cause of all human violence and suffering. A point that is returned to in the last century with René Girard's influential theory of the scapegoat based again on indifferentiation, this time on commonality of desire. Add in Maynard Smith's application of game theory to evolution and Dawkins' location of evolution at the genetic rather than organism level (Dawkins 1989) and you have a powerful nexus of ideas all of which proselytise the same message effectively. If one is not able to clearly differentiate the power or potency of two beings, and yet these two beings want, or indeed in evolutionary terms need, the same things, food, mates and territories, then conflict will inevitably occur.

The modern biopolitical problem therefore is summarised by one word: indifference. The body politic, thanks to universal human rights, is unable to differentiate internally which of its citizens are worth more than others, so all have to be treated equally. While due to evolutionary theory, even the idea of being human becomes indistinct because historically the identity and indeed political value of individuals and groups were determined by having some kind of heredity in common that differentiates this group from others, a process of separation from which accrue the rights of Prussians, for example. If the 'monkey theory,' as Darwin's ideas were termed pejoratively in the popular press of the time, demonstrates that we all share common heredity with each other and with all other primates, indeed all other living beings if your go far enough back, then suddenly not only can one not differentiate valuable humans from their enemies or can you define humans as more valuable than any other kind of beast. Indifferentiation of this order, literally being unable to differentiate one being or life from another, is the basis of biopower and in theory should also be the source of its pacifism. If no one person is worth more than any other, what justification do you have for punishing them or waging war against them?

Yet, as the mainstream of modern political thought shows, it is not inequality that is the source of conflict, but equality, indifference and indistinction. When a human being cannot be certain if they are stronger or better than another human or indeed any other being, the ontological uncertainty this promotes can only be solved by testing out one's power, usually by reaching out to another living being and striking it as hard as you can, often pre-emptively, mostly without any clear justification, hopefully with a mortal outcome. It is this pre-emptive strike against indifferentiation of species that killed Aylan Kurdi, not directly—this is not the way of bioviolence—but as collateral damage whose distance from the War on Terror is such that it is possessed by the quality of deniability. When we opted into this war, sharing the image and effectively, albeit unknowingly, signing the papers of our digital draft, it appears that this was for the right reasons. The Aylan optics on this reading turned against the post-Benthamite Panopticon of the surveillance state, placing the collateral centre stage and making the image so ubiquitous that the boy's death could not be denied. And yet as ever the state is one-step ahead of its subjects in that, in striking pre-emptively, the 20 million protestors were reduced to reacting post-mortem. When the state strikes too soon, then all our protests will be defined by their belatedness—a temporality of dilatory response that is remarkable considering the constant, omnipresent and instantaneous nature of the platforms at our disposal. It is one of the strong markers of our failure as a digitally mobilised resistance movement.

Race war and *immunitas*

Foucault, if you remember, came to realise that biopower was, in effect, the abolition of sovereign violence as it had been constructed as a tool of power. Yet he was willing to concede at least one violent effect of biopolitical pacifism which he calls 'race war.' What race as a construct allows is a means by which the indifferent mass of the population gathered together in terms of right to life and is then internally differentiated as regards their 'race.' As biopolitical states develop, it becomes increasingly difficult to justify war against other states due to the fact that, essentially, there is no fundamental bio-difference between Germans and Italians. Each has the same right to life, and a biopolitical power base cannot, in all legitimacy, wage war against beings that are essentially the same as its own citizens, a problem the sovereign of the Germans *qua* citizens did not have to concern itself with. This paradox of indifferential equality is, as I said, at the very heart of all Western political theory thanks, in large part, to Hobbes' *Leviathan* designating the origin of all human violence as an excess of equality of desires and means of attainment, a model we have rather unthinkingly swallowed whole and with considerable relish.

In a Hobbesian model of social contracts and sovereign guarantors, war is the natural concomitant of states' similarity to each other leading to pre-emptive strikes. In our biopolitical world, however, wars between states require a differential shortfall of another order to justify such aggressive incursions, especially in the 20th century with its penchant for world wars: an im-predicative state, the world cannot be separated from itself, which results in an unbearable contradiction, therefore it goes to war with itself. Indeed it is the conceptual, ontological pain of a contradictory tautology, world war, that marks the end of sovereign violence as the main drive of coercive power. After world wars, we now speak of cold wars, global conflict or wars on emotion such as terror. These new kinds of skirmish are the way we war now, typified by Ullman and Wade's conceptualisation of the modern warfare of shock and awe (Ullman and Wade 1996) of droning, the new ontological category of enemy combatant, the territorial indistinction of rendition and the reluctance of any state to put 'boots on the ground.' These new kinds of biowar are the natural development of the impasse of conflict between two members of the same species. What can encourage a world made up of indifferentially valuable human lives to go to war with itself, except some fundamental perception of an internalised threat to life, not so much in terms of direct threat to existence, but rather due to what Roberto Esposito calls the immunitory logic of the biopolitical? By this he means the viral infection within states such that one cannot make life unless one lets die certain members of the population whose presence, like a virus, threatens the long-term health of the body politic.

If, Esposito argues, we take the metaphor of the body politic seriously, which we must as it is a central pillar of the biopolitical bio-contract, then we are likely to come to appreciate politics as being like a body in line with what science is discovering about our somatic mechanisms, specifically when it comes to what he calls the idea of *immunitas* (Esposito 2011). *Immunitas* combines positive and negative elements so that yet again they enter into a zone of indistinction. Immunising actions protect the body from external incursions which may threaten its vitality, but auto-immunisations also have to concede that the very interior of any political mass will have to contain elements which threaten its sustained existence, as does our own body. On this reading, "immunity is the power to preserve life" that contains "two modalities, these two effects of sense—positive and negative, preservative and destructive" (Esposito 2008, p.46). What is unique here is that the negation of life is not the result of power applied to life from the outside, the Hobbesian scare-tactic, but rather a mode by which life preserves itself through internalised attacks on its own body, bodies and masses. "Immunization is a negative [form] of the protection of life. It saves, insures, preserves the organism, either individual or collective" by subjecting the organism "to a condition that simultaneously negates or reduces its power to expand" (Esposito 2008, p.46).

Staying with Nazism, it is this immunitory logic that permitted one SS guard stationed at Kharkov to believe that "anti-Semitism is like a disinfestation, Keeping lice away is not an ideological question—it is a question of cleanliness" (Esposito 2008, p.117). When the Jews were stripped of their German nationality and then systematically slaughtered, this was, according to Esposito and others, just the logical endpoint of the immunitory logic, a means of negating and reducing the power of an organism to protect its long-term health, an injection of a pathogen to immunise the body against future infection. A reduction that reached such a point of insanity that one of Hitler's final orders was the annihilation of the German people themselves, at this point having become a counterfeit German 'race,' as if the body was so infected that the only way to save its life was, paradoxically, to expunge it. This paradox of *immunitas*, the only way to save the body is to kill it, is the dark nether side of the supposed impossibility of bioviolence—how can the injunction make life—resulting in what Esposito calls 'biopolitical thanatopolitics' (Esposito 2008, pp.110–45) and Achille Mbembe 'necropolitics' (Campbell and Sitze 2013, pp.161–92). The key to their interrelation is the indifferentiation of life rights, giving way to the differentiation of race. Foucauldian race war, then, is just another way of speaking of a body politic at war with itself, cutting into its indifferent life with the scalpel of differentiated speciesism, which is allowed to become racism when degeneration indicates that some of our species are falling short of the mark, species-wise, and so no longer deserving of the constructive life rights afforded to them by the state. At which point, the best solution, considering they are part of the body, is to slaughter them *en masse*, gather them into camps or expel them from your borders.

Immunitas and the Aylan pathogen

It was *immunitas* that killed Aylan of course. The fear of the refugee is simply the fear of indifferentiation of large numbers. We privileged denizens of Fortress Europe know first that our wealth and our resultant ontological consequence are accidents of birth. We are also partially aware that, for example, the war in Syria is our fault, specifically due to the post-colonial and post-war creation and division of the Assyrian territories into countries such as Syria and Iraq that ignored ethic division in favour of financial gains for Britain and France particularly as regards the developing importance of oil and influence in the Middle East. Syria itself is, in retrospect, a biopolitical state of indifference. Never historically a nation of its own, modern Syria is differentiated from its neighbours through the creation of a nation state, yet with no recognition of the complex ethnic and religious divisions of the region. The diverse peoples of the region were treated as all the same, except where the artificial borders of the state were drawn by the European superpowers of the time. Civil war, in short, was inevitable, because when Europe created the Syrian body, the organs were carelessly distributed, the pathogens mindlessly scattered and the auto-immune system favoured, totalitarian states under the thrall of Western power, literally sui-cidal.

Finally Europeans appreciate that if the centripetal force of nationhood is weakened by life rights, post-colonial malpractice and the visible anachronism of totalitarian sovereign control, not just in Syria, but around the globe, then there is little to separate the three quarters of a billion Europeans from the many billions who would wish to share in their wealth and freedoms. We cannot say, as French or British, we are more deserving of life value. We have to concede that the abject precarity of the Kurdi family was something we had a direct hand in. And as digital soldiers we were indeed happy participants in the Arab Spring digital movement that led to the Syrian civil war breaking out (Morozov 2011, pp.1–31). Which means that we have no reason to exclude child refugees. Yet if we did not exclude them, then the final and most fearful indifferentiation of all would have to occur, the concession that universal human rights are irrelevant without universal access to the same sources of wealth and political stability. It is a realisation that we perpetuate precisely by our contemporary modes of warfare where we try to take development and democracy to failed states around the world, precisely so that we do not have to grant them access to our own privileges at home. Of course I do not mean here that the threat of the overwhelming hordes is real, but rather is part of our political imaginary regularly used by far-right groups to justify racist politics, while the more mainstream sense of this horde seems to pertain more directly to liberal guilt over the sense that global poverty is, at least in part, our fault.

These extra-immunitory wars, inoculating the surrounding bodies so as to limit infection of our own, obviously because of the indistinction between them and us, in terms of rights, colonial and imperial culpability and digital visibility, rather than allaying our dubious concerns over race inundation, have instead increased our own fear of infection. In inoculating Syria with bombs, certainly some of those infectious agents will be dislodged from the Syrian body, in this instance millions of them, and will therefore become a-somatic parasites, looking for new hosts. Aylan was one such parasite, or at least was viewed as such when he was allowed to die on the Aegean swell, collateral damage of a body politic at war with itself through its pre-emptive inoculation of places such as Syria, Afghanistan and Somalia. The effect of those photos was to differentiate the ontological and political indistinction of the mass called the 'refugee' or 'migrant,' transforming him from parasite and pathogen to human victim. In effect they cured Aylan of his infection, while inoculating the digerati at the same time.

Inoculating against Aylan

Hobbes' foundational theory of violence due to equality is very much based on a sovereign model, arguing for a governmental apparatus, the state as leviathan, and the social contract. When one enters a biopolitical arena, however, equality is of a different order. For Hobbes, equality leads humans back to an animalistic state of nature where we are constantly sizing each other up, looking for an opportunity to improve our situation. In this way Foucault is profoundly Hobbesian as both thinkers essentially ascribe to a theory of perpetual war as a basis for the development of systems of power, although for Hobbes these institutions are only positive, while for Foucault their role is ambiguous at best and genocidal at worst. In contrast, when the human is entered into the living realm as a living being, while this in theory opens them up to a Darwinian determination of survival of the fittest, in reality its effect is the very opposite. For biopolitical theory, the biological right to human life permanently separates the human from the animal realm where life appears more as a prelude to conflict. Humans then are granted a special privilege which is the right to a biological existence that is not prescribed by the conditions of biological existence, oddly, but rather negates the said existence by declaring all humans as equal, a profoundly non-Darwinian ontological state. This new concept of equality, defined as a biological indetermination of populations, does not totally replace the political classifications of subjects as citizens of states; after all, states are still fairly novel and powerful constructions up until our own globalised age, but operate as a kind of regulatory substrata. As a state you can do whatever you like, as long as it does not contravene the basic human right to life of denizens of other essentially similar biostates. Biopower does not, therefore, replace sovereign power, but supplements and regulates it within a mass, indifferential, life-population milieu.

Differentiation, however, is a fundamental aspect of the political, perhaps the foundational element, and rather like Freud's theory of repression, if difference is negated over here, it will manifest itself in another form over yonder—enter race. The designation of different human 'races' allows, according to Foucault, the basis for a new kind of modern warfare wherein states go to war with themselves or other nations as a means of protecting the blood, or what we would now call the genetic pool, of the healthy nation by eradicating the degeneracy of other races, or of regulating them for their own good in a kind of inoculatory war of imperial quarantine. There is no doubt that our current, open-ended War on Terror is precisely this kind of immunising war, as was the cold war it superseded in the late 1980s when America invaded Iraq. What this war has demanded is that we curtail the power of our lives and negate the lives of our fellow citizens, through a particularly pathogenic conception of the terrorist. The fear of radicalisation is really a concern over infection, the removal of the rights of citizens suspected to have links with terror cells, just another mode of disinfestation surely? Aylan Kurdi, along with many other children, was killed by a pre-emptive inoculatory strike against his potential as a carrier of the terror pathogen that is, let's be clear, assumed to be a 'genetic' part of his 'race'; being an Arab whatever you take that to mean. The pathogen is located, it is assumed, in all peoples from the Middle East, this by the way is the essence of what we tend to call Islamophobia, and can be activated through the indistinct process we call radicalisation, which on this reading is when the carrier of the disease of terror ceases to be asymptomatic and starts to cough and wheeze their ideology into your political air space and digital airwaves. Aylan had to be let die on a beach, just in case he began to sneeze in the crowded waiting room of the holding camp, banlieue or repurposed Kentish remand centre.

The formation of race and its relation to biopolitical violence is really only touched on by Foucault in the last lecture of the 1975–1977 lecture series, the real work had already been done earlier in the course, but it does at least provide a provisional answer as to whether or not bioviolence exists in a mode that can also be differentiated from sovereign violence. First we can say that central to the political imaginary of biopower is the negation of violence through regulation of populations. Second, it is clear that bio-rights indifferentiate all humans in a manner that historically, since at least Hobbes, has been thought of as being generative of violence, an idea made all the more powerful by Darwinian evolution. This requires that we cobble together a new manner of inscribing the human within the biological that permanently relieves them of their animalistic needs of survival. The state then finds itself in a problematic situation wherein their main tool for coercion and violence is now re-inscribed as the very negation of what the biopolitical leviathan ought to do. This means that third, within the indifferential state of universal human rights of life, internal differentiations must be developed. As the right to life is the result of the development of the scientific process of classification, allowing for humankind instead to become a scientific object of regard, the human *species*, it is natural that the nations will turn to the same institutions of knowledge, what Foucault famously calls *dispositifs*, to begin a process of internal, scientific classification of types or categories of humans based on the development of the ideology of race.

The science behind the idea of race, as is now well documented, is entirely fictive, but for a *dispositif* to work as a mode of knowledge as power, it does not need to communicate content that is true, but simply to make active and effective a series of depositions and modes of regulatory control. As Esposito eloquently describes, the idea of racial differentiation, because it emanates from social interpretations of Darwinian thought, finds it a relatively straightforward process to allocate invented racial difference into a very real social hierarchy. In that racial difference is pegged to an interpretation of evolution that presents humans as in some ways superior to other animals; it is obvious that if not regulated and monitored, that most precious of human commodities, the last sacred element of the human, namely, our special life, can degenerate into inferior, animalistic forms. And so begins, according to Esposito, the modern narrative of degeneration of the human race and the partial replacement of the idea of citizenship with racial purity. The German people become the German race, and hence wars against other nations are then conducted through narratives of racial degeneration and superiority. Wars between states for Hobbesian, sovereign or governmental reasons are now increasingly reconstituted as inoculations and pre-emptions against infection of a race by degenerate elements located in other inferior national blood pools, the Slavs, for example. Or against interior 'races' that threaten to destroy the purity of the blood from the inside, the Jews being the most historically powerful example, zombies the most notable contemporary reimagining of this state-created, yet communally imagined fear.

Foucault sums up his historically complex and at times problematic explanation as to why biopolitical states kill as follows: "In a normalizing society, race or racism is the precondition that makes killing acceptable … Once the State functions in the biopower mode, racism alone can justify the murderous function of the state" (Foucault 2003, p.256). Although Foucault's reading of racism as the basis for state aggression is as pertinent now as it was back in the 1970s, and his reading of the Nazis as the paradigm of race warmongers is supported by the other major thinkers of biopolitics, if we step back for a moment we can see that it doesn't quite solve our problem of the existence of biopolitical violence. It is clearly the case that violence is a fundamental component of contemporary life, and yet it is hard to say that this is mainly, let alone entirely, due to a race war. If Foucault's biopolitics is to be a viable description of contemporary coercive power, and we concede that the conflict in the world is not a reversion back to sovereign modes of statecraft, not least because they occur due to the forces of globalisation that are precisely the cause of the widely reported erosion of the power of the concept of the state in the 21st century, then bioviolence must emerge from biopolitics due to other forces, institutions and *dispositifs*.

Foucault gives us a hint in this regard when he makes it clear that 'killing' is a semi-metaphoric or rather metonymic term that includes indirect murder such as "exposing someone to death, increasingly the risk of death for some people, or, quite simply, political death, expulsion, rejection, and so on" (Foucault 2003, p.256). While this now includes and explains large numbers of acts of forceful harm broaching the possibility of an inclusive concept of bioviolence, we could and should go even further, although to do this we need to now open up our consideration of precisely how the biopolitical state operates through its regulatory rather than disciplinary modes. Which is another way of saying that while Aylan's 'race' was very much a part of the cause of his murder by neglect, his digitally enhanced responsibility shows us that his 'racial' shortfall as regards the index of his precarity can be more than compensated for by other modalities in which his becoming a meme supersedes his being a human or indeed a species, simply because, thanks to social media, we now all know his name allowing him to escape the threat of being massified into indifferential groups such as migrants. Sadly, to be named in this way and thus to be de-massified into a class of beings more valuable than mere humans, Aylan had to be neglected to death. It was only then that the world was able to name him, pull him out of racial indistinction and thus see him as paradoxically, indifferently and yet also singularly human, which the odd ontological state philosopher Jean-Luc Nancy notably called *being singular plural* (Nancy 2000).

Classification

The basic right to life is totally transformed in terms of categorisation and classification. We all participate in the universal category of humans with rights, but within that indifferentiated morass of more than 7 billion, the zombie horde, the state has to differentiate groups into sub-categories to make decisions about them. In the case of Aylan it was decided by Europe that the deleterious effects of mass immigration on its population of nearly three-quarters of a billion, meant that migrants attempting to enter Europe would be classed as illegal and thus have the regulatory protections afforded to European citizens revoked. To the point now where boats taking on water at sea full of human souls heading out of Libya are left to drown or subjected to the kind of port-to-port ping pong that we saw in the case of the ship Aquarius which attempted to dock in Italy in 2018. This mode of categorisation deals with large human populations, the mass, in two distinct ways. There are the masses under the regulatory rule of Europe say, the French, the Germans, the Hungarians and the British. How each mass is affected by migration is part of the common, woefully ineffective migration policy. Then there is the other mass, the swarm or indifferent mass of bodies, that makes up the group 'Immigrants.' A mass that can then be sub-divided into say 'Economic Migrants,' 'Asylum Seekers,' 'Skilled Migrants,' 'Young Males,' 'Muslims,' 'Women,' 'Children' and so on.

If you are unlucky enough to be placed in the mass, in the undifferentiated swarm of those who are not from here but want to live here because where they are from is going to kill them, then your life rights are revoked. Showing that although European agencies invented and enforced the idea of universal human rights in the 1950s, they are actually not universal if you try to make a claim on them in Europe and you are from Syria or Eritrea. Yet within this mass, there are other groups, sets or sub-masses. The so-called good migrant versus the bad. Some of the good migrants will be accepted, enhancing their life value and improving the regulatory protections of their life that they can enjoy. Modern immigration procedures then are both regulatory and immunising, regulating so as to immunise: differentiate the good ones from the bad ones, let the good ones in, exclude the bad ones and let them die. What Aylan Kurdi specifically appeared to enjoy was a liberation from his anonymous massification thanks to social media giving him something akin to mimic celebrity. He became a kind of gruesome undead influencer. Even within one of the masses that the state protects, you are still just one of the masses. But once your name is known the world over, you leap from anonymity to ubiquity to the point where you cannot be massified in the same way. Life value therefore—which is tied to access life rights, which means your precarity index is reduced, because if you were to die your responsibility value would be high enough to pose a threat to the stability of a state, and thus perhaps increase the precarity of certain precious masses—is determined by which mass you find yourself included in.

One thing #AylanKurdi reveals is that Foucault's conception of 'race war' as primary mechanism for an active and interventionist bioviolence is not quite correct. Aylan did not die from exclusion and neglect because of his 'race' degeneracy. However pronounced Islamophobia becomes, Muslims are not presented as a degenerate race. If they are not degenerating, then in what way do they pose a threat? It is because they are infectious. There are over a billion Muslims from many different sects, diverse cultures, often at war with each other. Yet in the West, according to our immigration policies at least and the propaganda of our populist leaders, notably Boris Johnson and his kingmaker Nigel Farage, all Muslims are assumed to be capable of radicalisation and are assumed to be Muslim before they are, for example, British. If one then allows oneself to be radicalised, one becomes a terrorist, the most despised pathogenic class in the world today. When one becomes radicalised as a terrorist, one's rights as a citizen, as we shall see, are revoked, and your life rights permanently neglected. This also suggests the assumption that life replaces citizen as the locus of rights is overhasty. Life rights are the reward for citizenship of a democratic, advanced economy. It is true that being British does not give you access to special rights, but to participate in universal human rights, being British is an unbelievable advantage and being a Syrian child an incredible obstacle. This is not because being Syrian or being a child is a lesser national or biological state, but that being such you are more exposed, as an assumed Muslim Arab (many Syrians are not Muslim by the way), to the infection of radicalisation that will result in your becoming a terrorist in our midst.

Race, on this reading, is a symptom, like a fever or a swelling. Nationality is another one. Legal refugee status is a symptom, being a child is a symptom. Anonymity itself is very symptomatic of potential radicalisation, as is gender. Emerging from a refugee camp to board a tiny dinghy is tantamount to saying, "I am probably carrying terror in my heart." Immigration agencies and policies are not methods of jurisprudence or bureaucracy, but medical checks and immunising shots. Yet being radicalised, being a carrier of the pathogen of terror is not necessarily fatal nor is it incurable. The logic of responsibility, represented by the 20 million who chose to identify and name a refugee, is also a curative *dispositif.* Each time the image was shared, it was like an injection into the arm of the anonymised mass of migrants, an antibiotic swallowed. The Aylan optic then, which was also a mode of omni-nomination—his name was, for a few days, literally everywhere—was not so much an act of mass protest, as of collective healing. Each time we shared the Aylan meme, we were attempting to de-radicalise the child migrant, to cure it of the potential for terror and liberate all such migrants from the beaches of collateral damage that flange our mega-state.

Morozov gets it wrong, I think, when he disparages the slacktivism of our online responsibility (Morozov 2011, pp.189–91). We are not slacktivists, we are quacktivists, fake doctors in the age of fake news, administering snake oil in an attempt to cure Aylan from his biohistory, the moment when post-colonial, Western imperialism coincided with the life value of one three-year-old child. In the case of Aylan Kurdi, for all our fake certificates and qualifications garnered from questionable university courses we completed via correspondence and bribery, remarkably, one terrorist was inoculated so that we became immune to his threats. Unfortunately, it is not a medical practice that can be applied widely because first it depends on a one-off elevation of one child to the status of net celebrity, and second the treatment itself is fatal. In the end, it was never about helping Aylan in any case, we knew he was dead, that was why we shared his picture. We were not, in our digital responsibility, inoculating the Kurdi child, but immunising ourselves against the threat of all future Aylan Kurdis washing up on our hallowed shores.

Aylan Kurdi and the end of the child

The immense diversity of political histories and contemporary experiences mean that the promise to make live, extendible equally to all living beings, is almost impossible to honour, even though the state has every intention of trying. Some inevitably fall by the wayside. It is a problem of categorisation. The equity of life negates all categorical division of ranking; that is the point of it. Everyone is equal, everyone is alive the same. Yet lack of categorisation can mean ontological indifferentiation on an immense scale. I can't get a grip on the lives and needs of the Rohingya of Myanmar, unless I admit they are the Rohingya of Myanmar and all that this implies. So we end up with what philosophers call a category error, you speak of one thing in terms of another. Only it is an error so immense that it is a fault line in the very idea of categorisation and universality itself. Can you honour the life rights of all? Can there even be a one-size-fits-all category? If so, does anyone actually meet the needs of such a mega-class of people, especially as the membership of the class is supposedly based on the unique diversity we each are assumed to possess, such that our lives are irredeemable and irreplaceable if lost? What we end up with is something akin to a modish concept of a life spectrum. Yes you are alive and so valuable, but your value is on a sliding scale. Some lives are worth more than everyone, many lives are worth less.

The case of Aylan Kurdi then is a salutatory lesson on the life value spectrum, how value is determined, how it can be lost and also how it can be dramatically gained. What is remarkable about contemporary slacktivism is that mass-action, in the form of mass-sharing, can free humans from the mass and digitally enhance their life value, literally overnight. This is a digital revolution in the ethics of relation that Butler speaks of, wherein relations can increase exponentially but in an instant, perhaps saving the lives of complete strangers in the process. Let us test if that is the case. Certainly Aylan Kurdi's death led to political action, not just clicktivist activity, but did it also enhance the life value of other humans in the same kind of category as Aylan Kurdi? If you are born a child of migrants who make a decision to flee their country, putting your life temporarily at risk, with the hope of dramatically enhancing it in the long run, if you are, in other words, like Aylan Kurdi, is it now the case that your life chances are enhanced because, after Aylan, you are more grievable, more visible, more responsible? Surely, after 20 million acts of grief, Aylan Kurdi did not die in vain? Surely, at the very least, child migrants have become a mass within mass migration, which states look out for, extending extra regulation, to reduce their vulnerability, to give them all a better chance to live? Not only is this not the case, regrettably, the obverse appears to be true. Of all migrants travelling the world at the present time, the most despised, the most precarious, because the most feared, are those victims of a global outbreak of what I would call paedophobia. Put brutally, if you are going to look for asylum in a Europe, Australia or the US, you had better not be a child. In this sense, Aylan Kurdi was the last child we could admit or admit to, the end of childhood in the world today, at least if you are an immigrant.

3

RISE OF THE PAEDOPHOBES!

Or the coercive power of norms, regulation, population and massification in the case of migrant children

The Trump administration gifted 2018 with several pinch-me moments. Perhaps the one I will find hardest to erase from my jaded mind was a press conference in June hosted by one Sarah Huckabee Sanders. It was the week that images were released of migrant children, separated from their parents, kept in Texan cages, with no adults to supervise or simply comfort them. Even by Trump's substandards this was a new moral low for the self-righteous nation clinging to the poetry of their constitution as if words alone were enough to define them as both the innovators and thus righteous defenders of freedom. Huckabee Sanders, Trump's outgoing press officer, all Trump's aides seemed to be outgoing, was defending the decision to cage innocent children, in what appeared to be a junior Guantanamo, based on the Bible, a great source text actually for the maltreatment of kids. When CNN's Jim Acosta asked where in the Bible it was written that it was right to separate children from parents, her retort was, it is very Biblical to uphold the law, and that that was all the administration was doing. You couldn't just hear a pin drop, you could make out the whoosh of its fall through the charged particles of the press room air. Pinch-me? Better to slap me across the face several times and check my pupils for psychoactive traces.

Investigative reporter Brian Karem could contain himself no longer and, speaking out of turn, literally pleaded with Huckabee Sanders, as a parent, to accept this treatment was not right. Clearly emotional, Karem implored Huckabee Sanders to step back from a moral red line. She not only refrained, she was contemptuous, insulting Karem by suggesting he was just after ratings. Disbelief permeating in a room full of hardened hacks already in a state of permanent incredulity since The Donald nabbed the most powerful role in the world and turned the Office of the President into a permanent cage fight. What had just happened? I will tell you what, because I have seen it before, in my own country sadly. Trump's administration had succumbed to a global contagion, they had caught the disease I will call paedophobia.

Paedophobia: a global contagion

In the same month it was reported that French Police had been observed detaining children as young as 12 in cells without food and water. They were spotted cutting off the soles of the children's shoes to make return more difficult and confiscating their sim cards, effectively denying them the digital rights of protection from distant family members. Then, at the end of this process, they were illegally deporting them to Italy, of all places, hardly a safe haven for refugees these days. During these vile procedures it was reported by Oxfam that the children were roughly treated, pushed around a bit, laughed at and intimidated (Giuffrida 2018). They were, in other words, bullied. This is another clear case of paedophobia which is surely coming to the point of being a global contagion. Where, I might ask you, are the French journalists overcome by emotion challenging the Macron administration? Where is the French version of Karem when we need him? Certainly not working for the satirical rag *Charlie Hebdo*. And where, for that matter, was the English Karem back in November 2016, when in fact it was the press themselves who were driving the paedophobic headlines, not the politicians?

I first reported on the global epidemic of paedophobia back in November 2016 (Watkin 2016). If you recall, this was one of the lowest moments in terms of the influence of the right-wing press on migration policy in the UK. Children at risk in the temporary holding camp in Calais, called the Jungle, were entitled to asylum in this country due to what was called the Dubs agreement. But, thanks to the toxic nature of debates about immigration, the government led by the woeful David Cameron were loath to take their quota, now that their sadness around Aylan Kurdi's death had been given time to dissipate. At the same time the tabloids, led by *The Mail* and *The Sun*, began to question the age of those few who had been admitted. Using photos illegally splashed across their permanently histrionic front pages, they claimed that it was clear many of these so-called child migrants were in actual fact, wait for it, adults! So commenced one of those Brexitised national scandals that historians will look back on in despair. At its most fevered and hateful heights, it led to calls from the press and right-wing Tories for dentists to be forced to check the dental records of child migrants, as the only reliable way of determining age. A measure many found reminiscent of Nazi Germany, not least because Lord Dubs, whom the Dubs agreement is named after, was a beneficiary of the Kinder Transport. Dentists, to their credit, came out in force rejecting the politicisation of their profession, leading to an astonishing moment in British cultural life, the ennoblement of those tooth-sadists we all otherwise try to avoid. Strange days indeed.

While it is true that this story was strongly critiqued by our quality press, all the same it originated from the right-wing popular press, revealing to what degree they were hand in glove with those in the UK, pushing with almost manic fervour to tear us from the European Union at whatever cost. Not just at the proposed cost of the dignity of dentists, and I never thought I would write that phrase, but potentially at the expense of the life of hundreds of children who were blocked access to these combative shores, and later were lost from the data-bases, most likely trafficked into various modes of sex work and slavery. And let us be clear, a significant proportion of these children are now dead. Paedophobia revealed to us all that nothing was sacred, not even the life of children, if it threatened to derail the national sabotage of the Brexiteers.

The American strain of the disease

That was back in 2016, and if they were in some sense late to the party, still when the US finally succumbed to their own home-grown strain of paedopho-bia, they embraced it with characteristic enthusiasm and razzamatazz. American politicians first started to show symptoms of the disease when Trump, at rallies in early spring 2018, called child migrants co-opted into gang culture 'animals.' Perhaps infected by standing too close to his leader's spittle-infected vitriol, in April 2018, American Attorney General Jeff Sessions declared a 'zero tolerance' policy for all migrants crossing a US border illegally. This kind of intemperate invective has become a depressingly common feature of contemporary political populism and during these toxic Trump years might have passed unnoticed if not for one fact. Because Sessions' new directive criminalised all illegal migration, actually only enforcing a law passed by Democrats back in the 1990s, then all such migrants were to be treated like criminals, which means, in the US system, among other things taking their offspring away from them, because it would be inhumane to incarcerate their kids right? By the same gesture these children are protected by the US law and so cannot be prosecuted. So far so jurisprudent, except that now you have a gang of kids without parents to look after them that you have inadvertently created, vulnerable children who have committed no crime of their own although having been press-ganged due to a loophole in the law, suddenly, according to Trump, these kids are also in the process of becom-ing animalised. What to do with them? The answer provided by Homeland Security was, because it was illegal to lock up the children with their parents as that is inhumane, the children were instead locked up *without* their parents, paradoxically placing them in much more inhumane conditions, apparently for their own good.

Sessions was expectorating his hateful, sputum-laced words all through the spring months, spreading his germs about the land, but the story didn't explode until mid-June by which time the whole administration, led by the stone-faced but fuscia-clad Huckabee Sanders, her name for me forever riffing on her politi-cal hucksterism, had caught a pretty severe case of the paedophobia virus. By then, over 2,000 children had been separated from their parents at the border, most notably in Texas where the majority of popular crossing points are located.

These kids, as young as two some reported, were locked in chain-link cages, with no relative or even adult to look after them, given a mere two hours exercise per day, admonished if they played rowdy games in the cage and, according to some reports, mocked and laughed at by the guards when they started to cry.

In that these are young children, their incarceration must be taken to be of a degree higher than the normal modes of punishment for criminal activities. If, for example, they were not in custody and their parents left them alone in these conditions, then the parents would be liable for prosecution. More than this, the children have not committed a crime, yet are treated as if they had, which means not only are they wrongly held, but are not liable to the normal protections against prosecution available to minors. Within the cages observers were able to see children with clear symptoms of anxiety, stress and trauma. Colleen Kraft, the former president of the American Academy of Paediatrics, who visited one of these holding camps, said she saw obvious symptoms of children in distress. "Separating children from their parents contradicts everything we stand for as paediatricians," she said. "In fact, highly stressful experiences, like family separation, can cause irreparable harm, disrupting a child's brain architecture and affecting his or her short and long-term health" (Kraft 2018). Put all this evidence together and we can see that the US had just opened up a new branch in their Guantanamo Bay franchise, this time not based on Islamophobia but paedophobia.

The pathology of the paedophobes

With the benefit of hindsight we can see that the disease has actually been gestating in the Trump administration for some time now. Trump clearly has a problem with kids. Aside from an 145% increase in the apprehension of undocumented migrants by ICE (Immigration and Customs Enforcement), leading to deportation of families whose kids were born and raised in the US, the the former president has also waged war against the so-called Dreamers, a programme offering relief for undocumented migrants raised in the States. You may have heard Trump sounding off against Daca as if it were a pact with the devil himself, when in fact it is a pragmatic and humane programme to protect the status of a million vulnerable young people, now left with no safety net when it comes to deportation. A million Aylan Kurdis, if you will, were made instead to seem like a million potential rapists and murderers by Trump's sustained anti-Hispanic rhetoric, use of terms like 'animals' and the portrayal of humanitarian legislation as a threat to the coherence of a country founded on populations of Dreamers. We should have known. Why didn't we spot the symptoms? I don't blame The Donald. If anything I blame myself for not raising the alarm earlier. Do you recall the incredible, noble, dreamy activism of the friends of the victims of the Stoneman Douglas High School shooting in Florida in February of the same year? How they were attacked by the right-wing press and were mocked in the midst of their trauma? Now, looking back, I can see what was happening: paedophobia in the early to mid-stages. Like in those zombie films, the malady begins with erratic behaviour and excessive rage before the victims succumb, like the Homeland Security guards, Sessions and of course Huckabee Sanders, to mindless cruelty. It is a truly awful malady that knows no abatement, as the attacks on activist Greta Thunberg in 2019 show.

I didn't invent the term paedophobia, as you might predict. If there is such a thing as coulrophobia, witnessed by the monstrous clown that haunts the netherworld of my dreamscapes, then there must be a related condition of fear of children, witnessed by the creepy kids that haunt the netherworld of the dreamscapes of my creepy clowns. Paedophobia is not just a metaphor; it is real. It is a recognised sociological condition that has been spreading for some time. In a 2006 article in the *Guardian* on a report from the Institute of Public Policy Research, Paul Lewis noted that "an aversion to young people, or 'paedophobia,' is becoming a national phenomenon" (Lewis 2006), while Letty Cottin Pegrobin, founding editor of *Ms.* magazine, is credited with stating that America is suffering from an "epidemic of paedophobia" (Cited in Zelizer 1994).

Paedophobia is a useful term to explain what I think of as a moral red line which, once crossed, shows your democracy is effectively broken. When your fear of terrorism, paranoia over loss of national identity and hatred of other people a little different to you reache a state where you are willing to treat children as objects of hate, or the basis of hateful discourse and policy, then you have succumbed to paedophobia. You have, basically, crossed the Rubicon that applies to the large majority of all people on the planet, that children should be loved, protected and cherished, at least until they are in a position to make their own way in the world, which may be till the age of 16 or 18 or could even be age 15. At which point it appears they are fair game.

For me, when politics overcomes this moral red line, then paedophobia occurs and a warning should sound in your parish: this time you have gone too far. It is not just wrong to separate kids from parents, cage them, cut off the soles of their shoes, mock them in their distress, 'out' them as not even kids in the national press and gang up against them so they have to face trafficking and other fates perhaps worse than death, leaving them with what Kraft called 'irreparable' cognitive and emotional damage; it is a symptom that something fundamental to the humanity of that culture has collapsed. Paedophobia is a warning: that which you should hold most precious has become the thing you most despise. Like the demonic spawn of a thousand horror flicks, their voice horrific snarls, their words profanities and threats and their actions cruel as if directed by darker forces, the demonising of real children in the real world tells you that something evil lurks in this place, get out before it possesses us all.

Why God curses the child

All around the world, in Western democracies, the combination of the fear of migration and the rise of a discourse of demagoguery is fuelling paedophobia. But the hatred of children is one issue; the specific fear of the children of migrants is another. The first aspect of the migratory paedophobia virus sub-strain appears to be fear of inundation. Children represent new life, numbers and a different future, things that the culturally moribund instinctively fear. Second, in groups, travelling free, unsupervised by parents, unaccompanied minors threaten our sense of order, making the transition from Aylan Kurdi on the beach to remembered scenes of boys on the beach in Golding's classic study of paedophobia, *Lord of the Flies*, a relatively easy one to negotiate. Third, they create a kind of ontological uncertainty. One day they are a child, and innocent, the next they are an adult and, by implication, culpable of acts of terror. Indeed their innocence may be the trigger for their radicalisation. I think the *Charlie Hebdo* cartoon of Aylan Kurdi's alternative future speaks directly to what Donald Trump Jr called the poisoned Skittles problem of migration in 2016 (Malkin 2016).

And finally fourth, migrant kids are a direct threat to the anti-migration discourses and policies of Europe, the US and beyond. Children are, after all, a highly emotive subject eliciting not only responses of suspicion but also unqualified love with an intensity that perhaps only the figure of the migrant can match in contemporary political discourse. As Aylan Kurdi's death and our response showed, it is enough for one young child to lose their life, and it be recorded and shared online, to completely change the political landscape due to the manner by which public opinion drives our new demagocracies, facilitated by the change from the rules of the public sphere, to the lawlessness of the Twitter sphere. There was only one Aylan Kurdi; there were 2,000 child migrants in cages at the US borders, all with their own heartbreaking stories ready for the billon-strong Facebook slacktivists to get apoplectic over. It was Christ after all, in that book Huckabee Sanders mentioned, the Bible, who said, "Suffer the little children to come unto me." This may yet turn out to be the most explosive political statement he ever made, at least if those children are born on the wrong side of a border.

Yet writing about a scandal that began in April 2018 and made world headlines in June, at my desk in October of the following year, with the scandal still jostling for room in a scandal-bloated press, Johnson returned with a historic majority, Trump to be impeached; there appeared to me no political fallout for the shameful paedophobia of Trump and his fellow paedophobes. True Trump was forced to back-track late summer 2018 and issued an executive order reversing Sessions' directive, but of the 2,300 children detained in cages on concrete floors in large hangers where the lights are never dimmed and toys were even withheld, still over 400 of these poor creatures remain separated from their parents and guardians. How can this be? Do we just not care? Have we all caught paedophobia or are we instead victims of an associated malady, paedoacedia or indifference to the child? Again we look to Foucault for insight and explanation.

Population and massification

According to Foucault, around the 18th century, coercion changed utterly. Instead of technologies of discipline directed at actual bodies, technologies of regulation were developed targeted to what we might call bodies of bodies, collections of bodies, or what he terms 'populations.' This incredible change did not of course erase the traditional means of sovereign violence, but rather added a new parallel mode of coercion that operates almost in secret, that indeed some may not call violence at all. This new, covert mode of control over bodies collected in populations is what we are calling bioviolence, a term that depends entirely on our understanding of the idea of the relation between Esposito's reading of the body politic and Foucault's conception of population.

In effect, if Foucault is correct in his assumption, the development of the concept of the population is the single most central switch in power as regards biopolitics. A population is not a people nor is it quite a collection of a multiplicity of bodies he says. So what is it? The simple answer is that a population is a tool, an instrument, a *dispositif* defined as "a set of processes to be managed at the level and on the basis of what is natural in these processes" (Foucault 2007, p.70). This conception of the *dispositif* encapsulates the diverse mechanisms the powers that be use as the location of their power, including institutions, knowledge structures and modes of administration. This conception of the *dispositif* is in keeping with one of Foucault's most central and influential reversals which is basically, say, if you are insane, you are not then judged to be so by expert knowledge and thus incarcerated in an institution designed to house you, but rather you are judged to be insane because you are inscribed in the discourse of expert knowledge of sanity and because you are incarcerated in an asylum. Insanity then is a discursive construct within which you are assigned a subjective place, meaning the knowledge, power and institutions of insanity thus precede madness, not only inventing madness as a concept or malady that can be treated by institutions and expert knowledge, but also creating you as a person if you are unlucky enough to be included as a member of its institutional purview (Downing 2013, pp.24–5). The same is more widely true of a population. You are grouped as a subject within a population, say the population of the insane, as a means of authorising the regulatory apparatuses which have collected you into said population. In short, you are not insane and then regulated, you are regulated so that you come to be called insane.

This is one of those ideas that literally appears to turn our world upside down. Imagine, there is not a group of people starving called 'the hungry' and then a mode of regulating this population by giving them food. Rather there is the regulation of food supply which includes within it a population called 'the hungry,' who are then regulated by the state, indeed allowed for as part of the risk management of sustenance. In lean years there must be 'the hungry,' and there will be lean years. This relationship is important for power, as a population is determined in large part by natural and economic circumstances beyond the control of any sovereign. Foucault calls this the milieu: the 2008 crash, the Anthropocene, famine and drought in developing nations, the Syrian war and so on.

Modern governance does not so much rule as manage the vagaries of the changes in the milieu, say, of insanitary conditions in 19th-century London and the subsequent outbreak of cholera, by controlling the population of that milieu, the poor with limited clean water supplies. In that a state cannot directly control a population, it is too large, nor control the forces of a milieu, which are currently beyond human ingenuity, it determines subjects into populations through regulation as its only means of power or even control, in truth.

A population then is not so much a collection of individual bodies but what Foucault calls "a global mass that is affected by overall processes characteristic of birth, death, production, illness etc." (Foucault 2003, pp.242–3). This mass represents a second mode for power to take control, not by seizing hold of bodies, say through disciplinary measures, but in a process that he calls "massifying" (Foucault 2003, p.243). Massifying, admittedly an awkward term, is, in fact, one of Foucault's most profound observations on modern power. Massifying or massification is a means of indifferential collection due to a differential apparatus: the poor, the sick, the insane. When you are massified you are forcibly given an identity which, at the same time, paradoxically, eradicates your individuality: you are just one of the indifferentiated poor now.

If massification is the single most important tool of modern biopower, which I believe to be the case, again it seems to undermine a claim for bioviolence or even biocoercion. For you are not, in truth, forced to be poor, rather you are designated as poor and thus massified through an apparently benign set of primarily statistical processes such as the ratio of births to deaths or the fertility of the population or number of deaths per capita of typhoid fever. Often with the stated aim of liberating you from poverty in the long run so that you are paradoxically massified as poor and that you can be de-massified from the population of the poor. I think perhaps the best example of the confounding logic of massification is Foucault's explanation of the historical shift from treating illnesses in terms of epidemics to regulating them instead as endemics or "the form, nature, extension, duration, and intensity of illnesses prevalent in a population" (Foucault 2003, p.243) These illnesses were treated as endemic to life and managed and regulated accordingly in terms of data and massifying. You do not cure them, you simply manage them. It is what we call today risk management, a central component of the modern state according to Brad Evans' lively book *Liberal Terror* (Evans 2013, pp.39–40).

A managed, partial immortality

It is not possible to live without risk, Foucault agrees, therefore power takes on the role of ameliorating risk for a population through the accumulation of data and the development of apparatuses which regulate populations so that the risk is reduced relative to the overall indictment to make live. For Foucault, the process of massification as the reduction of risk to a population through the application of data alters the very nature of death. Mortality ceases to be an accident that befalls a person or a population, say the plague or floods, but is rather intrinsic to life, an endemic disease if you will, and is therefore a mode of data that needs to be managed. Over time, as management becomes more effective and the massification of populations ever more sophisticated leading to radical new developments in biotechnology, there is even a novel kind of negative eschatology that emerges. Suddenly it becomes part of life that one could, one day, through proper management, live forever, leading to the end of death through the massifying improvement of life. As your ability to 'make live' improves, therefore, through regulatory massification and the ultimate aim of biorisk management, the removal of the threat of death slowly it becomes beholden on the state to manage your life such that you will not die, or live as if you will not die which is how we currently live, in the teeth of ecological disaster that is predicted to be an irreversible existential risk within 12 years. Isn't this in part the reason why we are fully aware of an ecological existential threat to the very species we have become, and yet do nothing about it?

If you don't believe me think about the slogans around finding a cure for cancer in the UK. Cancer is, after all, a milieu that is the direct result of our body's immunitory processes. A cancer is just the process of cellular life without regulation. It is also a concomitant by-product of increasing sophistication in the field of biotechnology. The longer we live, the more likely it is, statistically, to face death from cancer and, at the same time, to not die from cancer. At present one in two of us will get cancer. As the population grows older, that number will increase. If, therefore, we can cure cancer, the narrative suggests that many of us, perhaps even half of us, will not die of this disease. Certainly the backstory is we will die of something, but one implication as you watch those emotive stories and text some cash is that the removal of cancer from our lives means half of us will not die. Cancer then is the perfect biopolitical disease. It emerges from life, from cellular division, it occurs through failure of 'regulation,' it is the result of the extension of life expectancy so is a product of biopower and it appears susceptible to curing, meaning it participates in a wider 21st-century narrative proposition: do we need to die?

This incredible power of the state, what greater power is there than overseeing the regulatory incremental move towards immortality, is also a tremendous responsibility because, if a *dispositif* mismanages your life, let's say the currently underfunded NHS, then it is effectively guilty of your death. However, if we step back for a moment and remember the universal right to life which was the ontological, ethical and biological foundation for bioviolence, we can see this responsibility or covenant exists not just between a state and its populations, but between all states and the world population. For it is, after all, the duty of power to regulate populations to protect, prolong and enhance the lives of *all* human beings. Our anthropological exceptionalism demands a global indifferentiation in terms of the value of lives, a mythic and all-encompassing political imaginary that presents all human life as of equal and thus special value. If, therefore, the right to live is tied to a duty to make live based on a biological indetermination of all beings, all have equal rights to life whoever they are, then the process of letting die is essentially one of international neglect for which a concert of powers must be held mutually accountable. This is, in other words, the founding value of the UN, the NGO and, the most biopolitical *dispositif* on the planet, the World Health Organisation.

The three blows: acts of massification violence

The value of indeterminate life is naturally perpetually in tension with the differentiations and massifications that are intrinsic to biopower. We are thus left, thanks to Foucault's sketch of our contemporary biopolitical neo- or better bio-liberalism, with an irresolvable mismatch between universal biorights, massification of populations and 'race wars.' In this way, finally, we can say that massification is violent. In being regulated en masse to manage risk, it is central to the idea of risk that it can never be eradicated and of management that you are holding things together in light of this woeful fact. Which means that the massified populations are subject to two forms of coercion. The first is the forcible inscription of bodies into masses through statistical data such that they can be managed and their lives protected. A process that appears benign, it is in fact one of Foucault's greatest observations, made first in *Discipline and Punish* I think, that when a state manages your life through assigning you to a mass, thanks to testimony of experts, for example, you are a murderer of low IQ who was abused as a child so you should be spared the death penalty, such a benign intervention is actually hiding a sinister penetration of your innermost private being on the part of institutes of power (Foucault 1977, p.30). In the old days, when your body was tortured for the crimes you committed, at least what was being judged was only your crime, whereas now, if your sentence is commuted and you are placed, for example, in an institute because of your mental health issues, what is judged is your life or even your soul. If you survive punishment of a crime, you go back to being a private citizen, but if you are spared punishment due to personal circumstances, it is not your crime that is judged, Foucault claims, but your life. And there is no way back from that.

The second violence is statistical and milieu based and so naturally slips under the radar due to it being intentionally tedious. There are a lot of poor people out there, the number-crunchers admit, we will endeavour to feed as many of them as we can, but in hard times some of them will die of hunger, and all we can do is manage that tragedy as best we can, try to prevent it, support the hungry when it occurs, plan for the future and wait for better times. The third violence is the violence of exclusion, of not being massified, of being left off the list when everyone else is included for the food parcel held in warehouses in preparation for the inevitable, yet hard to predict, lean times. Which means that massifying is coercive in its inclusion of bodies, neglectful in its statistical inclusion of a group who will be excluded from the interventions of state due to circumstances of population numbers and vagaries in the milieu, and violent in its wilful or accidental exclusion of some groups from the mass altogether.

Massification is important because it allows us to realise that biopolitics is founded on a complex, anthropological, indifferentiated form of exceptionalism. All humans are special animals, sacred even (sacred just means separate), but they are not special humans. This then leads to a necessity for a specie-fication of the human such that a racially motived and invented internal differentiation called 'race' creates a hierarchical stratification of the races, as justification for war and other modes of violence. Finally, we encounter a third mode of collection and differentiation, massification into populations where the specificity of the social human is eradicated, so that they can be entered into large-scale studies of populations in response to unavoidable changes in a particular milieu—famine, disease and ecological disaster—such that their risk of death can be marked down through state-organised processes of regulation.

Hidden-in-plain-view-ism: numbering as regulatory coercion

The first act of bioviolence that Homeland Security took was to forcibly massify the 2,000 children of illegal immigrants into a new institution or *dispositif*, those holding camps of unique political status. In massifying the children they literally created a new kind of subjective position, that of the migrant non-criminal yet criminalised child. These children were unlike any kind of children we had seen before on the US territory. They were incarcerated as if they had committed a crime, but as children they cannot be incarcerated for a crime. Thus the state has to prove the innocence of these children. This was not ordinary innocence that we see attributed to the construction of ideas of childhood from around the 19th century on, indeed this standard concept of infantile innocence was most likely an obstruction to the making of the *dispositif*. Rather it was an innocence created out of a narrative of criminality. The parents of these children, in being illegal immigrants, did not pass on their criminality to their offspring but forced the state to demonstrate the legal innocence of the children by removing them from their parents because of the need of the massification of the illegal immigrants to be incarcerated. The parents then are placed in a prison of culpability, the children held in the incarceration of criminal incapacity. This *Alice through the Looking Glass* logic is a wonderful, if also disgusting, example of Foucault's greatest philosophical discovery, that meaning is not determined by what you say but what you do with your act of saying. Here, America was able to call children innocent, so that they could lock them up! Indeed, achieved the impossible task of defining their innocence through the massifying action of the dispositif of imprisonment.

This discursive transformation of the intelligibility of statements with real political effects, the basis of perhaps Foucault's most important philosophical works, *The Archaeology of Knowledge* (Foucault 1972), to such a degree that innocence can be made into a statement of guilt embedded in an institutional reality of incarceration, is not only Foucault's most significant philosophical observation, it is also perhaps the fourth and most effective mode of bioviolence he identifies in his treatise on massification. We shall call this kind of violence 'discursive violence' and define it not just as harsh words, but rather the means by which statements define subject positions irrespective of the facts or the truth, and then justify said statements by establishing physical, material and institutional spaces to prove the discursive imposition correct. We might then add into this a third element of discursive, what Slavoj Zizek calls less convincingly symbolic/systemic (Zizek 2009, p.1), violence in the form of retroaction. Although it is the incarceration of the children that defines their innocence by punishing them as if they were guilty, then by the magic of retroactive reasoning, they are then able to say they incarcerated the children because they were guilty, obviously guilty they are in prison, reversing the original narrative that they were put in cages to protect their innocence. This backwards running narrative discursive mode of reasoning, as we shall see, is absolutely central to discursive bioviolence running along the lines of "I hit you, so you must have deserved it or, I hit you, and in hurting you I healed you."

That said as we saw, the point of massification is not to gather together masses of people with something in common, but to create masses of commonality through a mode of massification that facilitates the detailed mechanism of subject creation, here the particular figure of the child of innocent incarceration. In other words massification is just a facilitator of the most powerful tool of bioviolent coercion: regulation. Indeed one of the key issues around the regularity violence of encampment of children due to their innocence in the US in 2018 was that of data gathering and regulatory failures. Megan McKenna, senior director of communications and community engagement for the NGO Kind explains, "What we are finding is that there is no mechanism, no policy, for communicating or even finding the parents once the child has been separated" (Holpuch 2018). On separation, she explains, parents and children were given separate case numbers and parents were not given access to the case numbers of their children. In trying to trace missing children later, Kind suggested putting in consecutive numbers, say if your number ended in 5 perhaps your child's ended in 6 or 4, hoping to score random hits on the system. Sometimes this worked, other times it did not.

As Foucault's work of the 1970s predicts, regulatory measures are a common feature in aggressive immigration policies brought on by fear of terror and the rise of nationalistic rhetoric. They are also part of a wider technical and legal process of determining the life value of children. On the surface, gathering data about children might appear to be a benevolent process, designed for their protection. Thus the assignation of case numbers has a legalistic ring to it. Yet through the simple act of skewing the process, purposefully or not, the child is actually inscribed into a regulatory nightmare of Kafkaesque proportions that puts their well-being at more, rather than less, risk. A little lesson for you all, regulation is not always in your best interest.

Aylan Kurdi's life value was dramatically increased by his visibility, his meme-worthiness, by the ubiquity of his name. It also seemed that he was grieved because he was a young child. In the case of the 2,300 children forcibly taken from their migrating parents in the US, however, perhaps learning from the Aylan Kurdi case, the Homeland Security forces not only dehumanised the children by giving them numbers but, through the simple act of assigning them different numbers to their parents, by definition allowed them to be permanently separable from them and thus much easier to lose. The number, then, makes them appear in the system, by dehumanising and isolating them in such a way as the system can process them in a manner that their parents have no way of tracing. They appear in the system, precisely so that they can then disappear, another brilliant example of discursive violence thanks to retroaction.

The violence of occluded encampment

Other elements of the case follow a similar, regulatory logic of visibility in the data set, invisibility in society at large. The cages they were held in were kept from the media for several months, and even after the story broke, while there were some images released of children in camps, nothing went viral like the Kurdi case. Even the logic of their incarceration has an air of hidden–in–plain–view, facilitating that most noxious of contemporary political values, deniability. It wasn't the Republicans who brought in the legislation, Sessions, Huckabee Sanders and their ilk bleated, but those pesky, evil Democrats. In finally enforcing the letter of the law, the Republicans were merely enacting legislation, not creating it. This was how Huckabee Sanders was able to claim that their actions were 'Biblical,' for which read evil. Even the process of incarceration used laws and regulations as if to accidently result in cruelty to children. As a philosopher I find their syllogistic reasoning as elegant as it is cruel. Migrants are criminals. Criminals are incarcerated. It is cruel to imprison their children along with them. Thus children will be 'held' in 'facilities' until they are 'relocated.' Aristotle would have been proud of such a syllogism.

I think that Richard Parker's piece on a specific camp in Tornillo, Texas, is powerful on this point of using regularity and legal language to hide a state's paedophobia by placing it in plain view, but also behind a shield of denial and occlusion. The camp in question sprung up almost overnight. Constructed of tents, it resembled a state–sanctioned version of our own Jungle camp in Calais. The facility holds hundreds of teenage boys, around 20% of whom have been separated from their parents. Access to the camp is all but impossible. The camp isn't a secret; journalists and senators alike are aware of its existence, but it is clothed in secrecy. Parker speaks interestingly of there being "something strange about a secret facility surrounded by dozens of journalists and camera crews" (Parker 2018). Again this camp is hidden–in–plain–view.

Parker then delves into America's troubled past to question the moniker of "detention facility" given to the camp by the government. Recalling the last times America separated children forcibly from parents and imprisoned them, he has to go back to the racist policies against Native Americans in the 19th century and before that, of course, slavery. Then there were the shameful internment camps full of Japanese during the Second World War, a dark stain on American history: "But even that camp was more humane," Parker muses. "Schooling was provided for children, who were kept with families" (Parker 2018). This leads him to prefer the term internment rather than facility, in that internment

> describes the confinement of prisoners of war, citizens of other nations and political prisoners without trials. With its troops, walls and arrests, the Trump administration is effectively waging war on a comparatively peaceful stretch of its own country … This is a 21st century American internment camp. For children.
>
> *(Parker 2018)*

Parker's rhetorical use of the copula here is simple and powerful, reminiscent of the passionate plea of Karem at the Huckabee Sanders press mauling. What it makes clear is that for all the regulatory language of facilities, processing and so on, surely there is one category of human that has rights to protection above all others: children. A state that forgets this is guilty, by my reckoning, of paedophobia. Yet as the case of child migration from the Calais camp called the Jungle on the UK shores shows, the language of regulation is not only not negated by simple moral imperatives like "suffer the little children," it is often the biological category of 'child' that is the basis for the combative nature of regulation, rhetoric and political action.

4

DEATH ON THE BEACHES

Bioviolence defined

And he grew and grew strong as a boy must grow who does not know that he is learning any lessons, and who has nothing in the world to think of except things to eat.

And what is a man that he should not run with his brothers? I was born in the jungle; I have obeyed the Law of the Jungle; and there is no wolf of ours from whose paws I have not pulled a thorn. Surely they are my brothers!

(Rudyard Kipling, The Jungle Book *2016, pp.9, 21)*

The Jungle Book

If we jump back a couple of years and one ocean, the scandal that broke in the UK about child migrants seems to be primarily organised around the issue of norms which relates directly to the regulatory abuses we highlighted in the previous chapter. At that time, an impromptu, self-assembling holding camp had grown up in Calais called the Jungle. The camp was populated by migrants trying to enter the UK. Many were economic migrants; there were a good number of asylum seekers and, by a conservative estimate, around 15,000 children. Although famously the borders of the UK are defined by its being an island, for the sake of immigration purposes at least, the real border is located in France where applications for entry are processed 'downstream' as securitised immigration parlance has it, creating, of course, a vexed, contested and displaced thick border which, as it thickens, becomes a territory all of its own called the Jungle camp. On a recent trip back from Brussels, my Eurostar trundled through this strange hinterland, outrageously fenced for miles, creating an eerie, post-apocalyptic feel, like a zombie film before the flesh-hungry hordes arrive. The fences were of stark white colour, maybe 3 metres high, following exactly the undulating contours of the northern French landscape sometimes to ridiculous, vertiginous inclines. It recalled nothing so much as the landscape art of Christo, perhaps filtered through a Banksy-shaped lens. As if Christo's inspirational work *Running Fence* had been reimagined for a securitised age.

In the Jungle camp of Calais, primary reason for this incredible, never-reported-on fencing of our national interests, officials and representatives from NGOs tried to work to process applications for entry into the UK. At that time, as I mentioned, thanks to the Dubs agreement, EU treaties and David Cameron's apparent change of heart after the death of Aylan Kurdi, a number of child migrants were given the green light, in principle, to be granted asylum. The total number was minuscule relative to the population of the UK but, in the heated post-Brexit atmosphere stoked by the right-wing press and the irresponsible actions of populist politicians like Farage and Johnson, even one child appeared to be the cause of resentment. And so began a conspiracy, really, to 'out' children entering these shores as being older than they claimed to be. Let's take a headline from *The Star* of November 2016 which screeched "Exposed: Immigrant admits he is 22." Why does this matter exactly? If you allow a number of people to apply for something, here entry into the UK, and some cheat the system, why is this so significant? What precisely does it prove? Didn't you ever steal stationary from work or lie a little on the CV that got you your current job? And who is *The Star* to throw stones at the mendacity of others when the glasshouse of lies they have constructed resembles a thousand crystal palaces stacked on top of each other? If the headline were something to do with the fact that this 'man' has jumped the queue ahead of the 1,000 kids still left in the burning remains of the Jungle, then that might be of interest. But we all know that is not on the minds of the tabloid press. So what is?

Many of us agreed with Gary Lineker, of all people, and Lilly Allen, of all people, that the press coverage was racist, but why is it racist? When you cover a story, you choose an angle. The Jungle is a massive story and has many potential angles. So what you choose to focus on tells your readership what is on your mind. Not in the words you use per se, the tabloids are assiduous in not using racist hate speech which is illegal, but in what your words communicate to your knowing audience beyond their simple message. So when *The Star* finds a 22-year-old pretending to be 18 or *The Sun* puts the words 'children' in inverted commas we have to read between the lines, only slightly, to get to the heart of the matter. Yet at the same time they always have deniability on their side. They are not saying anything racist and they may even be a reporting fact. So if you want to get to the racism of the tabloid press in post-Brexit Britain, you have to ask more complex questions. Let's do that.

Our first question is why were the press covering this minor story when the big story is right there on their doorstep? If you don't want immigrants from the Jungle washing up on our shores, say that, instead of illegally outing what you think must be adults pretending to be children. By the way, this trial by photograph is, as I said, illegal. You can't publish pictures of minors without their consent. And simply stupid, a photo of someone is the last thing you use to determine their age. It is also disrespectful to the authorities in Calais and the NGOs assisting them who have, at their disposal, a vast amount of data that is used to professionally determine the right or not of an asylum seeker. They don't have to rely on photos, they meet the actual child.

It is a minor, silly and actually illegal story, so why is it the lead story and not the wider issue of these abandoned 15,000 kids? Simple, you can't be seen to be picking on kids so you have to try to prove they are not kids so you can pick on them without too much blowback. People love children in the UK just as much as they appear to hate immigrants. If you say 1,000 minors shouldn't be allowed in, then you have to admit to the truth of the matter which is that many Brexiteers suffer from paedophobia. It is obvious that a large socially and politically mixed rump in this country of millions don't want to save the lives of 1,000 kids. Dead simple. We all know that. And most of those are also Brexiteers. That's clear as well. Even though Brexit is about free movement of Europeans and this is about the asylum applications of war refugees, completely different issues, no one thinks the two are separate and many don't actually know the difference. Even if they did, they would choose to turn a blind eye.

So what do you do, Nigel Farages of these isles? You don't want any more immigrants. You have won the battle on one front, Brexit, but for some reason Brexiteers seem unsatisfied with that. One reason may be that Brexiteers don't just dislike the Poles, they remain deeply worried about Syrian refugees as well. They can't deny their need, and in the case of the kids, they really can't, so they focus the entire story on a few who are cheating the system, possibly. That way no one has to talk about the fact that we are legally obligated to accept these kids, that the PM secretly supports this and that in the end the numbers are so small that it will make no difference.

By suggesting these few are cheaters of course, one is being racist. You want your readers to feel comfortable thinking Syrians are not to be trusted, that immigrants are cheats, that some of these cheaters will be cheating you in the UK, that some others will be terrorists and that they don't belong in the UK because we are a nation of non-cheaters. The implication is, all immigrants are potentially dangerous so don't let any in, not even kids, unless they look really young. In that we are basing our decision on how these immigrants look, you are basically saying keep out the ones whom we don't like the look of. There are literally no more steps to take to reveal that this is racist.

Yet the discursive coercion goes deeper than that. What we saw in the case of the US system was a wholesale disregard for immigrant children. In the peadophobic US, it would seem, being a child is not sufficient to protect you from imprisonment, torture or simply being gunned down in the corridors of your school. In the UK we may pride ourselves in not locking child migrants in cages, well done us, but in reality we chose to do something much worse. First, in placing our border 'downstream' in Calais we never had to face accusations of locking up children on British national territory. Second, in choosing to totally neglect the child migrants by leaving them, unprotected, in the Jungle, we actually exposed them to far greater danger than if we had housed them in cages. Third, while the Americans forcibly placed their child migrants with foster families, we left the children of the Jungle to the mercy of those adults who would bully them, steal from them, hurt them, abuse and traffic them. Finally, in a move that is remarkable in its way, the press decided to negate the very status that would be the kids' only saving grace, by questioning their claims to be children at all.

There is, in reality, no such thing as a child; it is just another *dispositifised* subjective construction. It will always be an arbitrary legal category. The word child is a form of figurative language, a synecdoche where the slight nature and emotional immaturity of a human being, also the way they speak, dress and so on, is replaced by one single term: children. To this is then added an arbitrary maximum age, 16 or 18. In the case of asylum seekers, the maximum age of a child is 18. Older than that you are assumed to be an adult and less deserving of our hospitality. Thus there are a series of regulations, measures, words and modes of thinking which stipulate what the norm of child is for asylum purposes. Cruelty to a child migrant is not only dramatically reduced if you show that child to be 22—you have less legal obligations, for example—it also suggests the migrant in question is mendacious and, by a process of infection, starts to undermine the whole brand 'child migrant.' Here then we see a different, more pernicious regulatory process underway. If the US authorities actively hate child migrants, in the UK we pretend to offer a hand of friendship to them, but only on the proviso that they equate with the norm of the good child migrant, a child that must be small, vulnerable and, dare I say it, like Aylan Kurdi, dead and poignant on a far distant beach. The best child migrant is, I am afraid, the young, dead and distant one. The closer the children get to our shores, and the closer their age gets to the maximum, the more our real hatred for them is allowed to show. Indeed we start to hunt them down, using cameras and tabloid journalistic dirty tricks to reveal them as legitimately hateful so that our instinctive hatred towards them is given permission to express itself. After all, if we learnt how to express tacit racism in the form of apparent concern from our national author Rudyard Kipling, we also learnt the law of the jungle from his creation Mowgli. A child left alone in the jungle, he says, becomes strong, in other words a threat, when he is exposed to unconscious radicalisation and forced to live and survive entirely according to his wits.

The coercion of norms 'n' forms

The use of the norm as a tool for regulation is an essential part of contemporary modes of coercion and control. If you are using data to regulate a population for their own good, here the population of migrants in the Jungle, then you will use these regulations to establish some basic data norms. Norms are the names you use to establish different kinds of populations to be processed in different ways. Economic migrants, asylum seekers, Syrians, families, migrants with relatives already in the host country and, of course, children are all norms. On paper, or rather on screens, they allow you to organise the confusing swarm, swarming is a collective defence mechanism in nature against predation, into groups that will enter the process of application for entry into the UK at different stages. What the norms say, in fact, expresses a classic law of every mode of rule by regulation. In a perfect world, all of you could be granted access, but we do not live in a perfect world. We have large populations already in Great Britain straining the services we have to regulate to protect our standard of life. There is also the issue of the terrorist. We need to avoid giving access to our country to them right? All of these provisos pertain to elements beyond a state's control, sizes and types of population, movements of populations and the world or milieu they are moving in also, a political milieu that a state will often present as beyond their control, precisely so they can increase the tools of their control.

As we have limitations of resource and so on, a state argues, we cannot save everyone and so, women and children first or, good migrants only or, Syrians or, in the case of the Dubs agreement, children first. A regulatory norm allows you to literally sort the wheat from the chaff meaning you preclude the entrance of the majority of migrants in the first instance by saying they are not children. Which is a good, exclusionary modality. However, you are left with the problem of those pesky kids, small in number but still unwelcome. Here the beauty of reasoning via norms is revealed. The normative label 'child' which granted entry for a small number so as to exclude larger numbers itself has a set of criteria which admit entrance to the normative population. These criteria are biological and so unquestionable but, in actual fact, all but impossible to prove biologically, depending entirely on documentation that migrants, typically, do not have, such as birth records. You can, then, turn biological determinism against the 'child,' questioning its right to be included in that group. In this way you use the norm to whittle down the small population into even smaller groups, as well as put the seeds of a suggestion into the minds of the larger population, do you love all children or only our own? Are these kids, who have covered thousands of miles and survived on the muddy streets of the Jungle vulnerable or, like our national, racially normalised wild-child Mowgli, feral and hateful or like Kipling's wolf-boy, worryingly strong? Do they really need protection or, schooled and possibly radicalised as they are by our own neglect of them, do we now need protection from them? In a version of Groucho Marx's famous "I wouldn't want to join a club that has me as a member," the very name of the club we devised to protect child migrants is, by suggestion, a solid reason to be more suspicious of children in holding camps than adults. It is the designation [child], meaning to be a normative, protective mode of regulation that, again through that narrativised process of retroaction, based on the fact that they are weaker, which means they also have more to lose and so will say anything, do anything and indeed may be ruthless in all areas simply due to the normative and statistical impossibility of their survival, while their allegiance, as Kipling explains, will not be to King and Country, but to their wolf brothers. To use Butler's terms, yes they are marked by precarity, but they are actually those who have survived their precarity, making them dangerously precocious in the ways of adulthood. Why, you muse, when you see a photo of a mature looking boy from the Middle East in Dover, are you not dead on a beach somewhere? Why, you wonder, did you survive and Aylan did not? How many Aylans, you perhaps ruminate, did you step over to get to Dover beach? Aylan Kurdi, at this point, becomes a regulatory norm all of his own. Aylan is what a truly vulnerable child migrant looks like. The ubiquity of his image becomes a global brand for the archetype or norm of the good, because dead, child migrant. All the rest are suspicious, all the rest are a potential threat, because all the rest are still breathing.

States no longer menace their citizens, rather they regulate them. Although aggressive regulation of the kind the Nazis used can, in certain circumstances, be called violent, on the whole while regulation may be intrusive and your rights of privacy infringed upon, no one in their right mind would call filling out a form a violent mode of coercion. But in a sense a form is much like a gun. Yes I did just say that. The old adage guns don't kill people, people kill people could be applied to form-filling as well. Data gathering, regulation and norms don't cause harm in and of themselves but they facilitate new modes of coercion, aggression and neglect. Forms don't kill people, neither do norms; think of them rather as the trigger of a weapon called the state that can be as lethal when it isn't pulled as it can when it is, when it does nothing rather than during those periods it can be found aggressively attacking.

Indeed, the paradoxical violence of not shooting, of not pulling, of not acting characterises the powers that be in their age-old quest to make you do what they want. In the case of the Grenfell Tower murders, we saw how social housing operates as a pledge on the part of the state to protect the very heart of what it means to be alive: dwelling. In neglecting their residents, in doing nothing, Kensington and Chelsea Council are guilty of the murder of omission or neglect. Here then basic life rights, handed over to power-structures, mean by implication that if those structures fail in their duty of care, they have let you die and are thus culpable at worst, complicit at best.

Next we considered the fiction of universal rights to life. We discovered a law of responsibility, upgrading Butler's thought-provoking but problematic measure of grievability, to reconsider how the value of a life, assumed to be indifferently of equal value, is devalued or dramatically enhanced by the responsibility both of a state to that life and also in terms of how the world responds to the precarity and loss of that life. The danger for states of responsibility is that as a value it is beyond their obsessive control. Social media, the contemporary world of value in terms of response, share or like, is not regulated by any state. Migrant stories can become powerful political narratives requiring governments to find ways of counteracting the bullishness of the child migrant emotional markets, by sowing the seeds of misinformation to make them resemble once more a bear-like recession.

America has chosen a legalistic route to achieve this. They have taken child migrants and created a mass of decriminalised criminals not dissimilar to the constructed category of enemy combatants which allows perpetual incarceration in Guantanamo Bay. The cages and internment camps of Texas are Guantanamo-Lite, child-friendly zones of massification, intended to allow the American population at large to see the children of illegal immigrants as collateral damage. It is not, Trump insists, his fault that the Democrats passed a law criminalising children. It is not his fault that gangs of migrant children form gangs. It is not his fault that the US cannot house a million Dreamers as they are called. It is not his fault that the law is the law. Indeed it is good that it is. Children should be locked up because their parents as so irresponsible as to put them in peril through acts of illegal transmigration. Those cages are there for the protection of kids let down by Democrats and migrant parents, two great evils in this world of ours.

I am never sure if British subtlety is really preferable to American directness. If Trump uses the term 'animals' to described child migrants, Cameron opts for the more indirect 'swarm.' If America locks up over 2,000 children separating them from their parents, Britain instead simply refuses to accept the same number, leaving them without parents on the other side of the channel. While the Trump administration is blatant in its paedophobia, British Brexit culture opts instead to show its hatred and fear by undermining the normative category of 'child migrant' by denying children that come to our shores the right to be children simply because they are tall, gimlet-eyed, insolent of expression, with a furze of hair on their upper-lip. The racist undertones of these assumptions sort of go without saying, one might as well call them 'swarthy youths.'

What is clear is that the European way of doing things shows us a final means by which the powers that be can use coercion, aggression, bullying, xenophobia, paedophobia and neglect, without appearing to. In setting up norms to allow the beneficial control of mass populations of migrants, the very norms and forms that are, on the surface, there for the good of those 'legitimate' migrants, actually open up the doors for a steady erosion of legitimacy through the questioning of a child's membership of that norm. Legitimacy becomes, in this way, not a regulatory measure of norms to allow for the allocation of a quantum of resource to protect, enhance and prolong your life, but the first step in a political process of de-legitimisation as justification for withholding that quantum of resource, such that your life becomes precarious, debased and curtailed. At this point, and here is the cruel irony of the whole process, from anonymous child-norm in the system, you become, gloriously, for a moment, an Aylan Kurdi, mourned by the very world which killed him through neglect. So yes, the form and the norm are triggers of an immense arsenal of resource that is like a weapon running in reverse, yet again retroaction, as in the famous section of Kurt Vonnegut's *Slaughterhouse Five* (Vonnegut 1969), where time runs backwards so that bomber planes miraculously suck ordinance from German cities and the Nazis benevolently release Jews from their concentration camps. In not pulling the trigger, you do nothing, and those humans whose life rights fall out of the norm, and are not then subject to regulation, are simply left to die.

Violence: a regulatory construct

When Foucault began the lecture series in the autumn of 1975, violence was very much on his mind. As the English title of the lectures *Society Must Be Defended* suggests, the central topic of the lectures is war. For Foucault, heavily influenced by Nietzsche, humankind exists in a state of perpetual war such that, even when at peace, we are at war, perhaps even more so. He says, "However far back it goes, historical knowledge discovers only an unending war, or in other words, forces that relate to one another and come into conflict with one another, and the events in which relations of force are decided" (Foucault 2003, pp.172–3). Foucault goes on to claim that history is never able to look down dispassionately on this war because historical knowledge, as a form of knowledge, is actually complicit in the conflict because "knowledge is never anything more than a weapon in a war" (Foucault 2003, p.173). For example, knowledge as statistical norms collated from impassive forms. Yet the very kind of knowledge power that typifies our biopolitical age seems precisely designed to undermine this very statement.

However, what we discovered is that biopolitical knowledge as power, in particular the data-rich regulatory powers of risk assessment and prevention, does not eradicate violence from the state, but rather changes the meaning of violence, deconstructs and reconstructs violence and remakes violence anew. Violence, on this reading, is no longer harm committed against the body through use of force, but duress allowed to happen to bodies and populations through neglect of authority, reading biopolitical compulsion as that of making live, or the forces that sanctify, protect, prolong and enhance the lives of certain citizens in certain states. Violence is, then, nothing more than a regulatory, massifying and normalising *dispositif* whose aim is, what else, to make live, a tricky task in our Age of Terror.

If what Foucault says is true and war is waged through knowledge, then it is no surprise really that knowledge wars, particularly those concerned with the biological right to life, will utilise different weapons but also different kinds of violence. Indeed, one might say that bioviolence is not so much a form of violence, as a mode of interpretation of the knowledge formations and institutions that encapsulate biopower, for even our knowledge, my knowledge is, according to the late, great Foucault, an act of waging war. Which leads us to conclude that violence, before all else, is a form of knowledge, not the application of force, which is all that being a *dispositif* actually means: knowledge integrated into an institutionalised set of processes which coerce subjects into massified classes within which norms can be established and regulated towards.

If I were to conclude that Foucault's most important discovery in the field of violence was that violence is a construct, you may recoil from that statement for several reasons, not least because Foucault himself certainly never goes that far. Suggesting that violence is a construct sounds a little like saying violence doesn't exist; it also seems to belittle victims of violence, making me sound like a member of a privileged class who do not have to live with violence in their daily lives. So let's qualify the statement a little to make it more intelligible and perhaps over time cajole a wider readership into finding it acceptable and communicable. What we are actually saying is that political violence is an essential *dispositif* in the modes of rule that define contemporary, global, neoliberal and late capital power. Unlike philosopher Hannah Arendt in her influential study *On Violence*, where she tries to separate power from violence to the degree that she actually defines the opposite of violence as power rather than nonviolence, in terms of the very biopolitical situation that Arendt herself was intrinsic in defining, biopower is inseparable from bioviolence (Arendt 1970, p.56). This is because Arendt sees violence as something that unquestionably exists, and which can be excluded from political action, and Foucault sees violence as something that only exists because of political action.

If violence then is not so much a construction as a *dispositif* then this means we can avoid the problems of ontological statements which fail to define what violence is, or is not, over and over again in all those books with 'violence' in their titles but which never actually say what they mean by the word, and instead we can focus on the idea of violence as a set of institutions and processes which does something, rather than just *is* something. This is in accord with Foucault's own radical definition of the nature of discursive 'statements' in his remarkable *Archaeology of Knowledge*, as meaningful not in terms of what they say but in terms of the fact that *you* can say *that* in this context at this time and it will be intelligible and communicable among a community such that one can say it is meaningful (Foucault 1972, pp.79–87). In other words, all meaning is political, which is why Foucault defines his own project as the politics of truth.

Violence is not something in the world that powers utilise, rather violence is something that power creates as yet another biopolitical tool of control or *dispositif*. To put it another way, bioviolence is an institution, and as such it behaves in institutional ways typical of biopower. At the same time violence is more complicated in that it is something á la Arendt, that good politics, especially solid *bio*politics should eradicate so, in that sense, it is the *dispositif* that should not be, a kind of self-abnegating process wherein its regulatory powers ought to be mustered to, ostensibly, regulate itself out of existence. It is this tension, between being an essential component of power that denies it, that makes bioviolence both difficult to spot and yet also peculiarly effective. After all, invisibility is an important weapon in the arsenal of the bioviolent state that should not ever be violent.

Bioviolence: an institutional *dispositif*

To sum up, biopower should not be violent. Its basic tenet is that it makes live, which is in a position of contradiction, surely, to the use of violent means which make life intolerable and curtailed. Yet this conception of the state as vital proph-ylaxis and arbiter of perpetual peace, because isn't world peace the easiest way to make live, is the origin of perhaps the greatest spate of genocidal war the West has ever known. These race wars, as Foucault calls them, are the result of the regulatory classification of the human right to life as, initially, universally, indif-ferently the same for all, followed by a necessary stratification of life value, based on a bogus 19th-century science of race.

We saw, however, how race war alone does not describe modern warfare or more widely contemporary acts of coercion. A second form of violence then exists. If a biopolitical state is tasked with making live or letting die, then state neglect is our second kind of aggression. State neglect merges with race war because of the indifferentiation between, let's say, valuable German lives and valuable French ones. This initially facilitated race war, but has subsequently resulted in international treaties meant to protect the sanctity of all human lives. These irksome treaties drag states into conflict not because of a network of legal documents, sovereign war thanks to the treaties of Westphalia, for example, or thanks to racially motivated genocidal wars, the surprising concomitant of 19th-century governmentality, but thanks to an internationally sanctioned demand to protect human life when under threat, even at the expense of national sover-eignty or racial/ethnic difference. If a Syrian child's life is in a state of precarity, it is the duty of the Germans to protect it, in Syria, Lebanon, Turkey, Greece and Macedonia, simply because it is a life, and because Germany is a signatory to the prerequisite international treaties from which it composes its own sense of nationhood and value. If Germany does not protect that Syrian child, it has committed an act of violence by neglect. If Germany turns a blind eye to how that child is mistreated by the French in the Calais holding camps, it is guilty of the violence of complicity. And what is true for Germans is true for the British, the Italians and so on because, you remember, we are all indifferently the same as regards biorights.

The imperative to make life comes with the collateral necessity to let some die. This is a violence of neglect. Who is let to die is the result of classification of life due to the speciation of humans: some are simply more valuable than others because they are more evolved, less degenerate, less animalistic, more civilised, purer of blood and so on. These initial classifications are explicit and genocidal in the last century, but increasingly these days they are of another order. It is not that the Syrian child is first classified as sub-human, quite the opposite, but as that child moves from a theatre of war and enters into a global office of regula-tions, they are increasingly asked to earn or prove their right to life against the limitations and demands of the milieu they are requesting entry into. To do so they are asked to fill out a form, which in a sense is akin to being told to palm a hand grenade and if you could just pull out that little pin here, here, oh yes and here …

Which brings us to our third kind of violence, that of massification. When a state massifies, they use data to allocate citizens into bodies which can be regulated along quasi-scientific lines. At this point governance becomes risk-management rather than rule, or rather rule through risk-management. There are two clearly identifiable risks that structures of power cannot control: the size of their populations and the vagaries of their milieu. Millions of people living in multiple milieus is a political problem. On its own massifying is coercive, of course; you are not asked if you are counted as a refugee, a terrorist or an asylum seeker. If you are a child migrant, you are not asked if you wish to be assessed as such, you are just asked for your data. But massification is also more clearly violent in other ways. For example, in terms of risk, there will always be subjects in that mass who are neglected in favour of the mass or because they might be seen as damaging to the overall mass. Massification then, because it is about inclusion for the sake of regulatory risk-management, is also just as much about exclusion: who is not in the mass, certainly, but also who is in the mass but whose status must be made precarious for the sake of the mass, or who is in the mass but whose presence tips the scales towards greater risk so they need to be excluded from the mass and so on. As our child migrant enters the processes of regulatory classification, is her life worth as much as, say, my own daughter's? She is of course also created as a subject through how she is massified, where she is included in terms of her data, what risks she faces and what risks does she expose us too. Is her life worth the risk to save it, making her, say, a 'good migrant' or not? The processes of massification and classification are interlinked of course, but not quite the same. Massifying implies no judgement beyond inclusion; classification then decides the value of the subject based on which masses she is captured by thanks to her data—data such as age, sex, country of origin, companions, history of association and so on. How she is massified, in other words, is how she will be classified, such that her life will be deemed valuable enough to be part of the make live regulatory processes, rather than the let die, unregulated 'out there.' But she is only massified because she is first classified as a valuable human subject.

Our final mode of violence then is determined by norms. Norms are not laws, although they often form the basis of the crafting of laws. Norms are statistical preferences of behaviour based on observation of populations reacting to their milieu such that risk can be ameliorated for that mass based on an implicit classificatory judgement, their lives should be protected more, because as members of the norm they are the most likely to be responsive to regulation. Norms are, in theory, impassive and neutral theoretical and scientific judgements but, of course, as the very name suggests, they also become ingrained narratives of good behaviour. Norms then become a means of social coercion, demanding that you behave in a certain way or be a certain kind of mass, not because that is the right thing to do morally or politically, but because that is the right thing to do to allow the state to make your life and avoid letting you die. As the name norm suggests, there will be those who are abnormal, and it is usually the abnormal that become the nexus of political decisions of neglect, exclusion, surveillance, coercion and so on.

The child migrant is significant for the manner by which she upsets the norm. As a child she is more pitiable and more vulnerable and so demands more resource and access, yet she is also more susceptible to influence and perhaps unpredictable, she needs more resource upstream, she presents a complexity of massification downstream, for example, proving she is a child, and so on. Her abnormality works in her favour, who doesn't want to save a child, which can become politically uncomfortable. Normative behaviour is an essential component of biopolitical coercion; it is also one of the most common reasons for the violence of the neglect. It is just so much easier, statistically and in terms of regulation, to protect the norm and so much simpler to neglect those deemed as outside those scientifically designated, and thus apolitical, norms.

There you have it then, violence, in biopolitics, is a regulatory *dispositif*, albeit one with a special nature which is that it functions due to the fact that it should not exist giving it that essential biopolitical quality, deniability. It is based on the right to life, which leads to classificatory hierarchies of how much right to life each subject actually has. It cannot be the case that all subjects have the same right to life, although as a bare universal indifferent right that is the case. In an ideal world we all have the same life value, but we live in a non-ideal world of vast numbers migrating through or settling in challenging and impossible to control milieus. To best make sure that the most amount of people have access to make live, a state needs to gather data about you so they can massify you and control that mass in terms of norms. To gain that data, they place you in a mass. These are all coercive processes disguised as benevolent bean-counting for you own good. An imaginary story which is totally convincing as long as you conform with norms.

But when you do not conform with norms, or populations become too unwieldy, or when the milieu becomes too challenging, unstable and unpredictable, then the invisible nature of the soft coercion of biopower becomes visible, violent and contested. In that we live in an Age of Terror, by definition we occupy one of those moments in history where soft persuasion has become insistent coercion that is spilling over to explicit acts of neglect, classification, massification and normalising which make the journey from being scientific to being political, and will eventually end up in what we should call regulatory wars. Which in a nutshell is the definition of bioviolence: the moment when regulation switches from being science to becoming politics. Violence then is a means of regulation—is better a perspective on regulation—such that pervasive regulation becomes invasive, cooperation with classification and massification becomes coercive, when norms alter from being about the good of the many, and start to be seen as to the detriment of the few. In short, contemporary bioviolence is a perspective, a process and a realisation that the regulatory processes of biopower, supposedly about making live, are actually about who they choose to let die.

The glib reaper

And so it was that Grenfell was lost, that Aylan Kurdi died, that the children of the Jungle were trafficked and that 2,000 innocent child migrants were first caged and then carelessly cast, like corn, across the stony ground of a nation that does not want them, lost in the cracks of the very system set up to regulate and massify them. In each of our cases, bioviolence has a particular role to play, not as a form of physical force, so much as an institutionalised process of inclusion, regulation, massification, subjectivation and normalisation. Bioviolence then is not so much a constructed idea, as an embedded *dispositif* or process, and it is in this way that Foucault's work on biopolitics abolished violence. Perhaps abolished is the wrong word; repurposed, reconstructed, relocated and re-affordanced, these all come a little closer. In truth what has happened is that biopolitics has indulged in an entirely new mode of coercion, aggression, threat and harm. Violence is no longer something that one subject does to another or even what a state does to its subjects or other states. Instead *bio*violence is a set of procedures whose wounding and intimidating aspects are accidental concomitants of its well-meaning data-harvest and its sad-eyed admission as the autumn leaves begin to turn and fall that, sniff, this year there will not be quite enough. Someone will have to go hungry, someone will have to be neglected and some of you who shouldn't even be here will have to be cast out. It is this entirely novel, mostly occluded, intentionally tedious, collateralist mode of coercion that allows the powers that be to make us do what they want, but it is a kind of violence by definition, that doesn't even exist, and so is all but impossible to perceive. Yet there are always glimpses to be caught, of the great figurehead of bioviolence, not the grim but rather the benevolent, if at times inattentive, reaper that is the compelling subject of one of our greatest ever poems, Keats' "Ode to Autumn." Speaking of our glib reaper, Keats sings:

> Who hath not seen thee oft amid thy store?
> Sometimes whoever seeks abroad may find
> Thee sitting careless on a granary floor,
> Thy hair soft-lifted by the winnowing wind,
> Or on a half-reap'd furrow sound asleep,
> Drowsed with the fume of poppies, why thy hook
> Spare the next swath and all its twinèd flowers.
>
> *(Keats in Wu 2012, p.1489)*

I think such sublime poesy contains within it two powerful images of global bioviolence. We are all sitting carelessly on our granary floors as the world around us goes hungry, and our nations appear asleep and harmless on the half-cut harvest, their reaping hooks innocuous by our recumbent bodies and by this very inaction, thanks indeed to the whole myth of the harmlessness of the contemporary, biopolitical process of governmental rule for the sake of well-being, the next swath is being lost, and the next, its twinèd flowers, all those migrant children, left to perish, precisely because we have chosen not to gather them into the great storehouse of rights we call advanced democracy.

PART TWO

Humanimals and bare life

5

#HARAMBE AND THE CONSTRUCTION OF LIFE

It was a busy day at the Cincinnati Zoo, 28 May 2016. Three-year-old Isiah Gregg was with his family enjoying the large gorilla enclosure. Isiah decided he want to get in with those majestic primates, so he climbed a fence and pushed his way through some bushes, before falling 15 feet into a moat that surrounded the exhibit. Thankfully he survived this heavy fall and almost immediately zoo-keepers were alerted. On arrival, they gave a prearranged signal to the gorillas to go inside their dens. The females complied, but one large male ignored the prompt and instead dropped down into the moat to investigate the small intruder, following a predetermined pattern of behaviour perfectly in keeping with the gorilla's genetic demands, behavioural norms and environmental situation. Taking Isiah by the foot, the male gorilla dragged him roughly through the moat water, clearly endangering the boy's life. And yet the same gorilla, at another point, appeared to nurse and protect the child. Make no mistake, however, there was nothing either cruel or caring about the animal's behaviour. As (Litchfield 2016) noted at the time, infanticide is a common feature of gorilla life, as is aggression towards outsiders. Both are strategies that allow males to protect and enhance the gene pool of the troop. It was, in effect, the gorilla's genes that were dictating the scene as it played out in front of an aghast audience above, an audience, however, not so appalled as to forget to film the incident and share it on Facebook and Twitter.

You might call the gorilla's response an example of necessary violence. Not necessary in the way that governments use the term when they justify their invasion of weak countries like Iraq or kill their own citizens fearing they may be terrorists, but in a more philosophical and Darwinian sense of the word. The gorilla had to attack Isiah, because in terms of its genetically determined behavioural patterns, to do otherwise would mean making a choice, the likes of which is far beyond the ken of any other animal than ourselves, as far as we are aware. This choice, to countermand the survivalist demands of one's biological–cognitive–behavioural make-up, is impossible for any animal except those which, around 70,000 years ago, were able to supersede the dictates of their genes and make decisions that had more to do with their immediate desires, than with the deep structures of their biological construction. If the gorilla really had no option when it came to its attack on Isiah Gregg, it appeared that the zoo authorities were also left with hands tied. Harambe the gorilla was shot dead, so that Isiah Gregg could be returned to his parents, relatively unharmed.

#Harambe

This incident is by no means the only case of a large mammal held in captivity that has been killed of late because it threatened a human, but it became an archetypal instance thanks to social media meme culture. In a piece written in *The Guardian* in August 2016, four months after the incident, Elena Cresci gives a light-hearted run-through of the extended afterlife of the #Harambe meme, which began with explosions of fury around the killing of the gorilla that simply refused to then dissipate, as is usually the case with memes that are typified by a combination of humour, tastelessness and evanescence. The meme spawned innumerable parodies, impinged on American and even Australian politics, and eventually led to the closure of the Cincinnati Zoo social media platforms because the workers there found the whole appropriation of the incident too upsetting. "Long to short," Cresci concludes, "Harambe lived on in the memes" (Cresci 2016).

From the initial exposition of clicktivism to the continuation of the #Harambe meme for the entirety of 2016, it is clear that Harambe came to stand for a set of issues which has transformed that lowland male gorilla into something more than an animal, something approaching a person. As Harambe cheated his untimely death and lived on in the memes, the essence of his life altered from animal to something else in a fashion that is profoundly revealing of where we stand on the biopolitical issue of human rights to life. #Harambe transformed an unknown animal into a nexus for contemporary anxieties about animal violence, animal rights, the limits of human, race and finally technology. It is perhaps no wonder we found that noble beast so hard to let go. Long to short, throughout 2016 we found new ways to grieve an animal until that beast's grievability, to use Butler's term, augmented its value to such a degree that I think it is safe to say, Harambe ended the year more human than his victim, Isiah Gregg, and certainly the victim's family. We also investigated new methods for what philosophers would call ontological potential. The appending of that little hashtag took a gorilla and made it into something else, something between animal and human, something we are calling a humanimal.

One of the initial reasons for the power of the #Harambe meme was access. As has increasingly been the case in the past lustrum, the entire incident was filmed on the smartphones of onlookers, which was then repeatedly shared online. As this imagery of Harambe and Isiah spread across social media and the shooting of Harambe was debated via various memes and modes of innovative, if suspect, clicktivism throughout the digital, global *agora*, one could almost plot in real time the digital transformation of Harambe from a mere animal into a human–animal cross-breed. Harambe, in death, came increasingly to occupy a hybridised or suspended state between animal and human, which appeared to retroactively increase the value of his now-squandered life. With remarkable rapidity, thanks to the feverish commitment that keyboard warriors, slacktivists and trolls have towards the augmentation and dissemination of their thoughtless outrage (does digital rage indeed ever sleep?), the killing of this particular gorilla caused a typhoon across the Twitter sphere and a frenzy on Facebook. If Harambe's promotion to personhood was thanks in part to Butler's idea of human value defined by grievability, what Butler does not grasp is a second affective state essential to subjective value in our age of responsibility, namely, mockability. Harambe was both a serious subject of concern, how we treat intelligent animals in zoos, and an endless source of jokes, lampooning the self-righteousness of the liberal animal–righters, while at the same time siding with them in terms of the suspect morality of keeping amazing animals in crappy enclosures for us to gawp at.

More than murder

This volatile mix of moral panic and merciless satire defines the nature of contemporary online discursive violence, defined by the term 'trolls' (Phillips 2015; Ronson 2015), and cannot be ignored as we try to get a grip on the precise nature of bioviolence or for that matter can the retroactive reanimation of a dead animal thanks to digitisation. Harambe was dead yet lived on, in fact becoming more in death than he ever was in life, suggesting that the hashtag not only confers a certain affective existence, albeit one that will be taken too seriously and not seriously enough at one and the same time, but also the potential to break the final frontier in biopower: immortality. Biopower's injunction to make live offers first to protect your biological existence, then to enhance its quality so as to finally extend it as far as is possible. The natural end point of this logic is immortality and certainly the hashtag raised Harambe from the dead, resulting in a zombie ontology that dragged itself well into the late summer of 2016. This process adds a whole universe of extra dimension to our initial consideration of digitised responsibility as a driver of upticks in life value that we addressed when considering the other animal raised from the dead by the net, namely Aylan Kurdi.

What was clear during the relatively brief initial period of the phenomenon was that for large numbers of vocal protestors, Harambe's life was worth more than other animals, as much as some humans, and perhaps, by implication, even more than the life of Isiah, the boy for whom the beast was sacrificed. Phrases like 'worse than murder' regularly began to appear on the #Harambe Facebook page which, at one point, had 150,000 members. Meaning at times Harambe, that lowland gorilla, presented in the minds of many as more-than-human, his death a unique legal category of violence for which we as yet lack the legal, regulatory vocabulary. 'More than murder,' the phrase hints at a mode of violence that exceeds normal human cruelty, perhaps a form of killing that, in its severity and moral vacuity, has the capacity to simultaneously destroy its victim and, in some way, by the same gesture, make it sacred.

The complex combination of animal rights, legal excess and sacrifice, for to sacrifice means to make sacred through violent separation, provides us with a kind of litmus test, or a better genetic swab, from which we can ascertain where the human stands in relation to the animal in terms of violence these days. In particular, if bioviolence is the result of biorights to life, transforming the discourse of violence from punitive to regulatory, as we have argued thus far, then the relation of the human to its animalistic life, in a century where genetic engineering, impending data and AI singularity, now-inevitable ecological disaster and a groundswell of net activism arguing for the extension of human rights to certain, perhaps all, animals, is surely where we must begin in our quest for the meaning of bioviolence. Hashtag Harambe, in other words, was one of the first truly significant meme texts of our current digital lustrum, and while it spoke to many disparate topics, as memes by definition tend to do, its overriding message was simple: the human right to life extends beyond the human, questions the concepts of rights and has no agreed-upon definition of what life actually consists of. In talking about shooting that gorilla, we collectively put a bullet in the *corpus* of the biopolitical state and damaged our own self-conception along the way. But how, it was just an animal after all, and we kill them in their millions every single day? The answer can only be found in a deeper understanding of the enigma of what I am urging you to think of as bioviolence.

Animal biorights

Bioviolence, you must recall is, in principle, impossible according to Foucault's initial formulation of biopower. To therefore account for the continued existence of violence in the world, Foucault had to think again about how biopower, which in principle is the eradication of violence in favour of preventative regulation, leads to, for example, genocidal world wars. His eventual answer, race, is, regrettably, all too relevant to the Harambe story, but that comes later. Our first question is rather to consider the problematics of the bioright to life and the claim by so many that it should have been extended to at least one non-human beast. Harambe's ability to live on as a meme raises a number of complex questions around our presupposition of the nature of life. Harambe's life, for example, is animal, so not protected by biorights. Yet in death his life was given a status that could be more-than-human, his killing being seen as more than murder, which means he exceeds the judicial realm not by being excluded from it, like all other animals, but by travelling through the entire legal architecture so as to exit it on the other side into a new, post-legal territory. It is as if, in death, through the net, he was handed the keys to the gates of the zoo and took off for pastures new.

More than this, his life, his extended life, is, thanks to certain discursive practices—being given a name, emotional rituals as it is clear he was grieved, and finally digital augmentation, he not only lived on digitally, he was not truly alive in the proto-human sense, that is in such a way as this life is sacred and pro-tected by universal legal rights, until he had died and been reborn online—was becoming or even exceeding the human. His augmented, grievable, responsible, digitised afterlife was, in other words, based on a discursive construction of a presumed biological truth: his life, in being taken, is worth as much if not more, as the life, say, of his 'victim.' #Harambe then is more than just a passing fad; it speaks to a fracture in our contemporary self-conception not just in terms of what it means to be human, a popular parlour game that the West has been playing for generations, but what it means to be alive or, more specifically, the significance of the granting of possession of perhaps the ultimate presupposition of all human existence: life! What, indeed, is life, when did it begin and of what is it composed, that it is now deemed so workaday, and yet of such incredible value? If we can trace, in just a few short months, the construction of a new kind of life, Harambe-life, can we do the same over longer periods in terms of our own constructed idea of the one non-constructed essential to human existence, our universal right to life?

The true history of 'life'

Most studies of the history of life begin around 3.8 billion years ago when a single cell organism experienced a dramatic error of replication and instead of splitting into two organisms, as it was genetically fated to do, became subdivided within the same corporeal confines and yet did not perish. In fact not only did the organism not perish, it began to thrive. Two cells soon proved themselves better than one, in terms of the absorption of resource, and soon those bi-cellular organisms began to better their mono-cellular cousins. Twice as many cells, all already carrying the genetic mutation that led to that initial separation, meant twice as many opportunities for further divisions, bi-cellular extravagancies giv-ing way to quadri-cellular baroque masterpieces and so on. Molecular organisms were 'born'; life on earth began. But is that ancient, multi-cellular organism that can be described as molecular, and which can replicate, passing on the infor-mation in each cell that permits and encourages further non-lethal divisions, information we now call genetic, really what we mean and understand by the term 'life'? Which, in truth, is more recognisable as a life to you right now, a billions-year-old molecule or Harambe the lowland gorilla?

After dipping its toe in the primeval swamp, the story of life usually moves rapidly towards complex organisms until it arrives, breathless, at one particu-lar, special species, Homo sapiens, which emerged around 70 millennia ago, although that figure tends annually to alter. At this moment, according to Yuval

Noah Harari's bestselling book at least, a second transformative event in the history of life began. He calls it the "cognitive revolution" where one species on earth began to form something we call cultures (Harari 2011, pp.3–86). On this reading the progress of life consists of two, temporally unbalanced ages: the molecular and the cognitive. The first commences life in terms of genetic necessity; the second invents 'human' life as that which prospers due to cultural desire, often thanks to, but increasingly at the expense of, our genetically encoded micro-fascisms. So it would appear that we have, at the very least, two kinds of life: life per se, and 'life' as the constructed self-conscious idea of life, created by human culture, from about 70,000 years ago.

Not only does this split life into two, diametrically opposed concepts, there is also a destabilising temporal disjuncture to contend with as well, in that scientific life precedes cultural life by billions of years, but was not discovered until the 19th century, by which time human cultures around the globe had all had a chance to give their version of what life is for 70 millennia. What this results in, in practice, is that culture had developed 70 millennia of desire around what we, as cultures, need life to be, for cultural not survivalist reasons, such that when the data finally came through as to the origins of 'life,' the choice to call those rather dreary molecular organisms 'living beings' was preselected. The result is two distinct phenomena: a cultural complex called human life and a scientific one that chose the term 'life' to describe what happened in the primordial soup, so as to be able to communicate to the culture, to participate in conversations by using a common language and, dare I suggest, to make obscure scientific discoveries appear of philosophical, even ontological, import. In the same way that Christian rituals were grafted on to already existing pagan ones, science has repeatedly appropriated the language of the pre-scientific to help its concepts bed down more easily. No more so than in the made-up concept of life.

For you see, scientifically speaking, there remains no actual, fully agreed-upon definition of life or indeed what its base unit can be said to consist of. Even Richard Dawkins, zealous defender of the doctrine of genetic evolutionary theory, has the decency to admit that the equation of life with genetic material is to some degree just an assumption, that the gene is taken as the smallest unit of life simply out of convenience, and further study may reveal that genes are just one of an infinite number of phenomena that manifest the true law of existence, what he calls the replicator principle (Dawkins 1989, pp.12–20). All of which combined means those lovely potted-histories of life on earth that head up any number of popular science bestsellers are at best, simplistic, at worst, representative of intellectual failure at a somewhat shameful level. For the truth is not that there was such a thing as life that began 3.8 billion years ago, and we recently discovered all about that, but rather, in a Foucauldian vein, there already existed regulatory institutions and *dispositifs* for whom the term 'life' was an essential component of self-justification including science, who then rapidly seized on the latest genetic data to found their essentialisation of a biological truth that supported a set of processes and normative regulations that already existed. Life, then, peered at through this more nuanced lens, certainly did not begin billions of years ago, but can only be located as either a product of self-consciousness or our cultural desires. Life announced itself as a worthy topic of thought and conversation somewhere between 70 and 30,000 years ago. By the time history encountered this concept, with the Greeks, it would have surely experienced tens of millennia of discursive chit-chat, all of which fed into a Greek conception of the human, the animal and life that we are still unpicking today.

Zoon Logon Echon

Since the Greeks, it has been clear that humans are animals or have an animal-istic element, but also that they are more than that, are in possession of that extra something that defines them as '*zoon logon echon*' or 'a living thing using language' as Aristotle defined us all those centuries ago (Watkin 2014, p.111; Agamben 1993, p.156). This realisation was probably a central component of what Harari calls the cognitive revolution, a discombobulation that puts an end to human dependency on evolutionary needs through what we might call the last mutation, from which a complex brain somehow evolved the capacity for self-consciousness, allowing humans to make decisions about their lives not sim-ply dictated by instinct and genetic selfishness alone. Historically it has been this human cognitive and cultural exceptionalism that has occupied our massive minds. We might call this the age of anthropomorphism.

However, since Darwin's theories of evolution gained traction about 150 years ago, Western culture has increasingly felt the pull of a powerful zoomorphism with our knowledge of genetics and the brain making it more and more the case that our arrogant exceptionalism resembles a vast tide that has finally turned, placing us on the cusp of a new wave of discoveries that are slowly washing away our self-conscious difference to the rest of those ambulatory beasts out there we generally treat so contemptuously, as waves around the world wash away the dreams of countless children, who thought the castles on which they had lavished such care would last forever. This, at least, is the hope of Harari's innovative representation of the human as a self-aggrandising, but ultimately lucky, bottom-feeder of the great savannahs of yore (Harari 2011, p.4). Indeed you might summarise the work of Dawkins, Harari and their ilk as typical of a movement towards human normalism which is pointedly Foucauldian. As sci-ence employs great storytellers to convince us that our specialness is not born out by the data, we enter the last, great phase of biopolitical regulation where norms are extended way beyond human culture, where indeed culture itself is normal-ised along genetic lines back into cruel numbers game of survival.

The pathogen of anthropomorphism

Aristotle's famous observation of exception, we *are* animals but we also have speech, was one that initially placed us above the animal kingdom, a position we have been holding on to for a good long time. But what is speech anyway, if not a tool of self-consciousness? In that many animals possess language of some order; our exceptionalism is not determined by the possession of language per se, rather it is what we did with language that matters. We used our words to invent the idea of an animal, precisely so that we could then define ourselves as different from, and superior to, those creatures, because we were animals with something more. You might want to think of this in terms of sticks, indeed why wouldn't you? Apes use sticks, birds weave with sticks and so tool-making is not the preserve of cognitively advanced human animals. Rather what sets us apart is what we used those tools for, specifically making more complex tools, such that we become not the tool-using but the tool-making animal. In both examples, therefore, self-awareness is not sufficient for our understanding of the human and animal division; the cognitive revolution is not the origin of our exceptionalism rather that resides within our cultural choices or, not with our tools, but with our tool-making tools, of which our self-differentiation from animals has proven to be one of the most powerful.

The moment we used speech, specifically narrative and argument, to ruminate on our exceptional animality, yes, we elevated ourselves, seemingly forever, above all other primates, but at what cost? For our initial elevation, like some fascinating late 19th-century psychodrama, was indebted to a secret debasement that we all knew would one day come knocking, demanding just restitution. A shameful flaw was inserted into all of us that insists on 'animal' as a word, a discursive construct, a figure of speech. Jacques Derrida puts it well I think when he describes the idea of the animal as simply "a word that men have given themselves the right to give … They have given themselves the word in order to corral a large number of living beings within a single concept: 'the animal' they say" (Cited in Bourke 2011, p.24). But in permitting ourselves the right to say animal to all those other beasts, it seems we could not help but be self-aware of the infection of our humanity that this entailed. For example, as we are the only animal that has speech, then we are the only animal able to say we are not an animal, because separating ourselves from animals is something only speech is capable of. Animals have no self-conception of being animals, nor do they have language sufficient to debate that point or, to put it another way, there is nothing more human than the idea of the animal.

At the precise moment we emerged from our animality thanks to this differentiation, what philosopher Giorgio Agamben calls our unique event of anthropogenesis (Agamben 2011a, p.251; 2011b, p.69), we introduced a pathogen into the human body of knowledge around our self-conception. If we are Aristotle's *zoon logon echon*, then we are the living thing using language to both differentiate ourselves from animals and at the same time admit that what sets us apart, language, is what drags us back down onto those plains of eternal, bestial conflict. To say we are human is tantamount to insisting we are not animals, which becomes an admission that we are but animals, animals with language, language as a mode of self-conscious, self-construction and deconstruction (Agamben

2004). In an observation that appears to be increasingly the case with all fundamental human categories, the distinction of human and animal demands a relational difference between human and animal; we are like them only exceptionally better, that, over time, obfuscates the essential sharpness of division we were looking for, such that the difference between human and animal results in an essential indistinction, human–animals, at precisely the moment when we are trying to differentiate, once and for all, the human *from* the animal.

As is the case with certain infections, the disease of the human–animal indistinction took quite some time to take hold of the organism, its effects manifesting for centuries in the form of inconvenient, but far from life-threatening symptoms: a kind of ontological indigestion or anthropological chronic fatigue syndrome. As philosopher Oxana Timofeeva admits, for the most part, humans have tended to describe the animal world in anthropomorphic terms, as a lesser version of our own, so that each mention of the animal was a means of humanising them rather than animalising us. Certainly this appears true of the Greeks she contends. The whole point of Ovid's *Metamorphosis* was not to show how close we are to animals, she says, but to make certain animals seem more like us (Timofeeva 2018).

Yet always ensconced within the historical anthropomorphism of the West, we can see the effects of the virus of *zoon logon echon* slowly infecting our every cell. In our fascination with the animal kingdom and our presentation of that kingdom as emotionally akin to our own existence, we were constantly raising certain animals up, while at the same time debasing the brand of human—our language, our culture, our emotions—by letting animals as lowly as pigs and dogs borrow it. If we are animals that 'use' speech then through our utilisation of speech, in particular literature, we habitually construct animals that are 'using' our qualities in the many famous stories from Ovid and Aesop to Orwell and Kafka that capitalise on anthropomorphism as some kind of allegorical key to unlocking the mysteries of human being or politics. Yet this was, for the most part, a slow, malingering malady, whose symptoms could be managed until, that is, there occurred a scientific discovery of such magnitude that it would alter our self-consciousness and our culture forever and have the power to not just halt anthropomorphism but, in one brutal gesture, reverse it.

The Darwinian revolution inaugurated a new zoomorphic relation between human and animals that could not help but impact on bioviolence, it being the regulatory violence of the neglect of human life, such that, in becoming just one more evolving life, our vital spark is, by definition, ultimately reduced to just another form of animal life. In a sense, contemporary biopower can be defined as the regulation between two opposing discursive forms, the enlightenment right to life and Darwinian indifferentiation of life on earth, as a means of establishing an essential difference between human and animal life rights, on the back of scientific evidence that seems to claim quite the opposite. At times this ontological fudge holds in place, at others, the mask slips and we see the simian stain indelibly smeared across our skulls. During these moments of life crisis, how states behave inadvertently lays their mechanisms bare for all to see, as if in holding up the mask with one hand, they have to let their trousers slip with the other. One such bathetic moment of human self-assertion married to embarrassment was our response to the shooting of Harambe the lowland gorilla.

The race war of petitions

The vitriol of the trolls was initially directed at the Cincinnati Zoo. Although Cincinnati Zoo is a research institution potentially involved in saving the entire gorilla species, the killing of Harambe was seen in those first days after the animal's death as an act of gross violence on their part. In that we kill animals in their millions every day, and that our consumerism and political complicity means we are all part-guilty of the single factor that threatens every species on the planet, destruction of habitat, then why did Harambe attain special status and why was the zoo seen as culpable, when it is obvious that they have done more to save gorillas than any of the 150k followers of a Facebook page? The answer lies in questions of animality and race, as soon became apparent as we entered the second phase of the Harambe story, what must be called the war of the petitions.

After the death of Harambe, a lady called, of all things, Sheila Hurt, was so incensed that she was roused into a bout of internet slacktivism. She put up a petition on Change.org calling for legal action. Not against the zookeepers themselves, for the act of killing Harambe, but against the parents of Isiah Gregg, demanding they "be held accountable for lack of supervision and negligence that caused Harambe to lose his life" (www.change.org/p/cincinnati-zoo-justice-for-harambe). The petition further stated that the boy's parents should be investigated by the authorities, because the parents' alleged negligence at the zoo was potentially "reflective of the child's home situation" (www.change.org/p/cincinnati-zoo-justice-for-harambe). Not only did this petition alter the terms of the debate from blame apportioned to the zoo, to the culpability of the bad parent, it also touched a nerve, gaining half a million signatures and igniting an already tinder-dry situation around questions of race in the US, fanned by salacious reports in the media in the US and the UK as to the criminal history of boy's father.

Because, you see, Isiah Gregg was black. And his father had a criminal conviction. Meaning, according to the tone of much right-wing commentary, they kind of got what was coming to them? Thus questions as to how Isiah got into the enclosure shifted from the limitations of the barriers used in the zoo to the responsibility of parents to keep an eye on their children, and the implication that black parents don't generally do a good job of that.

Although in a statement made later when the petition was closed, Sheila Hurt appeared to deplore the racialisation of the issue (www.change.org/p/cincinnati-zoo-justice-for-harambe), it was clear that blaming the parents simply gave vent to a presupposition that was already present in the US culture. It also resulted in a brief investigation of the Gregg family by the cops, and a nice cosy visit from socials services to their house. During the inevitable enquiry that followed, the enquiry is the bioviolent weapon of choice for regulation, it was made clear that the police were not going to charge the family for negligence and that their much debated 'home situation' could be given a glowing bill of health (BBC, 1 June 2016). This was surely one of the most notable moments of contemporary biopower during the whole sorry episode. The regulatory authorities, social workers, back-stopped by the punitive threat of the police, are given access to the domestic, private realm of family life to adjudicate on whether the said family fits the norms of human behaviour such that they can be exonerated of the death of an animal. Foucault predicted the influx of beneficial regulatory experts as methods of shifting legal judgement away from the crime towards the life of the criminal in his groundbreaking *Discipline and Punish* where he famously lambasts the so-called expert opinion as just another mode of state regulation. What he could not have predicted, however, was that regulatory control would be driven by a mode of massification due to norms that itself exceeds the control of states, agencies and experts alike, namely, the internet.

Yet it makes absolute sense. Who is in the best position to determine norms after all, observers or participants? What is a better way to judge norms of behaviour than to allow entire populations to publish, share, debate and attack each other's predilections, assumptions, prejudices and emotions and then simply respond to that? What the net proved, in this case and in numerous others since, not least the election of Trump, is that biopower has reached such a state of saturation that regulatory agencies needs must take a back seat to a massified online population who are regulating themselves, and each other, through their online participation. The mass demanded the regulatory testing of the Gregg family, the authorities were therefore responding not to the demands of a state that wishes to regulate a population, but a population that is demanding that a state regulate them, or at least some of them, namely, the poor, the black, the criminalised and the fertile.

For what was the message that was given out when the police and social services began dancing to the tune of the mob, other than poor black folks with four kids and criminal records are not good enough to visit zoos, because their home situation will manifest itself in bad examples of public behaviour and someone may get hurt? And who is that someone? Isiah Gregg, the three-year-old black child who statistically will grow up to be the most observed, abused and criminalised subject in any advanced democracy, or Harambe, the universally mourned gorilla? I think we all know the answer to this and certainly the Twittertariat did, for Hurt's petition's success immediately spawned a counter-petition calling for the first petition to be closed down on grounds of racism, opening up a new front in the ongoing race war that defines American political life.

6
HUMANIMALS AND THE ABOLITION OF LIFE

How did the death of Harambe lend itself so readily to accusations of racism? The most obvious and facetious answer, I suppose, is: isn't everything ultimately about race, stateside? However, thanks to philosophy, we now have in our possession a more powerful and revealing proposition do we not? First, we can say, after Foucault, that 'race' is the basis for the construction of the concept or discourse of the human as in sacred possession of the right to life, the foundation for modern biopower. If you recall, the process of specie-fication, begun around the 17th but which exploded in the mid-19th century, thanks to Darwin, social Darwinism and the bogus race sciences that subsequently emerged, developed a fictive hierarchy of classification of human 'races' with some being seen as more 'degenerate' than others, coming to be seen as a threat to the future success of the human race's blood purity (Esposito 2008, pp.110–45). This in turn resulted in the world race wars of the last century, with the Nazis being foremost in terms of using concepts like race, blood, purity and degeneration to justify a genocidal war initially against Jews, Roma, Slavs and so on.

Specie-fication, the fake assigning of race to Homo sapiens apparently backed-up by evolutionary science, facilitates the idea of a kind of genetic superiority for the human that also ties it in to the primates of our past, which allows for the construction of the idea of a racial hierarchy of degeneration that Darwin, to some degree, fuelled. This mode of racial classification is a necessary differentiation due to the indifference of the basic human right to life which, in valuing all humans as equal, creates problems for states that would use violence against humans to further their ambitions. Or put more simply, in being forced to give all humans equal life rights due to the development of otherwise impossible to control mass populations, states then had to find ways to differentiate these equal masses, to justify internal and external forays into necessary violence.

If we accept that the American state is, and has been, at war with its black population for generations, while at the same time consistently claiming to be the cradle of universal human rights, which are nothing other than the right to life written in different ways, then modes of internal differentiation are clearly needed to justify their treatment of the African–American population. American history has indeed abounded in a richly perverse vocabulary of regulatory methods to make it clear that African Americans are different and inferior to the rest of the population. All Americans are fluent in this language of racial segregation, as they are all native speakers. They know, for example, that yes, for many, black families are to be less trusted in public spaces than white families because their socio-economic domestic problems will be carried over into other arenas making them a regulatory abnormality. Indeed, the question of African Americans in public spaces is a profoundly vexed one, involving ghettos, gated communities, Broken Windows stop and search powers, modes of cultural representation, incarceration and, of course, the systematic gunning down of black males by a predominantly racist police force. If, the argument goes, the zoo had in place all the correct protections and procedures for their gorilla exhibit, then the Harambe incident can only be the fault of parents who have placed themselves outside regulatory norms of good behaviour, such as keeping an eye on their lively three-year-old, because, and let's be frank about this, they have too many children, an issue pertaining to biopolitical regulatory eugenics not lost on black radicals like Public Enemy who named one of their albums *Fear of a Black Planet* (Public Enemy 1990). And so it is that 'black folks' as a fake race can be mapped onto gorillas in ways which are shocking but, nonetheless, impossible to ignore. Leading to a terrifying series of implied, racial comparators. Gorillas should not be kept in cages and black families should not be let out into the open. Gorillas should be protected to ensure their gene-pool and numbers are strengthened; black families should be castigated for having more kids than they can look after. And so on. That's what the war of the petitions was debating, without ever saying it outright, deniability yet again. The petitioners didn't need to be explicit, it was all written out in the unspoken vocabulary of American, regulatory race violence.

Into the enclosure: human non-relation with the animal

But it goes deeper than that doesn't it? We can't ignore the fact that Harambe was a gorilla, that Darwin's theory was lampooned in the press of his time as 'monkey theory,' that monkey is a racist term against black men and women the world over and that the petition seemed more interested in the life of a gorilla than that of a black child. In other words, the personification of Harambe went hand in paw with an animalisation through association of the Greggs that is typical of the opening shots of any race war. Philosopher Andrew Benjamin in his study *Of Jews and Animals*, for example, is concerned with how Jews came to be vilified by European culture through being associated with beasts. He traces the philosophical history of the animal in terms of it being *without relation* (Benjamin 2010, p.34) or what Alain Badiou calls the non-relational (Badiou 2005, p.186; Watkin 2017, pp.10–11). By that he means that the animal is placed not just at one remove from us, a distant cousin that we have outgrown, but at the other side of a permanent and uncrossable abyss, rather like the moat of the gorilla enclosure at Cincinnati Zoo was intended to be. The animal is where the human must not and indeed cannot go: into the enclosure.

It is, I think, the non-relational nature of the constructed idea of the animal that is crucial to our understanding of violence and, by definition, who we are. Yes, we come from the animal, true we also invented the "figure of the animal" as Benjamin calls it (Benjamin 2010, p.34), but precisely as that which we have no relation to. Ironically, the more we concede that we are special animals, and the tendency we have to treat the despised other as an animal, the more we demonstrate that the animal exists precisely as that from whence we came, that is within us, and which for many of us will be our fate, such that we have sacrificed that part of us in order to live. It is typical of the kind of apotropaicism our culture abounds in, tantamount to saying we must construct the idea of a non-relational and thus animal life, precisely so that we can draw clear water between human and animal life, such that we can define our life, in relation to the non-relational difference between us and them. This is, after all, the very dynamic of post-Darwinian zoomorphism, bringing animals close by keeping them separate, as well as zoos, and, for that matter, inner-city ghettos and holding camps the world over. As we shall come to see in the second part of this chapter it is the paradox of the non-relational, bringing the other close by permanently excluding them, pushing the other away, through the ritualised act of including them as the excluded that, according to Agamben, is not only the basis of biopolitics, but the essence of bioviolence as well.

Sticking for now with Benjamin, however, he argues that racist biopolitical discourse has consistently defined the animal as that within us that we all put aside in order to live as humans, with the process of 'putting aside' the abject, as Kristeva famously describes it (Kristeva 1982), here often a euphemism for killing. There is nothing more non-relational than the living human and their dead prey, nor is there anything more intimate for, as the story of Harambe shows, humanimals, those queer beasts suspended between the differentiation of the human and the animal, stalking our every waking hour and populating our nightmares and our dreams. Benjamin's study of anti-Semitism comes to see the paradox of the non-relational relation between humans and beasts as a means of reversing all those centuries of anthropomorphism, demoting certain humans back to the status of the animal to rob them of the very relations to states, subjects, laws and rights that protect their humanised lives. The result is a combination of a fake scientific classification of race which allows states to push certain human masses towards bestiality so that the non-relational nature of those creatures provides enough emotional, moral and political distance that when the state then opts to genocidalise their relation to the said group, it will, by then, appear to most to be just another unpleasant but necessary day at the abattoir.

Our analysis of Harambe and race makes use of some of this reasoning, but it also appears to run in the other direction, concerned as it is with the according of the accoutrements of human existence to an animal such that this chosen beast becomes problematically relational and, in so doing, undermines our sense of self and our hidden assumptions about degeneration, regulation and race. It is significant, surely, that to raise Harambe up from beast to humanimal, the Gregg family, and more widely the 'black family,' has to be debased because specie-fication is the prelude to classification or the imposition of a hierarchy of lives onto the otherwise flat indeterminacy right to life in general. If gorillas get more rights, become more human, others need to be given less to compensate until 'black folks' meet the ascending gorilla as they make their way even further down the American food chain. The encounter of Harambe and Isiah, filmed and shared by millions, dramatised this hidden narrative of conflict between rights given and rights taken away: two humanimals at two different stages of their regulation, animals becoming less non-relational through the provision of rights, black Americans becoming more so through the extension of the regulatory questioning of their norms of domestic existence.

Animal personhood

Andrew Benjamin's work is yet another stark reminder that the definition of the racial other as animal is a typical gesture of racist states, placing a proportion of a population within a non-relational zone, wherein normal rules do not apply and thus the human right to life is waivered, while at the same time drawing an impossible correlation between animals and humans, by defining sacred human blood and genes as being radically other from the very animals we are forced to accept as our ancestors. But this is only half the story, for at the same time as the implicit yet readily legible racism of Hurt's petition points towards the ongoing race war of American society, allowing the animalisation of black families to justify their differential treatment, the petition effectively says ban blacks from zoos; it is also part of a wider impetus not to remove rights through animality, but of affording rights to animals. So that once the whole scandal of the petitions died down, a new dialogue opened up fuelled by the continued success of the #Harambe memes based on the question: should zoos exist at all? And if they do, shouldn't certain kinds of animals be banned from being held there?

There is a movement that has been gathering pace in the US in particular to recognise certain of the great apes with demonstrable cognitive and emotional capabilities as legal persons. If this were the case, as Richard L. Cupp explains, then these great apes would have their rights protected by being assigned a legal guardian, much like the rights of your kids are vouchsafed. If this were so, then the killing of Harambe wouldn't be *worse* than murder, as some said, but it could at least be called murder (Ohlheiser 2016). The recent film *Unlocking the Cage*

(Heggedus and Pennebaker 2016) follows the numerous attempts in New York to have chimpanzees in particular taken from zoos and labs around the world and placed in secure environments where, presumably, they would not be available for public perusal. The basis for these claims is that chimps are 'self-aware autonomous beings' with significant cognitive ability as are gorillas, elephants and dolphins. As such they should be granted legal personhood. Not so strange as it sounds, personhood, for example, has been extended to certain companies in the US (Heggedus and Pennebaker 2016). This is a movement that has parasitically attached itself to the term civil rights. Its natural habitat is of course social media. But is it so outlandish to ask that certain animals be treated as well as persons are supposed to be?

As a child who wanted to be a zoologist and was a vegetarian for several years I have some sympathy with the idea of certain special animals. I remember the effect the documentary *Circus Elephant Rampage* (Lambert and Moore 2015) had on my perception of elephants, in particular their deep emotional needs which appeared to me to be more profound than my own. I have also been fascinated by the doomed, yet revelatory attempts, to teach chimps like Nim to acquire advanced language skills (Marsh 2011). Yet at the same time there is a fundamental ethical illogicality to all of this which has a deep biopolitical aspect. Why should some animals be granted special status and not others? How is it that classification of animals includes some and excludes all others? Isn't the argument against speciesism simply the precursor to another mode of speciesism, where some species are higher in the hierarchy than others, shifting the idea of the animal down a few rungs and ramping up the potential for racism of an entirely new order up a few notches?

The motivation for this kind of selective speciesism is a very human one. Animals that are like us, get the rights we get. But, as Richard L. Cupp explains, genetic metonymy and visual simile are not the basis of ontological jurisprudence or the law of humans' rights (Cupp 2016). The crux here is that personhood is granted not based on intelligence, actual and emotional, but on what he calls "the human community's expectations of reciprocity from moral agents" (Cupp 2016). In other words, if we were to charge the zookeepers with the murder of Harambe, we would also be able to charge Harambe for attempted murder of Isiah Gregg. In recognising that humans have rights, we also demand that they are to be held responsible for being a part of our community of rights. Cupp puts it neatly: "Humans are the only beings that we know of where the norm is capacity to shoulder the mutual obligations that are at a foundational level related to legal rights in our society" (Cupp 2016). Animals, on Cupp's reading, can be protected by humans, but the same process of protection also, troublingly, gives access to our aggression towards animals in the form of incarceration, voyeurism, exclusion and regulation. More than this, it is because animals cannot take up the moral agency of humans that we choose some as special and accord them humanimal status, but leave all the rest to their fate at the hands of humans. Chimps, gorillas, elephants and dolphins are less intelligent, more vulnerable versions of ourselves, they are in effect child-proxies, Isiah Greggs in drag. Yet in treating them as special, because they are limit cases in terms of their anthropomorphic tendencies that are to be found genetically, behaviourally and culturally, we further bolster our right to treat the rest of the animal world as utterly dispensable. The formula is devastatingly simple. For every named gorilla mourned, 100 million chickens are tortured and killed. Is that fair?

However, the question of human rights for animals is far from simple. How can nations that systematically deny the rights to life of large proportions of their own population treat as dispensable the lives of other groups they either exclude at their borders or let die in their failed states and define as despised the lives of others who they decide are potential terrorists, and I am not just speaking of the US here, in good conscience at the same time argue for rights for dolphins? If moral agency cannot be granted to cognitively advanced animals, who are we to assign ourselves as fit moral guardians? How can we invite bonobos into our rights-enhanced enclosures, if at the same time we actively exclude the Greggs because they are black and poor? Hashtag Harambe exposed these questions to the digital *agora*, creating a unique moment in the history of humanimality wherein the potential for the personhood of the animal, an inevitable consequence of the direction of scientific normalisation of the human animal back into the genetic, clashed with the reality of the animalisation of the racial other, an indirect consequence of the same evolutionary sciences become cultural drivers. By which I mean the ongoing problem of our tendency towards cultural, now genetically inflected, Darwinism.

It was not just that we were asked to choose, Harambe or Isiah, but that we were unable to choose because the more videos were shared, petitions signed, positions trolled and memes created, the less able we were as a community to work out what it was we were debating: animals or humans, rights or racism, violence or regulation, lowland male gorillas or American urban black males. If a question seemed to be begged, thanks to slacktivism #Harambe's life mattered, where did that leave the status of another, simultaneous front of meme warfare, #BlackLivesMatter?

There is no such thing as life

It may seem like I have hung rather a lot of significance onto the passing #Harambe fad, which in the end was shallow, thoughtless, ill-intentioned, overblown, knee-jerky, trolly and temporary. After all, that was back in 2016 and, while it went on for a bit, nothing changed did it? So far it is true, nothing has changed for the Harambes or Isiahs of this world. However, to think of the net as a direct driver for political or social change is to misconstrue the nature of memes and social media as a whole. Social media activity is not about changing the world, but rather concerns itself with making a world, out of a new kind of interactive, instantaneous, durational, ubiquitous digital literacy. It is, for example, impossible to read a meme as you might a work of art, a book or even a moment in history. If you wish to 'read' a meme the only option is to engage with memeing; reading then becomes, at this point, a new kind of active participation, rather than passive receptive interpretation. #Harambe was, quite simply, a window into the regulatory narratives of rights, animality, race and, of course, justified violence. Memes may be evanescent, superficial, offensive, stupid and indeed meaningless, but it is their meaninglessness that is the opening up of their meanings paradoxically. We memers do not debate the issues around race, rights and the limits of the human, rather our meme actions perform them, thoughtlessly, and in so doing they lift a curtain separating us from the regulatory narratives that control us. When we share without thinking, we share the presuppositions, fictions, narratives and prejudices that biopolitical states use to regulate our behaviour by encouraging us not to think when all we have to do is live and leave the rest to the experts and the powers that be.

All memes are significant in their revealing insignificance and #Harambe is a particularly important 'text' when framed in this way I think. First, it taught us that there is no such thing as life. Could I ask you to put down Twitter and Instagram for a moment and think about that? There is no such thing as life. Certainly there are ambulatory, gene-possessing organisms, call them animals if you wish, but they are not alive in the way you mean it. Instead, there is a 70-millennia-long cognitive process of self-conscious activity on behalf of sapiens which means that a sense of life as a thing that we possess, can make and will lose became culturally desirable perhaps because it was in those early days evolutionarily useful. Initially, we bolstered this ridiculous concept with religion, now we back it up instead with science.

If life is a construct, as I am arguing, this allows for that fact that there can be different kinds of life, and, as is the way of Western thought, they are likely to be valued differently. What this demands is that instead of thinking of life as an object or force or whatever you want to term it, tied in to pre-discursive biological imperatives, you must reconsider life as a narrativisation of human value determined by biology. Animal life is not the life of animals, but that animal portion of our life formalised by the Greeks as the basis of human exceptionalism. While human life is a truly mobile concept which, at the present time, is making a transition from sacred universal right as a basis of humanism to a data-debilitated, zoomorphised, anthropocenic self-harmer, in preparation for the stark truth that, according to Noah Harari and Ray Kurzweil at least, it is set to be entirely replaced by genetic modification, automation, AI and, eventually, the total indifferentiation between human and machine called 'the Singularity.' My point being that life is not something that exists and which we in some way embody or possess, but that life is a concept used to regulate and distribute power. Life is not an 'is' but a 'does'; it doesn't mean anything, it does something; it does not exist, it rather facilitates, orders and controls different kinds of human existence.

First, the signature life allowed sapiens to establish self-consciousness away from other animals. Then it permitted the Greeks to define human exceptionalism based on cognitive prowess. In the 18th century it was the basis of a new political contract based on universal life rights. In the 19th century it was the justification of bogus race sciences whose genocidal end points then came to define the 20th century as the century of race war. With the development of genetic evolution and improvements in cognitive science, life is now being used to reverse centuries of religious and humanist anthropomorphism by insisting on a materialist zoomorphism to all aspects of human self-conception including consciousness, culture and our cherished powers of cognition. Finally, it is this materialist defining of life that is preparing the way for a potential eradication of human life as the waters rise, our genes get muddled, machines take over and our conscious minds become relegated to just one data set of information amongst a billion others.

Until that happens, let us content ourselves with the more pressing paradox of #Harambe, a meme war where the removal of rights due to racial difference is debated alongside a demand for more rights due to genetic similarity, because it is along these lines that much contemporary bioviolence is conducted actually. As Andrew Benjamin has already hinted with his theory of racial non–relationality and discourse of the animal, the animalisation of a human life, whose history has been the emergence of the sacred human life from its animal roots, is a central mode of racial discrimination in lieu of justificatory violence. Human lives are sacred, killing them is tricky. Animal lives are worthless, taking them is almost a human right in itself.

Yet while the racist element of the Harambe story confirms with this analysis, the personification of Harambe seems to suggest the opposite. A gorilla is a humanimal on the cusp of human life rights, just as an American black male is a humanimal living on the sharp edge of rights denial. Isn't, therefore, the image of the gorilla dragging young Isiah a perfect, memeable comment on where biopower, life rights, animality and race currently stand, perhaps explaining the success of this meme over all others? The pride of human rights represented by the power of the noble gorilla, and the shame of the daily abuse of those rights in the form of a powerless black child, dragged through the moat separating us from them, with no care or concern for its life, seems a more than apt 'meme' of where race, rights and violence currently stand.

There is no such thing as animal or necessary violence

#Harambe is a shorthand for a longer, infinitely more complex question which is: why are humans violent? Bioviolence is perhaps the theory of violence most affected by this ancient investigation of our worst forms of behaviour because, of all theories of violence, it is the only one that has to contend with the implied eradication of violence central to biopolitics. Indeed, as I write this, by far the most influential theory of human violence is that it is dramatically on the wane (Pinker 2011). That advanced societies have effectively regulated violence almost out of existence and, if we carry on the way we are going, in a few generations, the statistics suggest, violence will hardly be an issue in Western democracies.

Looking about us at the fractured wasteland that once constituted that advanced talking shop, the *polis* that Hannah Arendt held so dear (Arendt 1958, pp.22–78), this seems hard to fathom but like the hips, the stats don't lie. Perhaps it is a moot point, as to why humans are violent if they are no longer really violent anymore. Still, the reasons given for the downtick in cruelty are tied in to the question of a certain kind of qualified violence, what we call human violence. And if the question is one of *human* violence, then rest assured we are discussing both a constructed, cultural definition of violence, because that is what human-anything implies, and of course a non-relational relation of *human* violence to animal violence.

If we look one more time at the Harambe issue, we can say that a male gorilla will be violent if he feels his territory is threatened. But there is nothing spiteful about his behaviour, nothing violent at all really. Similarly, zookeepers will kill gorillas, whom they love and have given their lives to protect, if those gorillas threaten the life of a human whom they know nothing of. Again there is nothing malicious in this form of violence either or indeed anything legally problematic. Human lives are sacred, animal lives are worthless, so you must kill the ape to save the child. So not really violent either. This being the case, where was the violence of the #Harambe meme wars? First, for some, in the decision to incarcerate certain cognitively and emotionally advanced animals in environments where, due to happenstance, they can occasionally put a human life at risk. If this is violent, it is a singularly human form of violence; after all, no other animal imprisons different species for entertainment or research. However wonderful the research institutions like Cincinnati Zoo do; there is something malicious about zoos in general. Then there was the petition war. For all her denials, Hurt's invocation of racial norms of assumption, poor black criminalised families are not to be trusted in public spaces, was violent. It implied hate speech, it recalled the treatment of slaves as animals, it embodied prejudice against certain groups, it suggested their being ostracised en masse, it upset millions and it perpetuated the beliefs of racism. Yet no one was directly or bodily hurt. True the Greggs were briefly investigated, placed under suspicion, but physically Isiah was saved, and overall the family are all but forgotten about. Yet there was malice aforethought in Hurt's actions and all the signatories to her petition.

There is a clear difference between animal and human violence isn't there, which can be summed up in that one chilling phrase that the powers that be invoke when, regrettably, they are forced to take, restrict or devalue your life rights: necessary violence? In the animal world necessary violence is a tautology. To them, all forms of violent behaviour are necessary in that they are genetically determined modes of unthinking behaviour. Even the cruelty of cats with mice, and orca with seals, serves an evolutionary purpose and so is not, by definition, cruel. That we as humans even have the phrase 'necessary violence' implies, of course, that there are forms of violence that are not necessary. These are definitively human forms of violence but where do they reside? Is bullying necessary? We tend to think not, but it exists in chimpanzee troops and is a source of great stress. What about rape, is rape necessary? That is anathema but again in terms of animals, what we term rape is widely practised.[1] What about murder, surely murder isn't necessary? Yet animals kill members of their own species all the time. Harambe was set to kill Isiah, remember, because he thought the child belonged to a rival. What we can see in each of the above examples is that violence does not reside in the act of causing harm, but in the motivations for causing harm. Necessary violence means, in other words, post-evolved human cultures for which pure survival is no longer the prime concern. But even then you can, with just a touch of that social Darwinist magic dust, transform the machinations of Richard III or the crimes of Jeffrey Dahmer into necessities. Richard was just fighting for territorial advantage in a political rather than grassland environment. Dahmer was simply following the dictates of his genes, combined with deprivation of his environment.

What we have here is a series of mismatches of intentions when using the term violence, what philosophers call category errors. First, we mistake violent acts for violence. Second, we confuse, I think, human acts of violence with political acts of violence. Third, we muddle up actual beasts in conflict with animals such as we see them, primarily as human constructions. So that the very phrase human violence is as oxymoronic as that of necessary violence. Looked at from the perspective of animals, including humans much of the time, all violence is necessary and thus, on my reading, not violent. Perhaps we should describe these as physically forceful acts that can result in harm but which have no agency and thus no malice? Human violence, by the same reasoning, is just another way of saying violence, which is another way of saying non-necessary violence, which is yet another way of saying culturally determined rather than genetically pre-programmed physically, psychologically and discursively forceful acts that can result in harm that are determined by agency and intent due to cultural desires, rather than environmental needs. The problem being, with this definition, that the terms human and animal are contested and constructed, indeed facilitators of regulatory discursive and institutional *dispositifs* that are, by definition, coercive and thus violent. The violence of control, the violence of neglect, the violence of justified war, the violence of punishment and finally the violence of race war or genocide, if we read genocide as not the mass killing of an entire 'race' but the justification of murder due to the classificatory discourses of race. Which takes us back to Foucault one last time, and his contention that all modern wars are effectively race war born out of the phoney life science of the 19th-century social Darwinians.

Humanimal violence

The significance of the 19th century, evolution in particular but also the quasi-race sciences so perfectly described by Roberto Esposito's powerful *Bios*, is the manner by which anthropomorphism switches round to zoomorphism (Esposito 2008). What Esposito's work in particular shows is that after centuries of treating animals as demi-humans, our modernity is defined by when we started to treat humans as meta-animals. We are still special, but now that extra something is not really added to the human but evolved by them, and if one treats evolution properly, items such as speech or self-consciousness or just extremely large brains are not a means by which we can differentiate ourselves as being better than all other animals, but just modes of defining the human speciation as being relationally different to all other animals. This results in a crisis in the idea of the human animal, leading to a 20th-century hybrid of human and animal that I propose we call the humanimal. The humanimal is a confusing blend of anthropomorphism, animals are just like us, and zoomorphism, but we are actually just one of them, which lead to an almost impossible circularity, animals are like us because we are like them. A vicious circle that appears to negate the difference between animals and humans whilst simultaneously affirming it. The first result being if we are like them because they are like us that is because we are animals. The second however is if we are like them it is also because they are like us. We are not animals with an extra x as the Greeks insisted, but animals are rather humans which lack a certain y, as contemporary jurisprudence around the 'human' status of, say, great apes or elephants insists. Third, this conflation of human and animal, into the figure we are calling humanimals, appears to eradicate the difference, making the foundational separation of human and animal indifferent, yet at the same time its very basis is on the initial assumption that humans and animals are different. So that the oppositional pairing of human and animal becomes what Walter Benjamin calls a "dialectic at a standstill," Gilles Deleuze a "zone of indistinction" and Giorgio Agamben "suspensive indifference" (Watkin 2014, p.152). Confusing isn't it, the relation, precedence, relative value and non-relation between the basic ontological coupling from which all else migrates, populating, eventually, the entire territory of the problem what it means to be a human? Don't worry, for once it is meant to be an obscure and unsolvable enigma, a crossword puzzle with questions sadistically withheld, a Sudoku that just will not tot up. Because, you see, there are no animals, there are no humans, there are not even any humanimals. These are just words, forms of discourse, used to pin and mount the chimerical butterfly of our ontology as it flutters through the bee-loud glade of contemporary genetic theory.

I would like then to uncouple explanations of human violence from animal violence altogether. I would prefer if we used the word violence only sparingly to speak of political acts of coercion that result in harm that are presented to us as necessary. I think it essential that we separate the term animal from violence because it invites in the debilitating bloodless vampire of geneticised neoliberal social Darwinists who blame violence on genes to justify the liberal regulatory powers of our capitalist democracies whose data-camps claim to prove that neoliberal policy has dramatically reduced social violence, simply by distracting us with data from the real truth, which is what violence has always and will ever be, an accoutrement of political power, not a material, genetic pre-determination (Arendt 1958). But this is such a difficult ask because all theories of violence touch upon the animal at some point, finding common cause between hyena cubs and the Cold War, that sort of thinking. Yet when they do so they are also perturbed by the obvious difference in our constructions of violence, and remember we are arguing that bioviolence is nothing more than a regulatory construct, between animal violence and human violence. Animals, as far as we can tell, are not vindictive, sadistic, military and genocidal. Even the 'cruelty' of bonobos is just bonobos going about bonobo business. There is, then, a difference between animals and human animals, which is not speech, but rather violence, in particular the fact that human violence stands out from animal attacks in being both meaningless, sometimes we just like to repetitively kill and skin our victims then wear their pickled faces as pretty masks, and meaningful, invading Iraq in 2003. In contrast animal violence is, well it just *is*. It is not exactly meaningless, because it is always, for a clear end, predation, competition or defence, albeit a purpose beyond the real ken of the perpetrator. Yet it is not meaningful in the full sense of this world as an act that is imbued with some kind of discursive, cultural or political import. Animals chase other animals on the beaches of the Galapagos for the same reason that comets strike the surface of our planet and eradicate entire populations of creatures from the beaches of the Galapagos, on this at least Dawkins and Gould can agree (Sterelny 2001).

"Life" is but a signature

If the basic injunction of the biopolitical state is to make live, one has to come to terms with what this specifically means. It does not refer, as Foucault tends to emphasise, to the act of keeping you alive and enhancing the said life through the assignation of certain rights. For, as we have seen, there is, materially and essentially, no such thing as 'life.' Life is a construct of what Agamben (2009, pp.33–80) calls a signature. Signatures are those large-scale terms that organise the metaphysics of all concepts in the West. Life is one, power is another, violence is a signature, so too is the body and, of course, the animal. Signatures are fascinating in that they are words that organise our discursive constructs over long stretches of time and across various territories, and yet as words they are content-indifferent (Agamben 2011, p.4; Watkin 2014, pp.18–28). Life as such, as a signature, has no meaning per se. It cannot, as a sign, for example, refer to something in the world because, as I write this, there remains no scientifically agreed-upon definition of what life is. Life, therefore, is determined not by what it refers to, what it says, but what it makes or allows to happen and what it does as a concept, statement or signature.

Signatures develop from Foucault's conception of statements of intelligibility, which are meaningless in what they say, significant only in that they can be said (Foucault 1972, pp.3–17). Signatures certainly operate through dispositifs, but they differ significantly from them significantly as Agamben himself explains, using the term apparatus here, a typical translation of the term:

> Further expanding the already large class of Foucauldian apparatuses, I shall call an apparatus literally anything that has in some way the capacity to capture, orient, determine, intercept, model, control, or secure the gestures, behaviors, opinions, or discourses of living beings. Not only, therefore, prisons, madhouses, the Panopticon, schools, confession, factories, disciplines, judicial measures, and so forth (whose connection with power is in a certain sense evident), but also the pen, writing, literature, philosophy, agriculture, cigarettes, navigation, computers, cellular telephones and—why not—language itself, which is perhaps the most ancient of apparatuses—one in which thousands and thousands of years ago a primate inadvertently let himself be captured, probably without realizing the consequences that he was about to face.
>
> *(Agamben 2009, p.14)*

On Agamben's reading the operation of any apparatus is determined by the fundamentals of metaphysics itself, which contradicts Foucault's assertion that dispositifs are heterogeneous to each other. In addition, they are not subject to the material conditions of actual existence or a Nietzschean commitment to the basic law of life as conflict or war. Rather, they are determined by the philosophical logic of our categories through the truth of reality of the signature, rather than say the material realities of population, milieu and fear of actual death. All concepts then are controlled by the signature which does not express or represent the meaning of life or the animal, but is a means of expressing power through the ability of a signature to orchestrate stable concepts and maintain whatever the material conditions turn out to be. And instead of conflict, Agamben notices that all signatures are themselves engines or what my colleague Thanos Zartaloudis (2010) calls machines, which keep in play an oppositional or dialectical economy, or oikonomia as Agamben (2011, p.xii) calls it. These machines have three functions. First, they divide the signature into a foundational element and a specific example due to the foundation. For example, life as foundation and animal, slave, insect, bare life, humanimal as examples of life. Second. they allows these local examples of versions of life, Agamben calls them paradigms, to rise up the ranks for periods and come to define the content of the signature life. This gives the content-less signature something to talk about, and also means if this conversation runs into rocky ground, for example, life as vital spark, life as sanctity and life as racial species, the paradigm of life can be abandoned without life as such coming under question. It does not matter how many times we misconstrue life, human life, animal life and so on, we never blame the term life as much as our limited understanding of what it 'really is.' When a paradigm of life is mistaken for life as such, at this point the example becomes, paradoxically, the foundation which is the third purpose of the signature, to keep you confused. In trying, as a culture, to ascertain what is foundational and what is exemplary or paradigmatic, we have tended to ignore the truth which is life is a signature and that signatures are content-neutral, they do not refer to actual things in the world, meaning there is no such thing as life or, more accurately, there does not need to be.

The game that signatures play is a dangerous one. The signature life wilfully confuses human life or *bios* with animal life or *zoe*, so that there arise moments when we find it hard to remember which is which. These zones of indistinction of moments of conceptual indifference, in our case here between the human and the animal in the case of Harambe, are the points where the powers that be reveal the inner workings of a signature. In these instances of indifferential suspension—which is life again, bios or zoe, human or animal?—bad things tend to happen to the population at large. But they also present opportunities for us to point to the signature, see its logical impossibility (foundation is example which is foundational of the example etc.), realise the signature as such is content-neutral and non-referential and change the essence of the question. At this moment we stop asking what is life? And instead demand, why do we still pursue this meaningless world called life? This can be seen, thanks to Esposito, as a kind of conceptual autoimmune system or novel and complex mode of discursive violence. The coercive effects of the signature on our basic understanding of concepts like human, animal and life have clasped onto them a kind of metaphysical suicide vest. In trying to confound us, from time to time, they get befuddled themselves. When they do, people tend to suffer and die, but it is also at this precise moment that we, as thinkers/readers/activists, can render the entire discursive machinery of the powers that be inoperative. Or at least that is Agamben's hope.

From Foucauldian to Agambenian biopolitics

Like Agamben, Foucault does not see power as some thing; there is no such thing as the powers that be, but a means of doing something in a place, what he calls the deposition of power (Foucault in Burchell, Gordon and Miller 1991, pp.87–104). But unlike Agamben, it often feels with Foucault that there are external, material realities that power can do nothing about, and which it does not construct. In terms of biopower, Foucault often speaks as if life, fear of death, population, existential war and the milieu are in some sense actually real. This, of course, makes it all but impossible to escape from the depositions of power. In contrast, for Agamben, everything else is a signatory construct, even power itself, which is just a signature. In his work you find the metaphysical and historical construct of the term 'life' (Agamben 2004). His conception of power is not in a force hampered by some rather random large number when citizen becomes population as it is in Foucault. For Agamben, rather, both are just paradigmatic designations of the people. War is a signature, while the conception of constant struggle represented in our tradition by the dialectic, is constantly being suspended and so is far from necessary. Finally the milieu, as Foucault calls the reality of our environment, is entirely false as Agamben's book on poverty shows (Agamben 2013a). Even the regulatory means of biopower is a signature, according to Agamben, as his book on the office and duty explains (Agamben 2013b). Finally, the absolute frontier of the biopolitical realm, the 'body' both as biological essential, your body, and a modality of massification, these bodies gathered as the people, is, as the last volume of his vast homo sacer series *The Use of Bodies* Shows, yet one more signature (Agamben 2016). Which leaves the very theory of biopolitics in limbo if you insist on defining it purely in Foucauldian terms such that, from this point on, while retaining what is good about Foucault's concept of biopower, we will increasingly rely on dramatic developments of the conception of biopolitics, and thus bioviolence, to be found in the numerous pages of Agamben's immense Homo Sacer Project.

Complex methodological questions aside, you may be more curious as to what this conceptual shift from Foucault to Agamben tells us about #Harambe and the humanimal designation. Well clearly that the signature life is yet again held in one of its intermittent modes of suspension. The debates over the life rights of gorillas, the animalisation of the Gregg family due to race, the mode by which digitisation can confer a new life value, the problematics of personhood status and so on are all distractions from, and indicators of, the fact that there is no such thing as life and, as we will insist on demonstrating, the vital principle, basis of our universal right-enshrined lives, is not something that is sacred and true, but a set of processes and dispositifs that are made sacred and defined as true.

Life is not taught at schools or inculcated by parents, but rather assumed in advance and then re-enforced by culture at moments where life, on earth, is at stake. When a child on a life-support machine has their respirator switched off, when aid to the Sudan is cut, where NHS screening for certain cancers is deemed too expensive for its statistical probability of success, the moment a teenage boy is revealed as older than he seems and thus assumed, as a refugee, to be a potential terrorist, when plastic in the sea and emissions in the air threaten the very existence of life, as such, on the earth, and when proselytisers for its protection err into the language of anthropomorphism on prime-time TV to try to convince us to transfer some of the value of our human life over to the lives of all animals, because, zoomorphism now to the fore, that is all we are; these are the subtle and not unwelcome insistences by the biopolitical signature-sustaining machine that life exists as something sacred that ought therefore to be protected and, mildly and justly, regulated. A transfer of value that is all the more urgent because, when it comes to the treatment of animal life, basis for our own construction of sacred human life, we are, frankly, a force of such destructive and careless mundane monstrosity that in our quest for bioviolence, a violence aimed not just at lives but at the very existence of the concept of life as valuable, we cannot neglect the genocidal impact that the definition of the human animal has had, on literally every other animal species.

Note

1 On matters pertaining to the sensitive and important issue of rape I take my lead primarily from Joanna Bourke's exhaustive study *Rape* (2007).

PART THREE

Decapitation and the digital caliphate

7

ISIS AND THE ART OF DECAPITATION

Cursed be everyone that hangs from a tree

We should never forget that Christian culture commenced with an act of capital punishment. It may, then, have seemed fitting to some that it appeared to be embracing its much-touted eschatological endgame in the closing, autumnal months of 2014, when the first ISIS decapitation videos were streamed across the globe, and many predicted the end of the Western value system as we know it. Or at least its post-Reaganomical evangelical project to convert the world to its assumed-to-be universal rights (Curtis 2016). Not that decapitation promulgates the same message as crucifixion, which may have indeed been the point, but that the act of *capital* punishment, for that is indeed where the term gets its name from, the Latin for head, can both engender and destroy the state of affairs in a world. There was something about the sheer illegality of the act, an illegitimate stateless state, condemning innocent men to death in some godforsaken barren place and then publically broadcasting the moment, that made each decapitation appear a-legal, beyond the very reach of any idea of law or the nomos as our culture likes to call it (Zartaloudis 2019). The decapitations were brazen displays of anomie, of an anti-Pauline *klesis* (Agamben 2005, pp.29–34; Badiou 2003, pp.4–15), a radical break with the sovereignty of the rule of law that was a grim, negative echo of the manner by Christ's own death founded the nomos of the West.

Naturally, the crucifixion of a man called Jesus is not habitually presented in quite this way, not least because the other elements of his demise, for example, the not-inconsequential matter of his rising from the dead, have crowded out the bare facts of Jesus' rather shabby judicial status at the moment of his passing. Then there is the aesthetic fetishisation of the cruelty of his fate to overcome, which would require a complete overhaul of the entire history of our art.

Meaning the dry legality of the execution, or rather the statecraft of the crucifixion, always has to take a back seat to its more glamorous cousins: everlasting life and immortal works of art. However, the crucified God, as Luther memorably called Jesus' death, is arguably more important than cheating death and orchestrating paint, because it is archetypal of what cultural theorist Walter Benjamin famously called founding or constitutive violence. Founding violence, often termed necessary, he explains in his remarkable essay "Critique of Violence," is an act of brutality whose necessity is determined by the efficacy and solidity of the system which follows on from regicidal murder, slavery, colonialism, genocide, war or, in this case, the execution of a charismatic rabble-rouser. When we ask of our culture why this man Jesus had to die, believers might say he died for our sins, but political theorists are likely to present a more gimlet-eyed rationale. Jesus of Nazareth died because someone always has to die, for any new state or political structure to form.

Constitutive violence is invariably paired with multiple, subsequent acts of constituted violence, the name given to all regulatory acts of violence thanks to that initial constitution of power of the powers that be through the taking of the life of others. For example, it is because Christ died on the cross that Giordano Bruno could be burnt alive on the Campo de'Fiori in February 1600, or that Mohammed Emwazi be executed by a UK-sanctioned drone strike somewhere in Raqqa in November 2015. These, and countless millions of other acts of cruelty, are all localised moments of sacrifice honouring and protecting that first sacred eradication of a sanctified life. If, the argument goes, there is no great calamity at the commencement of a state or culture, then there can be no effective justification for any subsequently calamitous small acts of cruelty the powers that be are forced to commit, to both honour the blood sacrifice of those who gave their lives and to prevent reversion or degeneration back to how things stood before they chose or were forced to do so. So yes, someone always has to die.

In the early stages after a constitutive explosion of state-founding or legitimising malice and scourge, according to Benjamin and then Agamben's reading of him (Agamben 2005, pp.52–64), regulatory outbursts of cruelty might be termed vengeful but, over time, they are increasingly portrayed as a necessary means of keeping the founded state on the straight and narrow, to avoid reverting back to the even more perilous state of anarchy and anomie that existed before that foundational moment of intemperate, but purposeful, callousness. Indeed, the entirety of our political philosophy might be encapsulated in the idea of a move away from vengeful violence towards justified coercion thanks to a foundational moment of excessive force which, so the argument goes, aggressively alters the nature of aggression, away from bestiality and barbarity—or violence because we can't help it and we have an itch for revenge—towards the punishment and sacrifice of some, to keep the rest of us safe in our homes.

Necessary violence is an essential component of political states, explaining their bloodlusts and egregious periods of catastrophic neglect, and it is always pinned to an initial, partitive blow of founding attack. In fact, as an origins story, constitutive assault is usually organised around three types of interconnected yet clearly separate constructions of aggression. There is the anomic, animalistic melee that eternally rages before the state stepped in—sword in one hand, book of laws in the other. You have the one-off, decollative blow that separated the polis or state from its anarchic prehistory. And, finally, the reverberations of smaller scale mortifications of the flesh, often punitive in make-up, that are presented as regrettably essential if we are to avoid degeneration back to our animal or pre-civilised state. Walter Benjamin combines these three kinds of violence together in one neat package which he calls 'mythic violence.' Mythic because the animalistic state of nature is unprovable; the founding act of violence is usually a story told after the state has been founded as a justificatory narrative, and because this means the 'necessity' of those regulatory, punitive and constituent modes of violence, the only forms of harmful coercion most of us have direct experience of, is a lie, a myth, little more than an excuse for selective destruction. For you see we were not in a state of sin before Christ was killed, he did not then rise from the dead offering us all hope for salvation, and therefore you should not kill Muslims in the name of a man who did no more than what was expected of him, of all of us, suffering terribly under the duress of torture, bewailing his lot and, finally, shuffling off.

If Western powers encrusted by Christian values are, in some manner, founded on the act of execution, it has over the centuries become rather difficult to extrapolate precisely what ideas or concepts could be constituted by Christ's capital execution, not least because crucifying Jesus was intended not just to kill the man but also to humiliate and fatally humble him. Since time, immemorial crucifixion has been viewed as the most debased form of capital punishment, in stark contrast to decapitation, for example, that was often reserved for regicides. This is not just because it is unimaginably painful, physically humiliating and extended in its duration, in contrast to decapitation which is seen as comparatively demur in its rapidity (Moltmann 2015), but also thanks to the fact that it was marked out in the Bible as the most accursed of all forms of retribution. A person crucified was seen, amongst Jews, as rejected by their people, cursed in the eyes of God and, significantly for our purposes, excluded from the covenant of life.

The covenant of life was a demand from God to his chosen people that they not only live according to certain rules, but in living this girded lifestyle, each of their lives would testify to the singularity of God and be a kind of sermon or mode of evangelism to convince others to worship God and obey his covenant. You become, in other words, simply through living, an embodied manifestation of Godliness (Holmén 2001, pp.1–6). This model of religious observance where you do not live according to law, but due to an inviolable set of rules where, if you break but one, your entire mode of life is placed at risk, is, according to Agamben, the same adopted by the Franciscan movement in Italy during the medieval period. In the monastic movement, every element of your life, most notably the domestic dictates of dress, habitation and sustenance, was governed by a rule rather than a law. As Agamben explains, if you break a law you can expect punishment, but as a monk if you contravene a rule of dress or your daily schedule, you are not punished, you just cease to be a monk (Agamben 2013a, p.13). It is worth bearing in mind this difference between the covenant as rule, and the law as system, because it asks of its people that they merge entirely with their form of life, so that the rules do not curtail their behaviour but determine the very liveability of their existence (Agamben 2013a, p.25). To be crucified, therefore, was not just a punishment but more than this a radical exclusion of your entire existence from the mass of people you considered your own. When in both Galatians and Deuteronomy you find the same chilling malediction, "Cursed be everyone that hangs from a tree," what the curse is actually conferring on you is a kind of retroactive exclusion: to die this way means never to have lived as a Jew at all. Life as covenant therefore has a retrospective force which it shares with Benjamin's construction of mythic violence and his famous conception of *Jetzeit* or now-time, the past does not, in Benjamin's radical historiography, determine the present, rather the present reconstructs a vision of its past as a justificatory narrative of what is happening—it is name in the present moment (Benjamin 2010 pp.10, 462). Time runs backward, the present becomes our fate and the past a future potential of what can be shown to have been, so that what is happening now is what needs to happen. It is a mode of retroactive justification; it shares in common with all modes of what we called discursive violence, most notably the narrativisation of life typical of the *homo sacer*.

The malediction of crucifixion explains the dismay among Jews when early Christians chose to adopt the cross, of all things, as their symbol, but they were not alone in hating the crucifix. While Jews regarded the morbid attachment of Christians to this symbol with almost existential dread, the Romans viewed it in more superficial terms. Their main problem with Jesus on the cross was its affront to their aesthetic sense. For them, the crucifixion was simply unforgivably ugly and unsavoury. It was thought gauche to speak of Christ's death, a death fit only for slaves, in polite company and in as much as Christ was crucified for blasphemy, the attachment of his followers to the cross was seen as a perpetual blasphemy they carried on their person. As the great liberation theologian Jürgen Moltmann explains in *The Crucified God*, even once the tint of tastelessness around Jesus' death was replaced by reverence for the cross as a symbol of everlasting redemption, there always remained a remnant of this early revulsion (Moltmann 2015). To dispel this abject element which seemed to have been absorbed into the very pulp of the cruciform emblem, successful attempts were made to stress that the crucifixion was little more than a precursor to Christ's resurrection and so imbued with grace. In perhaps the most powerful act of mass semantic shifting of humanity has ever known, the cross, once seen as a badge of shame, came to be the most celebrated imago in the West. Even the vile process of crucifixion itself was transformed through its reiteration in transubstantiation as a weekly or even daily ritual, making the cross a cultic symbol rather than a material memorial or torture. The historical death of an actual man became instead the symbolic celebration of the resurrection of a god and, according to Moltmann at least, the message of Christ's life was obfuscated by the symbolic imagining and imaging of his death. And visual art, of course, was an intrinsic component of this movement from materiality to sacred cult.

Strange, isn't it, to reflect that there would be no Western art of any order without depictions of the crucifixion, no compositional sense, no conception of realism, no painting of the flesh, no "movement of the triangle" as Kandinsky called it (Kandinsky 1977, pp.6–9) and no moral seriousness at all, if a man called Jesus had not been hung from a tree two millennia ago and the nascent Christian church, when faced with the disruptive brutality of this fact, had not laboured long and hard to produce what I would argue is the real transubstantiation, the true miracle of the Christian church, that of exchanging memories of cruelty for a philosophy of beauty? Somehow, over 2,000 years or so, Western culture was founded on a combination of punishment, symbolic manipulation, the negation of fact in favour of ritual and, finally, aesthetics, all of which are combined in the image of a man suspended from a t-shaped contraption of rough-hewn wood, without which I know we as a community would be something, but I have no idea what that something would resemble.

I am also certain that without this transformation of capital cruelty to religious ecstasy, that simple aesthetic act of symbolism where the very content of the signs and images in front of you is reversed by the culture that surrounds them, the ISIS decapitation videos of 2014 would not have had the impact they did. Suddenly we were possessed with a collective dread that the Western value-state, founded in the exorcism of spectre of gruesomeness that loitered around Christ's ignominious end, would end with a sequence of decapitations whose aesthetic brutality almost woke us from the slumber of the beautification of executions that Christianity had induced with the narcotic of their incredible *freschi* and almost orgiastic painted *cupole*. Seeing those videos, it was almost like the symbolic meaning of the crucified god was scraped away to reveal the real painting behind the stucco. We saw that Christ was a man who was brutally humiliated in violent death in some distant desert, and in that sense he was no different than the stunned victims depicted in each unlovely, appalling and debasing film.

Those videos broke something in their pornography of explicitness when depicting capital punishment, a covenant that Western democracies had held with their God for two millennia, which meant that we were able to gaze upon crucifixion and perceive benediction. Specifically, the political benediction of our founding myth of accursed violence, thanks to a shameful artistic collusion which was more than willing to transmogrify the bare facts of an execution into a symbol of our redemption. Those videos, if they broke the covenant, had the power to break the Western democratic imaginary itself, because, as Agamben explains in relation to the monastic order, when you break a rule of the covenant, you break the order of the covenant as such, the rule-making possibility, the very concept of law. In being anomic, beyond the pale, outside the city walls of law and decency, each of them threatened to restage the crucifixion and remind us of our abiding political and cultural hex. "Cursed be everyone that hangs from a tree."

Those videos!

It began on 9 August 2014, when a video was uploaded and then widely shared online purporting to show the beheading of American journalist James Foley. Foley had been held hostage by the group Islamic State since his capture in 2012. The video showed him dressed all in orange, presumably as a comment on the habitual attire of the inmates of Guantanamo Bay holding facility. He was kneeling, hands handcuffed behind him, in a featureless desert. Standing over him was a man dressed in black, his face obscured, ranting for several minutes about the crimes and misdemeanours of the West and, particularly, the former US president, Barack Obama. The accent of the voice placed the fanatic unmistakably as a Londoner. The executioner, dubbed Jihadi John, by the media, came to the end of his sermon and then pushed a large, black bowie knife to the throat of James Foley and began to saw back and forth several times, as Foley appeared to groan. The video then ended with the camera panning across the decapitated body of Foley, his blood-smeared head resting at an angle on his back. Out from the neck a pool of blood and tissue oozed into the gravelly sand. Warnings and imprecations were written across the screen in Arabic and intoned by the voice of Jihadi John. Fade to black.

This video was first posted on YouTube, then shared on Twitter, from which it was then transferred to Facebook. No one knows how many time it was viewed but an estimate complied by *The Guardian* newspaper puts it at between 1.9 and 12 million views (Arthur 2015). Eventually, the video was taken down from at least Twitter and Facebook, and at one point just watching the video was deemed in the UK a potential terrorist offence, effectively making unwitting Jihadists of up to a million UK citizens, according to some estimates. But because it had been so widely shared, the video never disappeared from the net, indeed returning to this article five years later (Watkin 2015a),[1] I found it again within seconds. It is in effect a permanent, indelible stain on our digitised conscience.

This was the first video, others were soon to follow. In September 2014, a second video was uploaded showing the murder of Steven Sotloff, another American journalist. The same month saw the posting of the video of the first Briton to be murdered by the group, aid worker David Haines. The beheading of British aid worker Alan Henning was filmed and released online at the beginning of October. Each video was a reiteration of the first, a fact that, coupled with the regularity of the sequence of their appearance and a kind of holy dread that they cast over our culture during those months, emphasised a cultic, ritualistic side to the videos that they shared, in a sense, with the Christian recasting of the crucifixion as less a memorial of an actual atrocity, than a driver of a new kind of collective, cultic covenant.

The public response to these videos was as predictable as it was justified; a collective disgust at practices felt to be beyond the pale—of our ethics, our values, of our very modernity. We were shocked not just by the beheadings themselves but the weaponising of social media: Facebook and Instagram were now the Semtex and the Armalites *de nos jours*. We appeared to have entered into a new era of the image where actual snuff movies could be blithely shared, along with videos of our kids falling asleep in weird places and grumpy cat memes. Yet if the videos were illustrative of a new chapter in the great 'book' of digital literacy, at the same time, there was something immemorial about them also. It was this wedding of pristine digitisation and brutal decollation that cut us to the quick. Now we knew how the *Tudors* would roll if they were on Facebook, how Jacobins would troll if Twitter was to hand. They became, in some sense, a dark sacrament that we would habitually return to in the church of the internet, binding us together under the cloud of the threat of our cultural dissolution. The videos were totally new, unnervingly old, apocalyptic presentiments. We didn't quite know what to make of them, because it was what they were making of us that was the burning, if unspoken, issue.

For a while, mercifully, things went quiet. Then when Jihadism returned, it chose a new backdrop, not the desert but the boulevards of Paris; a different weapon, not a serrated knife but the dependable Kalashnikov and, perhaps most significantly, a different medium, a pre-digital one. When the staff of *Charlie Hebdo* were gunned down in 2015 for printing satirical cartoons of Mohammed, the issues raised were more classic; this was something we all understood, the power of satire, the freedom of speech. Everyone everywhere thought they knew exactly what to say about old-fashioned cartoons published by *démodé* means, awakening the perennial theme of the enlightened societies that we take ourselves to be. In contrast to the travails of politicians when describing the beheadings—was 'medieval' historically inaccurate, is 'barbaric' a little bit racist?—all those talking Hebdo-heads were eloquence itself. We were at home with our outrage, almost comfortable. These were Gutenberg atrocities, crimes against the body due to the power of the text. There was, accordingly, more than a whiff of the heretical bonfire about them. However, with unerring rhythm, just after the marching feet of our self-certainty that *Nous Sommes Charlie* came to a halt, the next video was released, and it was as if the ground fell away from our self-creation of the world.

Haruna Yukawa was by all accounts a troubled man, drawn from Japan to Syria by misfortune and, it would appear, misguided ambition. He was taken hostage alongside his friend Kenji Goto, a respected Japanese war reporter. Video evidence of Yukawa's beheading was posted on 24 January 2015, after the Japanese government failed to post the ransom set at 200 million dollars. We *Hebdoistes* were wrong-footed by this escalation, and for my part, the clarity of the issues became smudged. We were back with the fertile juxtaposition of the evanescence of digital imagery and the wet horror of the severed head, reminded yet again that Jihad has repeatedly been able to outflank the West in two of its most ardent pursuits, cinema and violence.

While we as military powers had, in the third millennium contented ourselves with a hieratic distance, the shock and awe of war as a permanent and ongoing *deus ex machina*, Jihad had opened an entirely new theatre of attack. It was focused on intimate, *verité*-style performances of close-fighting, meaty public spectacle and crude mortifications of the body. And again, while we lorded over the world with our complex technologies and our absolute control over images, the Jihadists won the media battle by more than a head. So that when ISIS followed up their *coup de théâtre* by hacking into the US military central command's social media accounts, the message was clear: in the war on terror, in the key killing fields of barbarity and broadcast at least, we couldn't hold a candle to Jihadi John, Kremlin-backed hackers and Macedonian clickbaiters. These guys just get it and we don't.

ISIS' formula was as simple as any high-concept Hollywood blockbuster. Take the latest in image technology and wed it to the most ancient, deeply felt human fears, then let the internet do the rest. It's a business model they may have lifted from Facebook, Twitter or Instagram, big tech companies whose huge profits come from the technological enhancement and then monetisation of basic human behaviours, not least because we know Jihadis are constantly chasing the digitised dragon. In that these companies purport to provide life-enhancing services in return for an unprecedented degree of surveillance, regulation and monetary exploitation of our day-to-day lives; they represent the cutting edge of what we might term biocapital. Seize hold of this biocapitalist model of life enhancement and reverse it so that it serves life curtailment, and a novel kind of bioviolence, a politicised realisation of the West's myth of snuff through graphic imagery of live beheadings, is spawned. A new event, a turning point in digital warfare or a second coming of an ancient dread? A rough beast was slouching towards Bethlehem, and it felt like we were just standing there petrified by its irresistible approach.

If the material means of production, reproduction, broadcast and sharing are original—these decapitations were the first concerted attempt to transform Web 2.0 into a theatre of cruelty, a snuff movie theatre erected in everyone's desk, purse and back-pocket—the novelty of their digitisation should not blind us to the cultural history of their subject matter. For if the West has created art out of depictions of capital punishment, it would be culturally illiterate of us to ignore the fact that Western art is not only wed to depictions of crucifixion. It has an equally involved relationship with depictions of decapitations. Indeed, the significance of the impact of the ISIS decapitations, which in turn might allow us to appreciate the inner workings of the incendiary device of your smartphone as a weapon of terror, may rest on our ability to look back and read a text not pinned to the symbolism of the cross, but the dramaturgy of decapitations. Could the art of beheading carry for us that dual threat of the ending of our covenant of power, and the quotidian matter of being in bad taste, that the cross had for early Christina culture? Is it possible that the ISIS decapitation videos were not only threatening our form of life, but also just deeply offending us in a manner that is, bizarrely and revealingly, intermixed? The answer, I think, is yes, and to understand these images you need to look back at not only the history of images of decapitation but, more than this, how the history of our conception of imaging, depicting, filming and publicising is, in some part, tied into a very long history of the reliance of visual art on the shocking visualisation of our heads as tied to and yet separated from our bodies.

The art of beheading volume 1: Medusa and the birth of cinema

During the 2016 American presidential campaign, a meme began to do the rounds. Taking an image of Cellini's famous statue of Perseus removing the head of the Medusa, some ribald Alt-Righter photoshopped Hillary's head for the Gorgon's and, cough, Trump's for the hero Perseus. Cellini's great work can be found in Piazza della Signoria in Florence. The less celebrated meme is located everywhere, but in particular you can get it on mugs and T-shirts. In the Greek legend, Perseus kills Medusa, whose hair is made up of writhing snakes and whose gaze turns living things to stone, by cutting off her head. In Cellini's sculpture, Perseus raises the Medusa head aloft by the snake-hair for all to see. His triumph appears, however, tinged with personal regret, as was Trump's by all accounts. Our hero's head is inclined, looking down almost in concern at the sculpted bronze form at his feet. Cellini is credited as the first artist to use the pediment of his work as a central part of the sculptural world, draping the half-naked and headless torso of the Medusa over the plinth, on top of which stands the victorious hero. It produces a sculptural motif of double, contesting dimensionality. The male form is vertical and extended, the female prone and convoluted. The male form is stable, perhaps even stiff, the female lithe and, even when dead and mutilated, unmistakably sexual.

Images of the Medusa myth concern Julia Kristeva's 2012 study *The Severed Head*. For the great French feminist, the Medusa is the phallic woman par excellence and her decapitation symbolic of the deep fear felt in Western culture of the threat of castration, in reality the removal of phallic power, that the phallic woman, or woman of power, presents. Because power is fundamentally gendered in our culture, and defined by the submission of the feminine other through highlighting her physiological difference as other, monstrous abject, as Kristeva calls it in her masterpiece *Powers of Horror*; these arguments make some sense. Yet, conversely, according to feminist historian Mary Beard, Medusa was not in fact a symbol of strong woman for the Greeks, not least because in Ovid's version of the myth she was raped by Poseidon then punished by the feminine jealousy of Athena (Beard 2018, pp.70–89). That may be so, but Cellini's choices, and the revival and distribution of the imagery via political memeing, suggest that whatever the Greeks thought, by the time of the Renaissance, the beheading of Medusa combined sexuality and power in a manner that we feel as horribly familiar. In Cellini's work it is the paradoxical duality of absolute abjection, decapitated, draped, left to ooze out of the noble bronze onto the more prosaic stone pediment, and the sexual power, stripped, shaped, manipulated and laid low, that makes this early manifestation of the art of beheading such a lasting influence in our culture that it became memeworthy. Hillary was regularly defined as shrill and difficult, snake-like even, in her untrustworthiness. Trump's aim was not just to defeat her but to destroy her: "Lock her up! Lock her up!" Crooked Hillary, Trump repeatedly memed and mooned for the cameras, crooked and twisted like the writhing of snakes and the contortion of the corpse in Cellini's misogynistic masterpiece.

Those snakes, they are an issue. None of the other images we look at feature anything remotely like them. They resemble nothing more than the female vulva, or at least they do to Kristeva who may have spent a little too much time looking at Caravaggio's famous image of the Gorgon (he gave great snake). The vulvic parallels, if you buy them, at least explain the horror of Medusa's monstrosity, a fear the French thinker traces back to ancient works of art where the vulva is either replaced by a face or exaggerated to the point of obliterating the visage altogether. "In short," she concludes,

> there is a choice between *vulva* and *vultus*, genitals or face, two fantastical equivalents that the myth of Medusa brings together again thousands of years later. Vulvar, phallic, necessitating, if not the erasure of the face, at least its decapitation so that representation can take over.
>
> *(Kristeva 2012, p.32)*

A great book in many ways, Kristeva's work however rarely avers from a mainstream psychoanalytical reading of decapitation as symbol of castration found in Hélène Cixous' foundational paper from the 1980 "Decapitation or Castration?" (spoiler alert, she chose castration) (Watkin 2000). Yet Kristeva's reading of the Medusa myth does appear to contain a theory of the history of decapitation's relationship to the power of the image that speaks indirectly to the ISIS videos. It was published just before they were broadcast. Whatever horror the Medusa represents, vulvic or otherwise, the significance of the story is entirely bound up with the power of the image. If one gazes on the snakes directly, one is turned to stone. Perseus' reflective shield, it transpires, is one of two safe means of looking at the Medusa full-on. The other is decapitation. Both are inscribed by a mode of visual reflection and separation that is the basis for modern film, ISIS' chosen medium. As Kristeva explains: "The Medusa-Gorgon only becomes bearable as *eikon*. Cut off the monster's head and offer its reflection for view, that is the only way to protect yourself from death" (Kristeva 2012, p.30).

The polished shield commences a process of self-separation that we call representation. What cannot be seen head-on is reflected through the interposition of a film that splits the subject matter in two, inoculating us against the corporal danger of unimpeded seeing. A form of cinema then is born back there in ancient Greece, out of the need to tame an image that, at the same time, we demand to see. The widespread, unwitting sharing of the videos reveals we are all still Greek enough that we want to gaze on death yet not be turned to stone. This is the logic of snuff movies that has been realised by the ubiquity of handheld devices and social media: direct access to the visual taboo of death that previously was only possible by being present at the act.

Reflective representation is the first cut but, as all devotees of decapitation know, if you want to sever a head from a body with a blade, according to Samurai lore at least, two slices are preferable, so as not to want to lose control of the head and have it bounce and spurt towards the emperor's new clothes. The second cut in the Medusa myth is the removal of the head with the phallic sword. Concentration on the gendered and sexual elements of this process blind us to perhaps the more central importance of Perseus' weapon which in Cellini's sculpture sticks out horizontally, only half erect. Read into that all you want, but the sword *qua* sword has the aesthetic effect of adding a third dimensionality to the work, occupying the distance between the work and the world out there, where you stand, on the Loggia dei Lanzi, just about where she must have stood, y'know, before he topped her? The crowd take a couple of steps back when they hear this, then recommence their selfies. If the weapon *is* phallic all well and good, but the sword also allows the hero to distance himself from the head he wants to sever. If a sword is a symbol of male phallic power, it is a power born of the distanciation of the intimate act of killing that tells the long history of violence as a means to an end for states and, in general, men of power.

What is significant in the Medusa myth and its many reproductions in Western art culminating in the ignominy of being memed on a mug is that the first separation, reflection, and the second, decapitation, reflect back on each other forming a profound exposition of the art of the *eikon*, the icon, the image of power. Memes after all are nothing more than a contemporary digitisation and mechanisation of the icon, the icon in the age of digital reproduction of your will, re-invested with auratic power, as I suggested earlier, thanks to their ritualistic, communal sharing. Due to the reflective shield, the direct power of the Gorgon is annulled. Yet in doing so the image has to be cut off from the real, losing all of its potency in the process. Thanks to the distancing violence of the sword, the cut of the head from the body is placed at one remove, this time anaesthetising the assailant from the horror of their actions. Yet this cut pulls the real back into the frame, so to speak. The shield is a deflection which cuts and the sword a cut which connects, as if Perseus wanted to push away the vulvic snakes with one hand and reach out to pet them with the other. It is this double impulse, attractive prophylaxis wedded to repulsing penetration that seems central to modern filmic media and to the long history of the art of beheading in the West. Is this history in some way transposed to the weaponising of the image that we can now see as typical of slacktivism and meme warfare? Are the ISIS videos both shield and sword? Is the Perseus' meme a jamming together of icon and sword? To answer that, we need to ascertain if the repulsion—attraction of the poetics of the Medusa carries over into the history of images of beheading in the West. There is, admittedly, an immense distance between the Medusa and ISIS. We need a shield to reflect, and a sword to connect, them.

The art of beheading volume 2: Judith balances the power equation

The importance, I suppose, of equating decapitation with castration is that it reminds us that beheading combines the duel forces of sex and power that are the dark heart of Western culture. If the Medusa myth is about fear of female, vulvic power and its curtailment through the act of decapitation, then our next collection of myths and tribal practices giving meaning to our cultural origins, a book called the Bible, ought to bear witness to the same phallic fears. In that the Bible sanctifies what are essentially ancient tribal rites, one would expect decapitation has a role to play there, and indeed there are numerous beheadings in the book. Of these, however, those of Holofernes and John the Baptist are head and shoulders above the rest in terms of the generation of works of art. In each case, carrying on the Medusan legacy, there is a decidedly 'feminine' principle at hand: the truculent Judith and the sexy Salome. Yet at the same time both are equally concerned with the political tension between states *and* a self-awareness of the power of image-making through head-taking. We begin with one Judith of Bethulia.

In the Book of Judith, relegated to the Apocrypha by the Protestants, the Abyssinian general Holofernes is poised to destroy the city of Bethulia. Judith, a native Bethulian and an attractive widow, uses her sexual allure to gain access to the general's tent. During their evening together, Holofernes, bewitched by the beauty of Judith, allows himself to be plied with so much booze that he renders himself unconscious. Judith summons her handmaiden and between them they behead the general. The head is then smuggled out in the servant's 'wallet,' a slip of translation or sad testimony to Holofernes' micro-cephalism, and the city is saved.

It would be so easy to read this story as the garish revenge of the Medusa. In this sequel, a man does gaze into the eyes of Judith and is effectively turned to stone thereafter with Medusa–Judith taking his head into the bargain. Certainly, such a reading would be in keeping with the manner in which the suppressed Judith has become something of a feminist archetype in recent times. As such, it is also fitting that the greatest in a long gallery of images of Judith decapitating Holofernes is that of Artemisia Gentileschi, one of the most significant female artists in the history of Western art. Her unflinching study shows Judith's maid holding Holofernes down, this is very much a handmaid's tale, leaning forward like she is scrubbing out a particularly recalcitrant stain. Judith pulls back away from the head, with a look of concentrated disgust on her face, similar to my own when I am occasionally called upon to gut a fish. With one hand she pulls Holofernes' head by the hair, the other saws at his neck. Her limbs are massive and phallically foregrounded. To avoid the graphic debilitation of foreshortening, they reach across rather than loom out, guillotining the painting in half as they stretch in parallel over the body of Holofernes, keeping him within arm's reach, yet pushing him as far away from her as she can, forming an improbable yet undeniable equals sign. Judith's arms have balanced the equation of power, the painting seems to say.

On the surface this work seems to have little to tell us about the shield and sword's tensile dynamic of separation and intimacy that we read into the story of the Medusa. Yet take another look at the picture and the entire power of the image is precisely the stand-off between repulsion and attraction that seems to mark the art of beheading. The great general is fighting off the women, yet it was his lust for Judith that brought her to this bed of destruction in the first place. The women are overpowering Holofernes, yet at the same time are repulsed by him and their own actions. The great equals sign at the heart of the picture says nothing other to me than that the political act of decapitation results in a suspension of power. One the one hand, violence is a prophylactic against destruction; we will call this Perseus' shield. On the other, it is an invitation to proximity between yourself and the other you most despise. This is the importance of the sword. It is also, of course, a graphic representation of the art of the *homo sacer*, of the included exclusion, of the inside/outside of the nomic–anomic logic of biopower since the dawn of the modern, political state, a thousand years or so before Holofernes' scalp was stolen.

There is a profound claustrophobia in Gentileschi's work, a tension that is almost unbearable. Everyone in the picture is simultaneously an aggressor and a victim. Most impressive for me, considering what I know of Gentileschi's history, is the sense of the women being forced into the role of sexual aggressor by the demands of the general. If you didn't know otherwise, you might think this is one of those myriad prurient studies of rape that had, somewhere on the way to the masculine viewing salon, gone visually awry. This is not as outlandish as it might sound. As is now well known, in 1611, Gentileschi was raped by the artist Agostino Tassi. After the rape she continued to have what we would now call 'transactional' sexual relations with the artist in hope that he would eventually marry her. When it became obvious this was not going to be the case, as Tassi was a womaniser and a fraudster, it was her father who brought charges of rape against him. During the trial Gentileschi was subject to a series of humiliations, including torture, to test the veracity of her testimony. Tassi was indeed found guilty and sentenced to exile from Rome, but the sentence was never executed.

It is impossible, I think, to look on Gentileschi's painting of Judith and not think of her own experiences of sexual assault. It was painted just a couple of years later. Yet if rape is about power exponentially more than it is about sex (Bourke 2007), then this supports our reading of the art of beheading as primarily concerned with a tensile stand-off between repulsion and attraction, in which two kinds of cut are enacted. The first is the separation of representation itself, the politics of depiction as such. The second is the intimacy of the act of cutting, what one might call the political intimacy of any act of violence. It would seem to me that phallic power is of less interest here than the power of representation as a dual mode of distance and intimacy, a power that has, for most of the history of the West, been in the hands and heads of men and so become unavoidably sexualised.

Intimance, apotropaicism and chiasmus

All acts of violence require an intimacy with one's victim that, simultaneously, one wants to distance oneself from. Death, after all, is the greatest span we can conceive of that, however, never leaves our side. In this sense, as Jacques Derrida explains, it is the ultimate dead end, the very essence of the Greek concept of the *aporia* (Derrida 1993). Such an intimate distance, or intimance as I call it, has a general effect of suspending traditionally assumed differences between friend and enemy we inherited from Aristotle (Derrida 1997, pp.26–48). In actual fact, all adversarial practice bears within it the paradox that repulsion of the enemy requires inviting them into your sphere of influence. The development of weapons over millennia appears to be the pursuit of ever greater degrees of distanciation to ameliorate the affective and ethical threat to the body politic that killing people poses. It would appear that this inability to differentiate between distance and intimacy, this indifferentiation of the most significant political difference there is, friend and enemy, citizen and barbarian, is accentuated when it comes to the practice and art of beheading.

One wonders if this indifferentiation of oppositional positions supportive of conflict is one possible origin for the fear and disgust felt around the world after the broadcasting of Jihadi John's capital crimes. A disgust so deep-seated one might even go so far as to say it was uncanny. Uncanny in the strict Freudian sense of something familiar made unfamiliar, a repulsive item that is also inexplicably attractive. Decapitation has an uncanny apotropaic power, to use the ancient Greek term for a charm to ward off evil that at the same time could draw you back into the sphere of its influence if only to prove the efficacy of the charm. Apotropaicism is the origin of what Freud called repression, leaving us with the emotive idea that anything you elect to repress will stage the melodramatic Return of the Repressed which, if nothing else, gave us the psychological basis of the modern horror film. Apotropaic repression thrives on the paradoxical tensions of its dialectic, indeed of the dialectic per se. That which repels also attracts because the true source of its repulsiveness is that it was once a part of you and perhaps still is.

The apotropaic tension of repulsion–attraction is the fundamental driver of the biopolitical act of supreme bioviolence, that of expulsion of the other to maintain the health of the body politic. It is also the very basis of the city state through the mapping of a territory whose very limits touch on those states it defines itself in tensile opposition to. It is a recurrent theme, indeed, throughout violence studies that the proximity of one's neighbours or closest relative appears to be a primary cause of conflict, war and revenge. What we find running through the art of beheading is that this apotropaic impulse is always prominent in the background, if one can say this. Perseus' shield and sword act therefore as ancient origin to a better understanding of the significance of the ISIS videos, apotropaicism and the intimance of bioviolent action. And it is a trope of course. Apotropaic means, in actual fact, a recurrent figurative mode of expression that divides or separates. Speaking of the enigma of the Sphinx, philosopher Giorgio Agamben says:

> Like the labyrinth, like the Gorgon, and like the Sphinx that utters it, the enigma belongs to the sphere of the apotropaic, that is, to a protective power that repels the uncanny, by attracting it and assuming it within itself. The dancing path of the labyrinth, which leads to the heart of that which is held at a distance, is the model of this relation with the uncanny that is expressed in the enigma.
>
> (Agamben 1993, p.138)

The image of Perseus' shield wedded to the sword haunted me with its uncanny, apotropaic power. It seemed a perfect parallel with the ISIS videos. The shield was clearly an early prototype for our age of film. Yet the shield reflected while cinema projected a difference significant enough for Kristeva to return time and again to the chiasmatic nature of self-reflection in head art. The filmic power of the shield came from its direct, literal proximity to the Medusa, and its ability to return back to us what we can already see. At the same time filmic representation robs the real of its power. Had the ISIS just been making a film, there is no doubt that the sword of that film would have failed to cut through. The weaponising of social media is not determined by the content of the imagery or its transmission. Cinema's earliest images were snuff movies by and large, one famous early clip showing the electrocution of an elephant for a few cents on Broadway, and mass market appeal has never been something the art form has suffered from. There was something else there, to do with social media, that made those videos the kind of lethal shields they had become. The Medusa myth and the phallus are a potent combination, but the Kristevan psychoanalytic feminism is not sufficient to unlock the meaning of this particular enigma, ISIS and the art of beheading.

The art of beheading volume 5: from the phallic to the acéphalic

But do we even need a head? Ruffling through my notes one afternoon I came across a forgotten work I had pursued on the figure of the Acéphale that crazed anthropologist Georges Bataille developed from an ancient Greek demonic myth, choosing it as the name of his short-lived but influential surrealist journal. Bataille was a theorist of violence, the sacred, ancient rites and the erotic. Acéphale is his post-surrealist superhero. In Andre Masson's drawing, Bataille's nightmarish vision comes alive. We see a headless body presented like Da Vinci's Vitruvian man. In one hand he holds a knife, in the other, fire. His intestines are on show, they spill like snakes, his genitals covered with a star, castrated or sexless perhaps. I would like to suggest Benedict Cumberbatch to play him in the film version; this would be Bataille's pitch to the producers:

> Man escaped his head like a prisoner escapes prison. Beyond himself he found, not God who is the prohibition of crime, but a being who knows no prohibition. Beyond what I am, I encounter a being who makes me laugh because he is headless, who fills me with anguish because he is made up of innocence and crime.
>
> *(Bataille cited in Jasper 2014, p.175)*

There is such a thing as intellectual fate, all thinkers sense that. Like the authors who tell you their novels or poems appear fully formed, dictated into their minds, so philosophy for me is not a mode of thinking but, primarily, of listening, then writing down what is transmitted. That said, this is not a mystical process at all. Where it originates, I think, is from always being open to ideas and cultural influences, and then letting the pieces fall into place of their own volition. It is the very opposite of the contemporary model of knowledge, however, typified by the intellectual evil that is Wikipedia. You see, I don't have access to all the information, and my access is filtered through the mind of only one person, not some god-awful, ill-informed hive-mind, the modern term for Pope's conspiracy of dunces. And it is this combination of limitation and prejudice, wedded to an openness and intellectual libertarianism, that sealed the fate of the Acéphale and this essay. When I first worked on decapitation, Acéphale didn't quite fit, so I cut him. Returning to the topic two decades later, he takes up his rightful place at the head of the feast.

The fit between Bataille's description of the Acéphale, and the imagery of the ISIS decapitation videos was uncanny. The hostages had been imprisoned for some time before they were murdered and, yes, decapitation is a kind of liberation from the somatic limitations of life. Isn't the power of removing the head the possibility, repeated ceaselessly if often covertly in the vast body of art on the subject, of freeing reason from the limitations and base demands of the flesh? Isn't that what is really meant by female phallic power, the power to be in a world without the phallus, even its negative presence as castrated?

And what is on the other side of this? The capital crime, a world without prohibition. The ISIS videos shocked us because they were beyond the pale, taboo-breaking, a step too far and yet, as Maurice Blanchot insists, not beyond (Blanchot 1992). What is most fearful in the world is not a state of lawlessness but rather a lawless state. In that a state is dictated to by its nomos, its laws; every state is also marked by a relation to an essential anomie, the trace memory of external lawlessness that it holds, however, within its DNA, its history and its midst, a dark, dirty secret of violence and statehood that ISIS simply broadcast to the world.

Bataille is right; there is something laughable in the worst sense in a headless body. It is the cold laughter of Baudelaire, upon seeing someone else's misfortune rather than your own in his famous essay "On Laughter" (Baudelaire 1972, pp.140–61). Bodies without heads are wrong; they are ludicrous, if they are bodies which once had heads. But the Acéphale is not a decapitated figure, but rather a body that never had a head or, more pertinently, maybe evolved to have no further need of one. The body that has no head is innocence indeed, for wasn't it the quest for knowledge that led to our post-lapsarian predicament? While for many cultures, the body with a head removed is the crime of crimes. The body without a head is also the internet without Google, Wikipedia and secretive algorithmic regulation as monetisation. Maybe I go too far but either way, this heady brew of innocence and crime, which does not disallow phallic readings of the symbolic history of the capital crime, seems to me to come close to the heart of the problem and the explosive impact that the ISIS videos amassed back in 2014. For what is power, but innocence founded on crime? And what is ISIS, but that rare phenomenon, the birth of not only a new state but a new kind of state, a stateless, lawless, quasi-Deleuzian, deterritorialised one. ISIS is the acéphalic state, a state without a head, both risible and terrible. But ISIS is also a reminder of the acéphalic power in all states, and as such their rise has shaken Western democracies to their very core. Perhaps I had been peering at the wrong taboo. Was it possible that it wasn't the phallic but the acéphalic impetus of the images that would unlock their secrets? Were they the end point of an art of decapitation or a new chapter in the apotropaicism of a-capitation?

Note

1 Some of the material from the *The White Review* article informs this chapter, but overall the two responses are dramatically different. Many thanks to the editor of *The White Review* for publishing my first response under the title "Uneasy Lies the Head."

8

BIOHISTORY

The human, the head, the tool, the cut and the tribe

The human skeuomorph

Like an unattended balloon in the hand of a distractible child I have allowed our original subject of bioviolence to float almost out of reach. It is time, therefore, to reel it back in, to ground it in the political realities from which the ISIS videos developed. If there is a biopolitics, a biopower, a biowar and a bioviolence, then there must be a biohistory as Foucault calls it in *Discipline and Punish* (Foucault 1977, p.23), and if there is such a field it will be marked by the dialectical intermittency that we identified in previous chapters as regards the creation of our bio-ontology through the hybrid monster I am calling the humanimal. Such a history should be composed of a culturally constructed and historically limited component laid on top of and alongside the evolutionary theory of how we came to be the animals we are. The head is the central component of this nexus of human history and a human, genetic, temporal, developmental recurrence from which the humanimal is composed. Biohistory is human history, tempered by the narrativising of inhuman, genetic temporality.

No wonder our ancestors worshipped the skull. Our capacity for self-reflexive reasoning, for all the fuss about dolphins and great apes, is not just better than other animals, it has taken us into a zone that no other creature can ever enter, that which we call culture but which it might be better to refer to as a post-evolutionary, non-necessary process of causation. This culture, ancient though it is, remains meaningless without technology. Studies now show that our brains would not have evolved without their prosthetic tools, a point that philosophers have been making for decades. Yet again there is an intimate link between head and hand (Tallis 2003, p.32). Increasingly cultural and evolutionary theory speak with one voice when they explain that our brains are tools developed in tandem with other tools, for example, the capacity for language and speech. To comprehend that, you have to come to terms with the coeval nature of the tool and the brain, explained by works such as Bernard Stiegler's trilogy *Technics and Time* (Stiegler 1998) and confirmed by recent work on tools and evolution (Ko 2016). This scholarship leads one to wonder as to whether there is any separation at all between brain and tool. A consideration of no small import as we teeter on the verge of the eradication of difference between human and machine (or tool) (Harari 2015). All of which leads to the conclusion that what matters in the imagery of decapitation is the uncanniness of head as seat of human reason, origin of human special animality and cause of the future eradication of humans by the very tools that came to define it as humanimal in the first place.

Take one last look at your smartphone. You probably regard it as the cutting edge of technology, and those cute icons as portals to an infinite array of virtual interactions. What I see is nothing more than a handheld, electronic cabinet of wonders; an anthropological museum crammed full of exhibits of the lives we once lived. Every icon on my phone is a visual prompt for the functionality of an app, based on the very technology it has eradicated. My email icon is a little envelope. The camera's, an old box kind. The calendar is made to look papery, by the corner being 'folded' up. Even Facebook has 'book' in its title.

These icons of a bygone age are called, in techy circles, skeuomorphs, a term inherited from anthropology to describe an object whose design echoes a functionality now lost. In skeuomorphs, a once essential feature, like the need for an envelope or the sound of a camera shutter, becomes merely ornamental. It seems obvious that these icons will soon have to be upgraded. My kids have never seen a real camera or an old-fashioned phone receiver, but one wonders if they will even get to that stage. Just as writing culture is being killed by image culture, so will image-prompts soon be superseded by speech activation and icons themselves will be skeuomorphic. This beautiful tablet I hold in my hands is itself on the verge of becoming a functional skeuomorph. A square box that had mass, that you had to touch, called a 'phone' how retro! Soon, all of that will be in a pair of glasses you chat with. Eventually, held in a chip in your brain that you think to.

At the point when the device becomes liberated from hands and enters our brains we will have completed not just a localised technological skeuomorphism but something more fundamental. Our sense of humanism, after all, is intricated in our relationship to our tools. You may possess a vision of humans descending from trees, walking upright, developing big brains, evolving good thumbs, learning language and beginning to use, then fashion, tools. If you do, this is a conceptual skeuomorph. We were tool-users long before we were Homo sapiens, and it is the creation of tools that promoted the evolution of the brain, not the other way around.

The human as apparatus

The crafting of a complex tool, an axe or phone, requires communication, muscle-isolation, certain kinds of hands and a lot of cooked food to fuel the increased brain functions that all the above demand. It could be that passing on the knowledge of tool-making led to what we call 'language' and gave us consciousness of time passing, portents of death and even the self-awareness that is the basis of consciousness (Ko 2016). As our ancestors fashioned tools many of the things we associate with human beings developed subsequently because of the making of those tools. We began making tools two million years ago; we became the Homo sapiens we call the first humans maybe 200,000 years ago. Our idea of being human is something we built from tools somewhere in between. Humanity itself, it transpires, is a tool-made technology or, as Agamben says with unfailing perspicacity, an apparatus. An apparatus is just his word for the *dispositif*. The *human* being, then, is not a creation of the philosophical science of ontology, but a tool, an apparatus, a dispositif. Contravening the basic law of ontology, the consideration of the 'is–ness' of existence, the answer to the traditional ontological investigation, what is x, the human as tool is not a thing at all, but a set of processes embedded in certain social and material realities, animated by the economy or *oikonomia* of the metaphysics of signatures whose primary concern is that tricky signature called life. It is not what humans are that concerns us therefore, or even what they do, but what they act on, allow, fulfil, comply with, succumb to and bully through. The ultimate tool, therefore, is power considered in this fashion. When humans began to use tools to fashion tools, the first apparatus they constructed was the powers that be themselves. The first weapon they hammered out, lathed and sharpened was the one they turned on themselves, not an elegant spear to transverse the distance between themselves and their prey, but a cage of such exquisite form and function one needs a poet like William Butler Yeats to best describe it:

> Once out of nature I shall never take
> My bodily form from any natural thing,
> But such a form as Grecian goldsmiths make
> Of hammered gold and gold enamelling
> To keep a drowsy Emperor awake.
>
> *(Yeats in Rainey ed. 2005, p.345)*

That emperor, by the way, can snooze because we are busy building ourselves into our own, golden penitentiary.

Around 70,000 years ago, according to Harari, sapiens began to spread out across the territories of the world using their tools to eradicate other hominid species and negate the evolutionary processes that gave them those tools. As they did so, already, they bore within each of them the beginning of Mezzadra and Neilson's differential inclusion (Mezzadra and Neilson 2013, pp.157–66) or what Vaughan-Williams speaks of, after Agamben, as a generalised biopolitical border we each bear within us (Vaughan-Williams 2009, 96–129), fulfilling Gilles Deleuze's and Thomas Nail's contention that we do not migrate from a territory but territorialise a pathway of migration (Deleuze and Guattari 1992, pp.351–423; Nail 2015, pp.1–17). As our nomadic ancestors disseminated, as Deleuze explains with his contentious theory of nomadoloy, they ceased adapting themselves to their environment and instead adapted the environment to themselves. Although this took some time to achieve, what this meant in practice was that almost everything about our bodies, including genes and brains, tools we needed to free ourselves from our Darwinian shackles, were ostensibly obsolete. These hard-won and hardwired apparatuses needed to be repurposed, new affordances for their ingenuity and instinctiveness attempted.

It has been pointed out by Dan O'Hara that many elements of the human body are skeuomorphic—the appendix, hair, men's nipples (O'Hara 2012). Couldn't we go further? Our physiology and biology was fashioned for a life led on the plains. These genes, hormones, synapses and emotions that modern scientific materialists reduce humans to, all originated in a hunter-gatherer existence that no longer pertains. Even language is effectively an autonomous tool-generating tool that sapiens took possession of and crafted self-consciousness from.

What is the human being itself but a tool-generating tool? Which is just another way of saying the human is a biological computer, a set of genetic algorithms subject to the same feedback loops, redundancies and self-reproductions as any other cybernetic system described, say, by Bateson's great study *Steps to an Ecology of Mind* (Bateson 1972). If this is true, some argue that in a few decades, when the internet of all things allows machines more intelligent than we are to talk to each other without us, then these new cybernetic systems can replace humans and we will hit an ontological skeuomorphism (Watkin 2019). If this transpires, the functionality we call human will still be needed, but the human being, that lanky, touchy-feely brain platform, will become ornamental, kept around for purposes of nostalgia only, like Yeats' transformation to a mechanistic songbird at the end of "Sailing to Byzantium," for the purposes of consoling the slipping crown of the somnambulistic powers that once were. When machines become not only cleverer than us, but autonomous tool-making tools like us, we should be able to finally jettison our biological container. After all, bodies are just a skeuomorphic hangover from that nightmare on the savannah before we could breed cows, get free Wi-Fi and merge with the machine.

If this all sounds like science fiction remember the skeuomorph as it should have already prepared the ground for your credulity. For example, we did not make our tools, our tools made us, so we should already accept an indifference between the human and the machine. We are not evolved beings; we are beings who evolved an escape plan from nature, meaning everything we needed to escape is skeuomorphic. Sadly, the human being is as obsolete as envelopes, box cameras and phone receivers. Our vital functions were reduced to hairstyles, nipple rings and lumberjack shirts aeons ago. It's taken us 70,000 centuries to twig but human beings are, by definition, organic skeuomorphs. Face it folks, we need a new science of being, an ontology not of essence, but of the ornament, for that is materially all we are. The human as ornament, the human skeuomorph, is not without a biohistory, that odd discipline I just founded where historical and evolutionary time have to be recounted simultaneously and relationally and yet in conflict. It began, I surmise, with possibly the first cultural moment, skull worship, and the remaking of the human skull into a work of art. To fully comprehend this momentous event, however, and how it pertains to ISIS, we need to go further back, to the historical development of the human skull itself.

We big-brained weaklings of the African plains

The most significant anthropological cut in the history of film remains Kubrick's remove from a flying bone to a falling space station in *2001: A Space Odyssey*. It is not your usual cut by any means, but something called a match cut. A match cut jumps from one thing to another unrelated thing, suggesting continuity by some form of visual similarity. It is the most poetic of all filmic techniques. It is also the most ideological. It wants to convince you. A straight cut, in contrast, simply moves from one scene to another and gets the audience to fill in the gaps of what happened in between so as to usher the story on a bit. A straight cut you can trust. It shows you something happening, and then something else just after. A match cut I am not so sure about. It has intentions on you. The jump from bone to spaceship finds Kubrick, for example, very much in professorial mode: "Listen, it shouts, I want to tell you something!"

In in the autumn of 2014, in the midst of the decapitation scandal, the first episode of Professor Brian Cox's series *The Human Universe* aired and I immediately realised it was little more than an extemporisation on Kubrick's idea. "From Apeman to Spaceman" finds Professor Cox somewhere in the Great Rift Valley. In front of him are lined-up various skulls. Brian the brain picks them up in turn, his eyes agleam. He names them, dates them, it is all very interesting. Then he starts to detail the cubic capacity of each skull. The first is 400ccs, about the same as a tall latte. The next, Homo erectus, is double that and so on until we get to the final skull. This one is 200,000 years old and has a capacity of 1500ccs which, Brian points out, 'is close to *my* brain size.'

The point Cox is making has something to do with a correlation between a rapid expansion in cubic capacity of the skulls and a set of extreme atmospheric changes made acute by the particular geology of the Rift Valley; a fascinating correlation. All I can focus on is this particular detail of the cubic capacity of the brain cavity. It relegates the role of the skull to little more than a container for stuff, soft raw matter, a litre and a half of mostly fat. I realise that when it comes to the human, the head and most particularly the brain, that grey matter, is all that matters, all that makes us matter if indeed we do. And mostly, according to the experts, we don't.

Up until the dramatic transformation of the human around 10,000 years ago when we settled the land to farm, as Harari never tires of informing us, we were insignificant foraging beasts. About 70,000 years ago humans were a marginal species with little impact on the world at large. Their capacity to eat meat had fuelled the expansion of a large brain, but the souping up of the brain meant refuelling was a constant problem. Our brains are using about 20% of all our energy at any one time, even when we are gawping at influencers' latest 'best me' on Instagram. In evolutionary terms, this is unsustainable. Not least because, back in the day, we humans were nothing more than the bottom-feeders of the savannah. Mostly too weak to bring down our own prey, we scraped an existence scavenging scraps from long-abandoned kills.

When Brian Cox fumbles with a lump of obsidian on the plains of Ethiopia trying to fashion a spearhead, he focuses on the need for language, social organisation and the passing on of knowledge necessary for our ancestors to create these engineering masterpieces a quarter of a million years ago. Actually, evidence shows that these spears hefted by my ancestral weaklings were pretty useless to the hunt. More likely sharp implements were used to gouge the marrow out of the reeking bone piles left by elegant apex predators, even worse, to crack open the skulls of our nearest neighbours, the Neanderthals, who were forced into extinction because we were the more hungry.

The fact is that our existence is meaninglessly material. Our presence on this planet is entirely due to the accidents of physics and the vicissitudes of environment. As a species we would be cosmically totally insignificant if it were not for one thing, our really big brain, the most complex thing in the entire universe so we are told. Yet in the end, physiologically, all the brain is is a smoothie of fat requiring an immense amount of energy and capable of providing a great burst of energy if you are clever enough to find a way to smash open a skull with something heavy and hard. For all its complexity, in the end, by far the largest part of the history of our brain has been that of an unsustainable resource drain that has resulted in one species turning on its neighbours and destroying them. And this is where it starts, the grim terror of the ISIS decapitations, with our reverence for the head, with the brain on the plain. Jihadi John knew this. Perhaps not consciously, for example, evolution is very not-Sharia, but at the deeper level, influencing his strategy, feeding his big brain replete with image-worlds.

You take the head to create the tribe

Kubrick's match cut is even cleverer than we might imagine. After all, there is a tendency to over-celebrate a bit of the cranal in an art form that is primarily dedicated to the carnal. In the case of the bone–spaceship mash-up, however, I don't think we have quite exhausted its full import. Kubrick's work actually dramatises a major shift in the history of our species from the material to the symbolic, from the plains to the flame-flickering caves, from victual to ritual. These days we still love our brains, but no longer as a main course. And before we came to love them on their own terms, we adored them as a central component of one of the most powerful symbolic remnants of our common ancient past, the head. Somewhere along the way, sapiens stopped using skulls as handy Tupperware for a brain-boosting snack and started instead to worship them. This shift from the material to the symbolic is surely what Kubrick is getting at as he transforms film-making from merely showing, to deeply saying. This same journey from the material to the symbolic is what allows skulls to become works of art and Homo sapiens to become recognisably human. What I mean by this is simply that whilst we relied on heads as diet supplements, we were still held by the chains of our evolutionary fascism. Eating heads didn't 'mean' anything in that whatever we do out of instinct in order to survive has no meaning beyond what it is. However, the very moment that we took heads, removed them from bodies and displayed them, putting them on a plinth or marking them in some way, we became symbolic beings. Symbolic beings are special as they have transcended their genes, moved beyond the brute dictates of their appetites and indulged in that act that makes them recognisably human: they did something unnecessary. It is, after all, what we do not need to do in order to be the human animal that we are, that defines us as more than the human animals that we are.

The oldest human skull found in Europe dates from around 300,000 years ago. Sapiens had left the Rift Valley and were on the move, looking to exploit new resources to feed their brain habits. This is about the same period as the first spearheads were fashioned. The skull found is not a work of art but it has been 'worked,' the flesh stripped clean, the back caved in. We don't know if this working was a ritual or prep before a meal. Around 35,000 years ago, skulls were made into drinking vessels and appeared to have been displayed on slabs. About 10,000 years ago, when the human comes into its pomp, domesticating cattle, contracting new diseases and intractable metabolic problems, skulls are collected and stained red. Pretty soon after that they are augmented using plaster and adorned with things. They have become aesthetic objects. Using a skull for some other purpose is simply practical, but doing something to a skull that is ostensibly useless is in some way suggesting that a skull can be made, once more, to speak. Skull-art these days, after Damien Hirst and Alexander McQueen, may already be old hat, but it coincides, pretty much, with the most interesting thing in the universe emerging from the most complicated thing in the universe: our post-evolved cultures of meaning.

Skull worship cannot be separated from headhunting and more widely cannibalism. There is ample evidence that many cultures consumed parts of the bodies of their enemies after battle to absorb their power. In *The Severed Head*, Julia Kristeva argues that these acts of decapitation were no longer for sustenance but were ritualistic. Speaking of the likelihood of widespread use of exocannibalism among prehumans such as Australopithecus, Archanthropus and Neanderthals, she says, "It is *human intimacy that is established* through these barbaric practices, an intimacy that blends the fear of the other … with the desire for identification, continuance, and power over one's kind" (Kristeva 2012, p.12). Something very important has changed here. The simple biological need for humans to feed their brain, with the implication being they would eat anything that gave them a fat-flush, including carrion, their neighbours, at times each other, is now usurped by cannibalistic decapitation as a means of feeding a society's sense of self. We have stopped lopping off heads to make something happen and have started removing them to produce meanings.

These meanings are themselves instrumental, tools of a kind, but what they make happen is of a different order than stupid spears. Eating brains simply stopped us from becoming extinct. We were only one of a number of well-brained, vertical beasts competing as things got colder on the steppes and not even the one best-adapted. We worked together in groups because it was the best way for us to get food. But when we started to worship the skull, our human society stopped being simply social like that of Gelada Baboons. It became, in fact, cultural, and it is this cultural component of the human that meant at the end of the last great ice age we sapiens had survived, and all our competitors had not. Not because we killed and feasted on them or because we were the better hunters, but because we had made the single most important discovery in the history of the universe. Human beings had invented complex communal forms of meaning. What some people call, misleadingly, language. Naturally, the head was at the heart of this development.

Capital punishment: a public safety measure

I suppose the answer to the enigma of the simultaneous attraction and repulsion of decapitation, represented by the Islamic State videos, can be made so much easier if you only stick to the facts as I initially promised, ignoring the kind of cultural match jump I have this far indulged in. Rather than rummaging around in ancient history, psychoanalysis, art theory and technological prophesy, trying to bring together the edges of what are, in reality, immense temporal and cultural chasms, why not start with the obvious? After all it is not surprising that ISIS, seeing themselves as a new kind of state, launch with a 'public' display of sovereign violence. Of all forms of capital punishment, decapitation has remained popular throughout the ages by oppressive states of all kinds as a means of performing their absolute power.

For millennia decapitation has been a common form of state violence. It has a direct relation to state power. The term 'capital punishment' originates in the Latin term *capitalis* or pertaining to the head. Beheading was often reserved for those in positions of power and has a natural alliance with regicide. This is because in general capital punishment was a long-drawn-out public spectacle of torture with death being simply the natural conclusion of the show. The humiliation rained down on common criminals was seen as politically threatening if applied to noble enemies or even, from time to time, royals themselves. So instead we neatly took their well-coiffed capitals.

Yet if beheading has been a special form of execution, it is also a favoured means of mass killing, as the decapitations of 70 soldiers in Idlib in March 2015 shows. Mass decapitation began with the French Revolution and the presentation of the democratisation of death as allied to the scientific development of the guillotine. Death by decapitation was now a fit death for all citizens, not just kings and lords. If beheading was an enlightenment form of state-sponsored murder due to its impassiveness, it was also of its time due to its scientific efficiency. The guillotine was the lethal injection of its day, a medicalised, scientific and pain-free mode of mass dispatch.

It is the 'efficiency' of beheading that lends it to genocide. The Nazis used it for a while until their ambitious outstripped it. In both cases, the killing of kings and the eradication of the other, decapitation is not seen as taking another human life. Robespierre summed up the trial of Louis XVI with the words: "You have no sentence whatever to decide for or against a man, but a public safety measure to take" (www.bartleby.com/268/7/23.html). There is, in other words, some consonance between the taking of the head, the formation of a state and the removal of one's basic humanity. Beheading, it would appear, has a heightened deathpower. The victim is not just killed, they are ontologically annulled, their humanity removed.

In trying to address the sudden resurgence of beheading as political violence, commentators have stressed that the use of decapitation by Islamic State is typical of a new state trying to assert its authority. Naturally, the shadow of the French Revolution looms large over this idea. It has also been said that the videos are more intended to rally supporters of Islamic State than to strike fear into the hearts of its enemies. This would certainly be in accord with the ritualistic power of headhunting for many ancient societies. When the brain feeds the tribe, the tribe just gets by, but when the head symbolises the human, the sustaining power of the image of the head becomes fecund enough to allow us not simply to feed, but also, due to symbols, to dream. And what dreams we have had: Cellini, Caravaggio, Gentileschi, Moreau, Redon, Flaubert, Mallarmé, Bataille, Cronenberg ...

Yet whilst I am comfortable with what the head means, and how our cultures have developed due to the head's material and symbolic weight amongst us, carefully composed canvases hanging on the salon wall are of an entirely different order to the visual immediacy and ubiquity of cheap digitised images. Paradoxically, at the very point that we have the means to both capture and communicate actual acts of beheading, it remains the power of what we don't see in the videos that is their real significance. And few if any of the commentators at the time noticed that.

Headhunting on the dark net

Did I mention that the films are fake? All four videos show the same four scenes. The hostage in question dressed in orange overalls reads out a prepared speech outlining the culpability of their leaders in what is to follow. Then a figure dressed in black, widely believed to be Mohammed Emwazi, expresses his ideology, one, troublingly, not that much at odds with my own. This figure subsequently attempts to cut the throat of the victim with a knife. At this point the screen goes dark and the camera cuts to a headless corpse shown lying chest down with what appears to be the head of the victim placed on its back. And that is it. The camera pans across the image reminiscent of the movement across a still image that any basic photo-editing software can reproduce. It seems this is an animated still image. Why? Perhaps because they are easier to photoshop. To me the head sits awkwardly on the body. Is that because that is how a head sits on a corpse or is it because even this image is not real?

In a recent interview Donald Trump declared that he invented fake (Salmon 2017). When you stop laughing you should consider taking everything he says seriously. If Trump fundamentally can't tell the truth, this doesn't stop his utterances from being a form of truth. Truths are created by the communicability and intelligibility of ideas, and fundamental to the communicability of any idea is power and, increasingly, control of a tech platform. If this is the case then Trump's statements are all truths in an apodictic sense, if you train ourselves in Trump literacy. When he says he invented fake he is simply demonstrating the self-belief of the faker. If you are still thinking of something as fake because it says something false or inauthentic, then you remain mired in the dregs of the Gutenberg perspective of the late, last century. Faking is a process, an activity, a belief in the falsity you are promulgating. When Trump says he invented fake, and we know he did not, all that proves is that he did indeed invent fake, for he is the only faker who fully comprehends what faking it is all about.

The ISIS videos are possessed with the same, demonic self-belief as the sociopath president Trump. Some of the more perceptive critics have suggested that these videos are fake but, strictly speaking, this is not the case. 'Fake' presupposes that there is some possibility of authenticity that we could attach to the footage. It hints at an attempt to convince. Some commitment to authenticity of a kind. In a Baudrillardian world, the fake usurps the real by being more real, to a degree where real and authentic become indifferentiated and the very concept of the real collapses for good. This is not how technology has enhanced the fake in reality. What was central to the ISIS videos was not that they were convincing as films of acts of brutality, but something other, something to do less with the content of the films than their communicability and intelligibility. As with Trump, it is not what they say, but that they can say this that is the source of their meaning, the meaning of intelligibility in Foucault and communicability in my own work (Watkin 2017, pp.19–20). In both instances of Trump and ISIS, you witness the invention of fake. Fake not as false statement, but a false belief wedded to false intention combined with access to a platform from which to launch your fake world truth and make it true. Whatever else we can confirm about the deaths of these particular hostages, we can be clear that at present, there exist no videos of their being decapitated available anywhere online. As regards those videos you saw of those hostages being beheaded, I can confirm you never saw them actually being beheaded. It was a sleight of hand, more accurately a *trompe l'œil*. The videos are not, on this reading, truly fake. While they do not show the actual act of beheading, they reveal with devastating aplomb that ISIS are willing and able to do that at any time. As with Trump and the sense he will say anything, especially as he realised as president he cannot do anything, so does ISIS show that they will do anything and broadcast it to the world. The videos are not fake; they are the invention, exposition and foundation of fake. The decapitation videos are the political and bioviolent authentication of fake.

All of which leaves me even more confused as to why an organisation like Islamic State would shy away from simply showing the beheadings, if they took place. I have raised this issue with my students many times and they have directed me to 'real' versions of various beheadings, but not a single video of decapitation uncontested by the denizens of the dark net appears to exist on the dark net (Bartlett 2015). This is absolutely in keeping with the peep-show logic of snuff and the contestable nature of every fact online. Fake is the very basis for the communicability of the truths of the troll. Even more perplexing is why it was widely accepted that these much-reported clips did show graphic scenes of decapitation even by those who have seen them. Watch them for yourself. Don't be afraid. You won't see anything much. *Lord of the Rings*, *Walking Dead*, the brutally violent *Logan* all show much worse. What ISIS videos open a window to are two men, one of whom looks like he is trying to cut the throat of the other. Then a straight cut. Then a headless corpse. A straight cut, as simple as that, from one scene to another, suggesting the basic illusion of cause and effect that all films depends on.

It really is all rather unexpected and perplexing. The first time I saw the videos I played them over a few times. Then I sat at my desk for an age, feeling a mixture of relief and, to be honest, an unpleasant sense of betrayal. The point is that I came to see, it is my digital right to see all that there is that can be seen, in an instant, whenever I demand it. My electronic imperialism had been thwarted and I didn't like it. ISIS had enticed me into the peep show then left me alone in the tent, in the dark feeling, frankly, foolish. Is this, I wonder, Jihadi John's last laugh? In a world called the West, where everything is reduced to the visually obvious, the readily available, the painfully explicit—pornography, shopping and gossip—is it that not showing the decapitations mocks us more effectively than any actual image ISIS could have released?

Social media and the blind cut

Philosophers have worried about new technology primarily in terms of its effects on our grasp of reality. Baudrillard's hyper-real theory of the simulacrum was in response to data-rich simulations of the real world through the use of digital technology (Baudrillard 1994). CGI is the end point of this logic. This has been the dominant theory of the fake that we have applied to the contemporary visual world we find ourselves in. In truth Baudrillard got on his moral high horse then promptly got it all wrong. CGI has changed little beyond ruining French-style film-making. The great French maverick misconstrued the nature of the perceptive field. The manipulation of our reliance on vision is not down to the richness of the scene presented at all. The cheap, tawdry rope-tricks of ISIS videos have regularly been pointed to as a kind of cutting edge in the bioviolence of new media. Anyone familiar with their work must find this bizarre. The state of the art represented by ISIS' cinema of cruelty is not because their videos are good, they are not, but due to the fiendishly intelligent way they are used. In particular, I think, ISIS understood that video's power is not in the image but between the images, so to speak, in the art of the cut.

True their videos use very rudimentary, if effective, causal suggestion to convince the world they have seen something they didn't. But their cuts go deeper. An intrinsic understanding that social media is also an art of the cut allows ISIS a deep purchase on our imaginative uncanny. Again, we thinkers got this wrong as well. We thought the net's facilitation of jumps from hyperlink to hyperlink would present an exploded, disseminated, democratic new kind of meta-text. Imagine a film you cut yourself, where you can cut to whatever you want! In reality, it is not the click that sends you somewhere else that has dominated the age, but the click that sends your content somewhere else through the power of sharing, while you stay put on your platform feed. This cut is a special kind of cut. Where cinema depends on a visual consonance between the scene watched to the one cut to; social media depends on a blind cut. What you click on is sent from you for others to see when you are not present. True you know what they are going to see, but you don't know ultimately who is going to see it, or, and here it differs from film, in what continuum-context of communicability. And in that most meanings are discursive constructs based on what we want to see, facilitated by the director's control of what we see in the case of film, effectively you click the image out of its meaning-context, when you share, and hope for the best.

So much has been written about the filter bubble and the echo chamber, so many wasted words until you understand the blind cut of the net. The echo chamber is not the result of a closing down of our social interactions to only those who agree with us, but a prophylactic against the high-risk strategy of blind sharing. We are starting to realise the threat of sharing and thus have begun to only share amongst our own kind. That way we have some control on how we think they will respond. The misconstrual and subsequent reaction to the ISIS videos are a watershed in the history of sharing, a history yet to be written. We need it with some urgency. Did we really watch the videos? Statistics and anecdotal evidence suggest not. People were aware of the images, but they didn't watch them, even if they shared them. And so it was that fake videos of people being decapitated became real videos of people being decapitated, not through the technological attack on the real but rather due to the technological enhancement of the social. In that these videos become global news; they are perhaps the first systematic use of social media to create what we now call fake news. The videos had little or nothing to do with seeing and everything to do with sharing. If there is any cut that matters here it is not the match cut or even the straight cut but the blind cut that you instigate every time you click share.

We all watched these videos of men not being decapitated and saw men being decapitated then went online to register our disgust. Whose side were we on? In the war against terror, every click of a key is the squeezing of a trigger, now that the newest theatre of conflict is the net. Theatre is apt because the decapitation videos are all about illusion and, dare I say it, a kind of titillating entertainment: *grand guignol*. When we shared and tweeted about the videos I imagine we thought we were speaking out against ISIS, but in reality we had been drafted to their cause through our insatiable voyeurism. Fact is, we are digitally enhanced and yet totally illiterate. We possess the greatest text ever known to humanity but it comes with no instructions and we have no idea how to use it. Until we grab hold of social media with our great tool of tools, our cultures and our brains, then the net remains the most powerful weapon in the arsenal of bioviolent coercion. As long as we remain slaves to our lesser tools, all emotions and fingers, clicking share every time we see something that upsets us or makes us laugh, we will never be free from the other metaphoric potentiality of the net, not a network of communication, but a mesh to capture those creatures dumb enough to shoal together, thinking there is safety in numbers. Based on current online behavioural patterns, we have allowed ourselves to become grouped into just such shoals by big tech on the one hand, and terror hackers, on the other.

Bioviolence of decapitation

When I began this project, ISIS was seen as the greatest threat to democratic states in a generation. Reviewing this piece for publication just a couple of years later, that threat is all but nullified. ISIS' stronghold Raqqa fell in October 2017, and Russia has reassumed its traditional mantle of global super-villain number one. All the same ISIS will remain a salutary lesson on how biowar will from now on be increasingly conducted through bioviolence. Their wedding of cutting edge social media savvy with 'medieval' cruelty is a paradox that was the basis of much of their early, dark glamour. The digital caliphate understood that 9/11 was an attack on another kind of culture, the society of spectacle. We don't do spectacle so much these days and Debord's influence should now be permitted to wane (Debord 1994). In a new millennium of new media, everything must be reduced in size so as to be shareable, handheldable and immediate. If 9/11 was the terror of spectacle, Jihadi John is the terror of the meme and this shift in media is significant. It is not even clear if Emwazi killed James Foley by cutting off his head with a bowie knife or if Foley was executed by normal means then his head removed after. Pardon me for saying so but it really doesn't matter. A meme is only partially composed of content, the rest of its significance is found in its activity: sharing.

People see what they want to see is a cliché isn't it, and in some sense, this is true of the videos. But with their phones in their hands, scrolling through Facebook and Twitter, people now also see what they don't want to see, and they watch it anyway, and they also don't yet behave as if they do. Confusing isn't it? A more illustrative adage for our age of bioviolence might instead be people see what they want to share. Many shared the videos of the beheadings as evidence of their outrage without watching the videos. In the shift from spectacle to meme, the content of what you share is only of limited concern. More important is what you can get that meme to do for you, a little dopamine hit here, a brief chuckle in your lunch break there or a few bucks of click-through on the weekends. That's what a meme is for. ISIS' digitisation of terror and violence was, for me, a significant watershed in this history of waging war through the composition of violent imagery precisely because it is memeworthy. A better definition of contemporary bioviolence you could not ask for.

Rereading this piece for inclusion in this book I am struck by how far I was from getting memes back then, just a couple or so years ago. I was still very much wedded to the content of the videos, in particular the amazing scoop that no one picked up on, which is that the decapitation videos were clearly fake. Over time I have been asked to write more on this topic but have been loath to as slowly I came to appreciate that the content indifference of memeing, its defining feature, is obfuscated by our desire instead to focus on what memes say and show, not what such imagery does. I now see that bioviolent digital content in the form of memes must be wedded to action to make sense or be effective. What you see is meaningless without what you do, when it comes to the digital draft's weaponisation of meme culture. Neat it would be to drop this espousal, seeing and doing or content and action, onto the paradox of digitisation and bloodletting that the videos themselves represent. Certainly the digital is the seeing: the making of a film using the language and grammar of mainstream Hollywood and the YouTube generation. And the execution is the doing of course, hands-on, Foucauldian *Discipline and Punish* kind of stuff.

I would love to leave it there, but I can't because I am not so sure this neat fix is entirely correct. My question is one emerging from my own developing understanding of the world we have created for ourselves, the world of bioviolence where we submit to small acts of violence, here the violence to our senses, of being assaulted on an almost daily basis by images of horror, so that we can live our lives the way we think we want to. Social media is an operational, not a representational, mode, and this shift marks the move from modernity to social mediality that I am trying to capture. Seeing is, quite simply, a doing. All poiesis is effectively reduced to praxis which is what the meaning of the term originally was for the Greeks, the lifting of the veil of truth (Watkin 2010, pp.69–86). The difference between watching something and participating in it has been suspended by social media's utilisation of memes, of which the videos are just a more extreme version. Or rather, online, nothing is truly seen until it is shared.

Bringing the matter to a head

What does decapitation, the archetypal capital punishment, performed by a rogue state, committed to video following the conventions of Hollywood snuff movies, and like all snuff movies being essentially fake, then uploaded onto social media, causing an international sensation or wave of collective disgust which, ironically, recruited all us slacktivists to ISIS' cause, laying out a blueprint for how to pursue biowar through the bioviolence of dark net trolling strategising, mean?

We began by trying to locate the videos in a larger cultural history. What we discovered is that the art of beheading is marked, from Medusa onwards, by an apotropaicism of repulsion and attraction, symbolised in the myth by Perseus' shield and sword. The shield has a filmic quality that separates the image from its reality precisely so that we can approach the taboo, or even the life-threatening entities. This is the typical dynamic of representation; in bringing you closer it also places that object as a permanent remove, in a never-to-be-recuperated zone of authenticity, self-presence and reality. The sword instead conveys the intimance of the technology of harm. Naturally violence is a repulsive mode but to kill someone you have to touch them, bring them close enough to injure them.

Thinking more broadly we came across a second history of beheading, what I tentatively called a biohistory. Such a history has to suture human time to evolutionary time, accepting the humanimal constructions around these ideas. The biohistory of the head, it transpires, goes back 2 million years to our conception of ourselves as special animals, special because we are tool-making tools. As we saw, the brain is coeval with the tool to a degree that it becomes impossible to differentiate brain from tool or, more pertinently, inside from out. Jumping forward to about 70,000 years ago, the head is also central in our self-conception as the animal that escaped from evolution through the creation of that super-tool, culture. These primeval intimations seem part and parcel of the power of decapitation both as image and as cultural activity. Indeed, the ornamentalisation of the head is always a political act: it brings together the tribe in a ritualisation of a common enemy.

The ISIS videos however are not just barbaric, and backward looking, they are also hi-tech and forward looking. What was noticeable when one took a good long look at the videos themselves was how the culture of spectacle that had typified terrorist acts had given way to a new culture. In a sense 9/11 was terror as Hollywood, while ISIS hails from another part of California, Silicon Valley. It was not what the videos showed so much as what they intimated, our self-definition through the imaginary of the head, and what they did, transformed film from a medium that we watch together, to one that we share in isolation. Film is very much the technological enhancement of those ancient skull-worshipping cults, gathering together as tribes in the flickering light of a cave. Social media, ironically given its name and ideology, creates a community of alienation that I tried to capture in the idea of the blind cut. It also reminds us that 2 million years ago, when we commenced the evolutionary path of tool-making tools, we also began crafting the material and genetic basis for idea of the special human, the humanimal, which maybe only bedded down when we became sedentary nomads, according to Deleuze, around 35,000 years ago. At the same time, we instigated the negation of the human soon to arrive, in that sense already here, when our tools will outstrip both the cognitive and the biological powers of human beings, and our animality will finally become surplus, a skeuomorph.

The removal of a head, shared by a billion-plus social media platform publishers, broadcast by a state with no history, no territory, no institutions and thus no body politic, telescopes the history of the body as head, collapsing our 2-million-year history as tool-making tools and our 2-decade-old history as social beings in digital networks without bodies into a single, portent of total political and possibly ontological skeuomorphism. The question the videos almost inadvertently pose is: what is now the meaning of the head, now that the brain can exist online alone? If the brain is the tool-making tool, that tool is the human being, and that human being, an animal coming to dominate a territory, is soon to be superfluous. Don't the ISIS decapitation videos speak to that, and isn't that why they filled the world with unholy dread?

For me the meaning of the videos resides in the duality of the immemorial and the unbearably contemporary, in the videos being both "The foster-child of silence and slow time" as Keats memorably puts it, and the very epitome of 21st-century dromology, Paul Virillio's term for the contemporary technological war of speed (Virillio 2006). The videos are a stuttering dialectic of intermittent exchange between our ancient history, the emergence of the human from the animal on those African plains becoming cultural beings for whom the worship of the severed head was central and indicative, and our current trajectory. As I said, we stand on the cusp of two suspensions of difference or indifferentiations, both of which threaten to eradicate the human race, each of which is directly addressed by decapitation videos.

The first is the suspension of difference between human and animal, central to bioviolence and which I am calling humanimality. The second is the indifference between human and machine usually called the cyborg, which is the latest front in a new kind of bioviolence facilitated by social media and the rise of the violence of cognitive digitisation and gene editing. In a sense, the videos dramatise the entire history and destiny of the human, those tool-making tools, who both despise and sanctify their animal part, to the point where their biological life and their conceptual sense of special difference, Aristotle's *zoon logon echon*, the talking animal, is about to be eradicated entirely by the tools they created.

Yet this history, an animal that creates tools to differentiate itself from the animal only to be superseded by its tools and, in a sense, forcibly reverted back to being mere *zoe*, mere animal, did not occur back in autumn 2014. It commenced the moment that the differentiation between human and animal was instigated by an indifferentiation we have yet to grasp between the brain as the manipulator of tools, and tools as the creator of the brain. Either way, the videos are the very archetype of bioviolence, and their message is simple: the human skeuomorph is upon us, not because humans are being overtaken by the tools they make, the internet is no more powerful than a honed piece of flint bound to a stick by animal gut in this regard, but because the very idea of the human is about to be exploded, pulled apart by the dual demands of humanimality and cyborgism (Harraway 1989). This human being, in a body made by genes and animated by the ghost of consciousness, will be left in bits on a desert ground. Western culture began with a man being executed in a desert. Are the ISIS videos of a man being executed in a desert, portent of its end, not thanks to ISIS, they were never anything more than a sideshow, terrorist hucksters, noisy snake-oil salesmen, who we have finally run out of town, but thanks to deeper forces, set in motion millions of years ago, whose meaning is only accessible and thus communicable and intelligible and therefore effective now, thanks to the impossible overlay of the biohistory of the human, the tool and the head?

PART FOUR

The global camp

9

DAYS OF RAQQA AND THE
BETHNAL GREEN GIRLS

One February morning back in 2015, three school friends, Amira Abase, Kadiza
Sultana and Shamima Begum, surreptitiously left their homes in East London
and made their way to Gatwick International Airport to board a plane to Turkey.
Digitally altered CCTV footage shows the three of them crossing the airport
concourse, backpacks bulging with the stuff they had bought against the cold
in the Westgate Centre the day before, confidently striding best foot forward
through the milling crowds, looking like so many young people heading off
for a bit of travelling, a school exchange programme or maybe to visit distant
relatives. It is an image often used these days to indicate the incorrigible intent
and disconcerting transgression of this trio of terror brides who have come to be
called the Bethnal Green girls.

From Turkey the resourceful young women managed, or better were allowed,
to cross the border with Syria with the help of a probable spook name of 'John.'
From there the inexperienced teenagers managed to find a way across rough,
war-torn country, to the notorious city-stronghold of Islamic State, the terropo-
lis called Raqqa. What a sight Raqqa itself must have been in 2015, having only
fallen to ISIS the year before but already transformed into a totalitarian terror
factory. It was a town that had taken on a mantle of malfeasance, representing
to the wider world an urban experience unique on this globe, the political,
religious and military centre of an entirely new mode of de-territorialised statehood called Islamic State. ISIS had begun as a state of the mind, but with the
capture of Raqqa was in the process of terraforming inhospitable geopolitical
landscapes to literally make a land liveable for the life of death, perpetual jihad
and bio-thanatocism.

I wonder how much sightseeing the teenagers were able to fit in? With a
population of a million, and thousands of years of history, the conservative but
bustling northern city was dotted with historical sites and local interest, before

ISIS' reign of cultural extirpation put paid to all of that. I think those initial few days were probably thrilling for the rebellious young teenagers striking out on their own for the first time. Based on first-hand testimony of others who took the journey to the Raqqa of ISIS, the Bethnal Green girls would have been welcomed with open arms and treated with respect, smiling faces, kind words and gifts of food. I tend to conceive of the girls not so much as the fanatics of the British press than the angry, disaffected young people of Azadeh Moaveni's wonderful *Guest House for Young Widows* (Moaveni 2019), whom she describes as looking forward to a brighter future, away from the frustrations, poverty, petty racism and low expectations of life among the predominantly Bangladeshi community of East London. These three besties were impressionable women who were duped by manipulative women and men to take the wrong path. As such, thanks to that doctored airport image perhaps (Moaveni 2019, p.154), the Bethnal Green girls occupy a kind of demonic rebooting of *The Wizard of Oz* in my imagination, the three of them arm and arm, skipping towards the emerald city of Raqqa, not yet fully aware of the subterfuge they and their ilk were to be victim to, the ideological wizardry they had been fooled by, and the alacrity and craven-ness that their own country would succumb too in rapidly disowning them.

Within days of arrival it seems probable that all of the underage girls had been married off to murderers they didn't even know, who used them flagrantly as biotools in the production of ISIS offspring. Six years on from those bitter nuptials and Kadiza Sultana has been killed in the apocalyptic and shameful shelling of the city by ISIS' many enemies, reputed to have resulted in the most devastated urban fabric in the world today (Chulov 2017). Her friend Amira Abase is missing, presumed dead, like so many thousands like her. Which leaves us with the last Bethnal Green girl, the unapologetic, unsympathetic, sulky Shamima Begum, currently imprisoned in a Syrian holding camp, illegally stripped of her UK citizenship, mourning the premature death of all three of her children and begging to come home to a land she has no desire to live in and who will do almost anything to make sure she is kept out.

Shamima Begum, the name will live on in infamy one suspects. At the present time she is probably one of the most widely disliked even despised of all living UK citizens, hated by most for the crime of allowing herself to become married to an ISIS fighter and for not apologising about it afterwards. What happened to Shamima Begum to transform the normal 15-year-old from Bethnal Green into the 19-year-old bride of terror, what went on in Raqqa to radicalise her to such a degree that she has been deemed totally unwelcome on these isles even though, in truth, she has yet to be found guilty of any specific crime or indeed complicit with any particular atrocity, aside from saying that her own home culture was not good enough for her? Now that Raqqa has fallen and we have first-hand testimony of what life was like in our modern day Gomorrah, perhaps we can begin to piece together a picture of the process of Raqqafication that turned Shamima into such a 'monster': Bride of Terror!

Days of Raqqa 1: like a Hieronymus Bosch brought to life

In the few years they were in charge, ISIS transformed the culturally rich centre of Raqqa into a theatre of cruelty. One eyewitness has literally described the staging of executions as like being at the theatre, before ISIS closed them all of course (Yassin-Kassab 2017). Imagine a Hieronymus Bosch painting brought to life, not by CGI, but thanks to the old-school efforts of Islamic extremists, inexpertly and ignorantly imposing their false view of Sharia law and strict observance of the Quran, and you come close to the abominations that were committed against the poor people trapped in the vast city-prison from 2013 to 2017.

Violence was so regular and public that it is inconceivable that Shamima Begum did not witness the executions that habitually took place on Clock Tower Square, for example, not least because ISIS used loud hailers and threats to make sure a crowd always mustered there. Although, in that infamous interview with the *Times*, she denied witnessing any atrocities except once seeing a head in a bin, which left her unmoved (Loyd 2019). From 2013 until the city fell, it seems there was an average of 13 executions a month and it would have been difficult to avoid them. "If you were a spy they cut your throat from the front," one source explains. "The same if you were a blasphemer or murderer. Magicians were beheaded from the back. Women were always shot" (Chulov 2017). Crucifixions were not uncommon. Gay men were thrown from high buildings. Some victims were burnt alive in cages. Other cages they submerged leaving their denizens inside to drown. Heads were hung from lamp posts or impaled on park railings. Also dropped carelessly in waste bins it would seem. Often these executions were filmed. Some were broadcast on social media to intense international outrage, the snuff-imagery seen as a new mode of digitised terror that yet had the whiff of how things got done by states in ancient times, before we had independent regulators and the possibilities of public inquiries.

As things got worse outside city limits, with ISIS in retreat, the regime inside Raqqa became more violent, 'medieval,' totalitarian. Surveillance was the very air that every citizen was forced to choke down. The cursed city slowly began to turn black, literally, as the black flags of ISIS proliferated, women were forced to wear dark niqab from head to foot and whole building complexes were crudely daubed with stygian paints like some sulky adolescent's room. Ironically, this inky architecture later became a series of black beacons for Western, Syrian and Russian drones, resulting in many being redecorated with incongruously jaunty candy stripe hues to avoid detection (al-Raqqawi 2015). Maybe that was all the paint they had left, or perhaps it is a rare example of jihadi irony.

In those early days, inking the urban environment must have appeared apt as the city itself came to possess a shadowy glamour for those who believed in the cause. ISIS were brilliant manipulators of their image as the most evil of all terrorists, seen by some as a powerful pull-factor for radicalised Muslims from around the world. The sense that ISIS were not ordinary men and women, but somehow personified as an ancient evil has been hard to dispel. Ahmed Issa, a

25-year-old student from the city, speaking after the liberation and annihilation of his home town, said: "We are haunted by bad spirits here. Something needs to cleanse us" (al-Raqqawi 2015). That something appears to be first Russian, then American and Syrian bombs, as all three bully states showed themselves willing to kick a man when he is down. This is not just local superstition. Our fear of Shamima Begum, Mohammed Emwazi and their kind surely borders on an irrational trepidation, otherwise why not bring the converts back home to face trial, serve out their punishment and dispel the enchantment cast over them by the ideologues and rogue clerics?

Perhaps attracted by this awful, yet fascinating, reputation for optimal depravity, many already brutalised or alienated young Muslim men and women flocked to Raqqa ignoring the images and warnings on social media and MSM. Most of the fighters who arrived from the outside came from beyond the nearby Arab world, drawn by the false advertising of the eternal benefits of martyrdom during jihad (al-Raqqawi, 21 February 2015). A wide variety of languages were spoken on the streets of Raqqa, different ethnicities mixed and the vibrancy of diverse cultures, all moving with a common purpose towards an uncompromising goal, would have been tangible in the cafes and mosques, something definitely missing from the Nandos and Dessert Cafes of Begum's East London manor. For those willing to sign-up to the terror-state package, a kind of Air BnB for extremists and holy fools that for the ISIS brides at least soon became the *Guest House for Young Widows* of Moaveni's book, you cannot ignore the fact that the power that they wielded over ordinary citizens must have been addictive, especially for the many individuals recruited with learning difficulties, mentally-ill illiterates suddenly elevated to important administrative duties with life and death consequences. Surely Shamima, a working-class 15-year-old from a traditional Bangladeshi Muslim family living through the diurnal microaggressions of our burgeoning Islamophobia on the streets and online, was caught up with the same feeling of empowerment, even if it were purchased through her rape and abduction? No one had ever treated these marginalised peoples so seriously or even paid them so much attention before. Is it any wonder that to Raqqa they came and, for a significant time, stayed, even when things which were already bad, became unspeakably worse?

Ahmed al-Raqqawi, a 25-year-old anti-ISIS fighter talking to a journalist in the devastated centre of his home town, seems to put his finger on the psychologically corrosive effects of sudden immersion into untrammelled power that the brides and lackeys of ISIS readily launched themselves into. "When they were here, they used to think they were kings. Even the women" (Chulov 2017) Even Shamima? Why ever not? Raqqa cast its glum necromancy over everyone drawn there for the myriad desperate reasons that one leaves security and enters a self-imposed precarity. I think Begum has been victimised, made into a feminine fiend, neurotically scapegoated by her troubled, micro-racist and macro-misogynist home nation, but at the same time I am convinced she must have enjoyed being so potent, so included, so feared. Does that make her an abomination or just a humanimal like the rest of us? In so many ways she reminds me of Robert Browning's Caliban, whose cruelty to crabs is not so much sadism as passing on the hate of his domineering master Prospero. "Am strong myself compared to yonder crabs," the mooncalf boasts. "Let twenty pass, and stone the twenty-first. / Loving not, hating not, just choosing so" (Browning in MH Abrams ed. 1962, p.1402). Just choosing so; perhaps Begum had become drunk on the potent distillation of her expanding options, a sad indictment of our society, when a young girl finds more liberation as a bride of rape in a totalitarian caliphate, than as a teenage girl in growing up in London, E2.

Days of Raqqa 2: toking on internet heroin

When ISIS was not decapitating suspected informers or stoning women busted at the bazaar for being ill-attired, life in Raqqa was, well, pretty boring. Many of those who had lost their way, possibly even their minds, and yomped the almost mythical journey across the desert to the city were to be disappointed when confronted with the realities of the life promised to them by online propaganda, family friends and the unscrupulous clerics who groomed them. They would have found that while it was rather easy to get into the city, the Turkish border guards appear to have been uncommonly accommodating, perhaps because they worked for the security forces and wanted a number of ISIS brides to get through, but it was impossible to get out as passports were immediately seized on entry. And when they weren't fighting, and mostly dying, the jihadists had little else to engage them or occupy their time. Raqqa, Abu Ibrahim al-Raqqawi reports, was never an exciting city at the best of times and would-be international jihadis, zealous freebooters hunting for adventure, often found themselves more than a little disappointed by their precious downtime on the concrete boulevards of the city (Worth 2016).

With most forms of entertainment banned, smoking and drinking punishable by lashes and the streets and cafes often unsafe, especially when the Western shelling intensified, the shrinking population, reducing rapidly from a million to less than half that as those who could get out took the arduous journey north through the hills, became captured in the thrall of a kind of stupefying obsessive attention disorder. The only real source of information was a heavily controlled and monitored internet which, when the electricity was on for a precious few hours, the populace would obsess over much like the rest of the world only probably with more desperate intensity of directionless pursuit. Al-Raqqawi explains about his fellow Raqqanis, "With no work, they mostly just stay at home watching television or using the internet. Ordinary people cannot live without internet and ISIS cannot live without the internet; it's like the heroin trade here, everyone is addicted" (al-Raqqawi 2015). And so it came to pass that the new way of waging war by what has come to be called the "digital caliphate" (Atwan 2015), transpired to be just as pointless as the unbelievers' digitally decadent life of peace on the outside. Many, I imagine, may have wondered why they even bothered to come, flicking restlessly through their Facebook feed, re-checking their WhatsApp for the fifth time that hour, nervously glancing at the empty reception bars and their unmoving notifications prompts, once the initial thrill of battle started to fade and the dysfunction of its effects began to bite. My point being, I suppose, for most of the time, ISIS extremists are just like the rest of us, unwitting junkies hooked on the digital crack of social media, albeit perhaps more hungry for the dopamine than your average office worker, thanks to the intense nature of their particular choice of lifestyle.

I can imagine even for the leaders of the movement, reality fell so far short of their fanatical recruitment videos that at times there must have been some sense of embarrassment. Surely even jihadis get the blues? As the West turned the screws on the regime and their city-stronghold, the familiar malodorous miasma of war-induced poverty and hunger settled over the ancient streets and squares as tedious corruption began, predictably, to replace egregious extremism. Islamic State became beleaguered with the same managerial and regulatory concerns of any modern nation, its believers transformed from murderous jihadists to petty bureaucrats as they tried to keep their nascent stateless state up and running. One could argue that it was at precisely this moment that ISIS approached real statehood, as it bickered over competing demands for shrinking income streams that were steadily stymied by international efforts as they tried to burble over the borderless badlands of our global launderer's economy (Kottasova 2015).

Lack of ready cash meant fines slowly replaced amputations and lashings for minor incursions. Shortage of blood for fighters at the front resulted in everyone being mandated to give blood, a biotax to be paid along with real taxes and the klepto-tithes of all those bribes (al-Raqqawi 2015). Basic infrastructural concerns began to occupy the facetious minds of the leaders of the city; electricity, food, water, all the boring stuff of life taking precedent over the sadistic pleasures of their culture of death. In so many ways appalling, for the outside observer the collapse of Raqqa into bureaucratic micro-fixes for banal local-authority style problems, also took on an element of schadenfreude. One wondered what the Raqqa health and safety or planning office might come to resemble once the atrocity exhibition had closed its doors and things settled back down to some kind of normality.

Personally, I was as transfixed by the biopolitical fate of Raqqa, as any doe-eyed TV scientist able to witness the miracle of a new star forming in the tiny eyepiece of some multi-million pound piece of kit. Here was the birth, development and maturation of a modern biostate over a period of a couple of years, rather than a couple of hundred. Islamic State was founded, as they usually tend to be according to cultural theorist Walter Benjamin, by unconscionable yet deemed necessary acts of founding violence (Watkin 2015b). To keep the whole machinery of ruling up and running, daily attacks of what Benjamin calls constituent punishment and coercion were demanded (Agamben 2005, pp.52–64). To bind the disparate aggregate of international misfits together into something resembling a nation, an external enemy was elected to enter into a Hobbesian perpetual war with. Initial sovereign violence was accompanied by public displays of spectacularly cruel mortifications of the flesh, dubbed by many as medieval, perhaps in their Eurocentrism and historical myopia betraying a forbidden sense of ISIS as our close cousins, rather than being truly beyond the pale, until the all-pervasive rot of Foucauldian managerialism set in, and fines took over from torture as the punishment of choice for most crimes.

Finally, from being ISIS the terror state, where even a wrong word spoken in public could result in decapitation plus crucifixion, we ended up with Raqqa, the local authority, overwhelmed by questions of hyperinflation, sanitation and blood-banks. So much so that the rulers of the city came to spend as much time making live the half a million citizens they had chosen to lord it over, as they did acting as brutal arbiters of life and death over the much smaller number who chose to rebel. Perhaps what Caliban did not learn on Browning's Setebos was that it is rather easy to crush every 21st crab, but much harder to herd the remaining 20 into manageable masses that can be regulated through statistically supported and institutionally embodied functioning organs of the state that are well funded and transparent to internal mechanisms of scrutiny and accountability. It is easier to cut off the hand of the thief, is it not, than to enter into discussion on what they took, from whom, why, what kind of reparation is in order, is any of that evidence inadmissible because it was acquired under duress, what does international law say, what judicial treaties are we subject to thanks to membership of the EU and so on? One wonders if it was envy in the West of the neatness of some of ISIS' solutions to petty misdemeanours that inspired us to start to murder our own citizens such as Mohammed Emwazi by drone strikes (de Londras 2015), and illegally strip others, like Shamima Begum, of citizenship, it being so much easier to do that than follow legal due process.

Days of Raqqa 3: city of rape

It was Hannah Arendt who spoke memorably of the banality of evil (Arendt 2017). What she should have added in to the mix was the tedium of totalitarianism. Mostly life in the northern Syrian city of Raqqa was a meaningless, sordid grind just to get enough cash through complicity and quiescence to feed your family for another day. Rather than a city of Islamic fanatics, Raqqa increasingly came to resemble an urban sprawl of exhausted survivalists, with little commitment to any kind of fundamental law beyond the most primal of all human dictates, shortage of food and who you have to flatter and cajole to get sustenance and a handful of worthless banknotes. This is not to downplay the fear that the populace felt or make light of the personal loss they all experienced, it is just an attempt to get to the truth of what it was like to live in Raqqa, month after month, year after year, for someone like Shamima Begum. Too much violence, too much hunger; the entire population started to get a little numb, inured to their own predicament, unable to share with the West the view of themselves as some kind of fascinating episode of *The Walking Dead*. One could speculate that Shamima Begum and her Bethnal Green friends were pretty let-down by the whole rigmarole of daily hand-to-mouth; this wasn't, I am sure, what they envisaged escaping to. Indeed certain details might lead you to concede that for all their sense of themselves as queens, it may have a good deal worse for them than many others.

Let us not forget that Begum's case counts as statutory rape under the UK law. She was 15 when she was married off to an ISIS fighter and, please appreciate, still a British citizen at that point. We tend to forget that the Begum story is primarily that of a vulnerable teenager who is manipulated by forces far more powerful then she can imagine, turning her social alienation into the so-called radicalisation, but which in truth is better described as coercion through digitally enhanced brainwashing. Begum is then tricked into leaving her home country, coerced into staying in Raqqa, raped by her forced marriage to a randomly chosen ISIS fighter a mere ten days after her arrival in the cursed city and then used as a biological resource to swell the ranks of jihadis by bearing three children for the cause. If this were a novel written by Margaret Atwood, rather than a news story manipulated by Britain's so-called free press, I suspect we would be thinking of Begum as more akin to a feminist archetype, than a terror threat.

It is estimated there were around 5,000 ISIS brides between the takeover of Raqqa and its fall who gave birth to the children of foreign fighters alone. Of these perhaps 250–500 were Westerners (Moaveni 2019). We are, therefore, talking about rape on an industrial scale for a clear, biopolitical aim: to grow the state. Although Begum gives the impression of being unapologetic of her actions, life for women in Raqqa during ISIS' reign of misogynistic terror, was cruel, exploitative and highly sexualised. Sexual activity appears to have obsessed the movement, with ISIS fighters regularly raiding pharmacies for Viagra, of all drugs according to source al-Raqqawi. Rape being primarily about power, there was also a strict hierarchy of sexual abuse in place. The Yazidi women from Iraq were taken prisoners as concubines for the upper echelons of the party, many as young as 13 or 14. When they had outgrown their use, they were summarily executed on the spot. Many fighters had multiple 'wives.' The city became a prison for women young enough to bear children for the cause. The marriages themselves, well you can hardly call them that, were a sham. The young women were often not told the real names of their husbands and so effectively had no idea who they were living with. And what kind of a life was it, locked indoors, forbidden education, no freedom to move around, severe restrictions on dress and behaviour, slight infractions punishable by death? "Magicians were beheaded from the back. Women were always shot." They were also routinely stoned. And their children forcibly conscripted to fight from a young age (Yassin-Kassab 2017).

During the intense bombing of the city from 2015 until its fall in October 2017, civilians and ISIS militia alike would scurry for shelter in one of the hundreds of tunnels that had been excavated beneath the crumbling cityscape. ISIS has a passion for tunnelling apparently. But, one activist noted, the ISIS brides seemed to find the bombardment liberating, almost refreshing. As the bombs fall, "You see them going on their balconies and windows, to breathe the fresh air and look at their city" (Hawramy, Shalaw and Shaheen 2015) What kind of a life was it for still young, clearly impressionable Shamima Begum, when lethal ordinance dropping from drones is seen as "a brief opening of freedom"? A life that is perhaps best summed up by the words of Raqqa Is Being Slaughtered Silently activist "Tim Ramadan," not his real name of course: "The life of a girl was itself a violation" (Hawramy, Shalaw and Shaheen 2015).

It was this already violated life that Begum carried inside her, along with that of her unborn son, when she finally fled the ruins of the rape camp they call Raqqa, and found herself in the noisome and lethal al-Hawl holding camp on the edge of Jordan in 2019. A young girl, tricked into sexual servitude, who experiences unspeakable brutality, who lost two children to illness and malnutrition, whose life, the very sanctity that we hold dear, had become defined by its daily violation. Why was it then when Begum asked to come back to the UK and face the consequences of her actions, like any British citizen who has committed a crime, her request was refused, her citizenship revoked and the nation shrugged its shoulders? I think the answer lies deep within the knotty problem of life itself, the different kinds of life, of the dynamic interchange between the violation and sanctity of life, of its very history as a concept. It is a biopolitical problem certainly. What is biopolitics but the politics of life, but one which cannot be solved from the pages of Michel Foucault alone. Foucault understood the importance of life in formations of the deposition of power, but he seems to have spent scant time actually asking what life is. To address this shortfall in the theory of biopower we need a new thinker for a new kind of bioviolence, not the Foucauldian coercion of passive neglect, but a different order of aggression born of active, often forcible, exclusion.

What was it that was able to transform 15-year-old Shamima from child victim of rape and abduction to 19-year-old Begum, someone so disreputable, dangerous and disgusting that we would rather let her and her unborn child rot in a holding camp, than bring her back onto these shores to face justice? What pathogen did she carry that was so dangerous to us 65 million that we could not countenance her ever setting foot on these shores again? How did she go from being victim to scapegoat in a mere four years? The answer to this local question is, it transpires, the basis of a wider understanding of the role of violence as a whole for the modern biopolitical state. Or at least that is the argument of Italian biopolitical theorist and philosopher of life, Giorgio Agamben.

Homo sacer

Sometime towards the close of last century, Roman-born philosopher Giorgio Agamben was trawling through obscure classical sources held in one of the many ancient libraries of his home country, possibly the Vatican libraries located just a short walk along the Tiber from his marvellously appointed yet modest abode, when he came across a reference in the work of Pompeius Festus to a *sacer mons*, or sacred man. This discovery was not only set to change the direction of Agamben's life but, like Foucault's concluding lecture of 1976, was to prove to have world-disrupting impact and influence. The sacred man, Agamben read on, or *homo sacer* as he is most usually called in the literature, was someone convicted of a crime who, however, is then confusingly deemed sacred rather than despised. This apparent definitional reprieve actually places our sacred man in a rather sticky situation for, as the learnéd Festus explains, "It is not permitted to sacrifice this man, yet he who kills him will not be condemned for homicide" (Agamben 1998, p.71). As such, the sacred man or *homo sacer* finds himself juridically suspended between life and death. There is a solemn interdiction on his murder, yet also a legal impossibility: killing him cannot be called murder. It is this paradoxical double state of sacristy and debasement that provides Agamben with the ornate, rusty key to unlock the secrets of our confounding biomodernity, committed as it is to the protection of life, yet also author of the greatest genocidal acts of war possibly in history. You can imagine the scholar putting down his pen for a moment, looking up at the Roman light slanting through high-placed windows, the many-moted air of a venerable cache of mouldering tomes appearing to sparkle and fizz before his tired eyes, and thinking, "Ecco! This is it!"

As Agamben, the perfectionist, over months and years, pursues the various references to the *homo sacer* in a dizzying array of forgotten or neglected texts in multiple languages, like some metaphysical Montalbano, he opens up a whole vista of obscure scholarship around this double enigma: a person whose killing is unpunishable but whose sacrifice is banned. Intrigued by this paradox, Agamben digs ever deeper, days passing into weeks in the fusty Vatican air. Trains taken to distant provincial Italian libraries in the north turn up new leads. Hours spent in Paris at the Bibliotheque Nationale Français help to cement the case. Slowly but surely the evidence accretes and forms into a coherent and explosive thesis. As the philosophical clock-maker tinkers with his conceptual machinery, so, ideas already on his mind pertaining to power, Foucault, the Holocaust, Hannah Arendt, life as such, scapegoating, coma patients and Walter Benjamin begin to coalesce into what we now can see as the second chapter in the history of biopolitics. It is an episode concerned less with the question of the implications of our *right* to life, as Foucault insisted in the 1970s, but on the very conception of the *nature* of life as such as Agamben defines it in the early 1990s.

Giorgio Agamben is, by all accounts, the very opposite of the charming racehorse of a man that was the Michel Foucault phenomenon. Although he has achieved some kind of global success, it did not result in his becoming a national treasure at home, let alone the world's most famous thinker, as Foucault came to be described. Agamben enjoys little or no celebrity in Italy and a certain unwillingness to travel, coupled with a diffidence in his make-up means there is no exciting story to tell about when he changed everything in front of everyone in a famous lecture hall, but change everything he undoubtedly did in his own idiosyncratic and wilfully circumlocutory fashion. Sometimes the most exciting story in my field goes like this: someone works for years in obscurity and then publishes an amazing book which people eventually read, and that is precisely what Agamben did in 1995 when he released *Homo Sacer: Sovereign Power and Bare Life.*

As the title suggests, it is an investigation of the relation between old-school sovereign power and Foucauldian biopower, suggesting not that biopower over-takes and part-replaces sovereign power as Foucault would have it, but that power as such in the West, since at least the Greeks, is defined by an articulated relationship between sovereign power over life and death, and the biopolitical injunction to make live and let die. A dual, uneasy, ever-shifting, tensile rela-tionship of potency and powerlessness captured by the weird juridical suspended being of that ancient *homo sacer* figure who made himself known to Agamben one day in a dusty library. The book was translated into English in 1998 and almost immediately had an impact across many diverse fields. I think it is credible to claim that there would have been little of the excitement around Foucauldian biopolitics without Agamben's book. There would not have been, for example, an instalment of the Kassel art festival documenta curated by the great Gerhard Richter called "Bare Life" in 2008 (Lagnado 2008), a key term from Agamben's 1995 study. And it is not just art that felt the impact of Agamben, think also about political science, international relations, theology, literary, theatre and film stud-ies and, of course, philosophy without *Homo Sacer.* It is pretty hard to do now.

Unlike Foucault's lectures however, *Homo Sacer,* brilliantly written though it is, was not intended for a general audience and in fact suffered for more than a decade from misreadings and misunderstandings. After years of activity around the book, there remain aspects that escape the wit of even the most talented and willing readers. Whatever else you can say about the tome, and it is one of those that has such profundity that it supports a whole industry of interpretation, it is resolutely *not* a book about violence and yet, it is also unmistakably nothing *but* a book about violence, in particular bioviolence, or what I am calling bioviolence at least. All of which encapsulated in the question of an ancient Roman figure, the *homo sacer,* and a 20th-century conundrum: how did democratic states flip so easily into totalitarian ones, such that their biopolitics of life management became Esposito's thanatopolitics of genocide?

If Agamben's work was instrumental in the development of our appreciation of Foucault's biopolitics, it is actually a rather devastating critique of his great forebear. Agamben agrees with Foucault, certainly, that biopower defines our age, and that the idea of life is now the basis of all political action. But he does not concur with his hero that this began sometime in the 18th century. Rather, in excavating a forgotten figure of ancient Roman law, he sets out to demonstrate that power as such, all political action, since at least the ancient Greeks, is defined by the politics of life. More than this, the idea of life is very much just an idea, a discursive construct. Unlike Foucault, Agamben does not appear to view life as, say, an objective part of the milieu, in the form of illness, birth rates, hunger and the fear of death, but as something that is somehow produced by language. 'Life' is certainly something like a *dispositif* in Foucault; it has a regulatory rather than defining or indicative function, for example, but unlike in Foucault, in Agamben's work, the term 'life' doesn't name a materially delimited institution but is something approaching a meta-concept, Agamben's theory of the signature. As a signature rather than an institution, life is able to move across time and space allowing it the power to manifest in a wide array of institutions, most of which are simply too ancient to be regulatory in the data-based Foucauldian sense. If all our politics is biopolitics, therefore, Agamben's work argues, it goes far beyond the limited sense of the term in Foucault and results in a richer conception of bioviolence for us along the way.

The two lives: *zoe* and *bios*

Agamben's first point on the first page of *Homo Sacer* is an attempt to shock us out of assuming that life is a word we use to refer to an objective reality in which we all participate that began 3.8 billion years ago. Lover of the past though he undoubtedly is, Agamben doesn't relish going that far back and indeed studiously avoids evolutionary theory for the most part leaving the nexus between Darwin and biopolitics to his compatriot Roberto Esposito to unpick. Instead, Agamben's magpie-mind alights upon a section of German philosopher Hannah Arendt's *The Human Condition*, where she mentions that the Greeks had no single word for life. Instead, she explains, they spoke of two aspects of living, *zoe*, which is your animal, genetic, private life, usually located in the realm of Greek existence called the *oikonomia*, the domestic or private sphere, origin of our word economy. And *bios*, not, confusingly, the biological aspect of life, but the public, lived element of existence, enacted in what the Greeks called the *polis*, or public sphere, origin of our term politics (Arendt 1958, pp.22–8). Suggesting that if we were being really accurate, and perhaps if Foucault had read Arendt, we should speak of zoepower, zoepolitics and zoeviolence.

Arendt, as a German Jew who had to flee Nazi Germany and take up residence in the US, who is famous for her cold-eyed study *The Origins of Totalitarianism*, currently enjoying a bounce thanks to Trump, who coined the famous phrase "the banality of evil" when reporting on the trial of Adolf Eichmann, and wrote her major works under the threat of nuclear war, remains refreshingly optimistic in her many considerations of the essence of power and the political. More so than the mordant Agamben, for example. For her, there was an ideal version of Greek politics, where your private, biological existence, your *zoe*, was kept out of public political discourse, a healthy separation that only began to break down as Greek politics started to take the *oikonomia* as a place of interest and in doing so also transformed the language of politics making it more confrontational, personal and violent (Arendt 1958, pp.28–37). It is touching, but also philosophically astute, of Arendt to trace the origins of political violence to politicians being rude to each other in an old Greek town, for after all violence as a regulatory principle is a discursive and social construct with real, bodily outcomes: harsh words will inevitably lead to harsh acts. There is in Arendt's masterpiece a clear link between violence and *zoe* although she appears uncertain what it is composed of precisely. This irresolution however does not hamper her from arguing in *On Violence* that politics and violence are not inevitable bedfellows but, in fact, anathema in that, for her, the opposite of violence is not non-violence, but power itself. It is clear, she says, that states use violence in pursuit of power, but, she argues, there have been no successful states based purely on violence because violence is but a means, while power is about human ends, and you cannot have a state of pure means without ends (Arendt 1970).

Whether Agamben accepts this final position, well that seems unlikely, he is profoundly influenced, I think, by Arendt's historical realisation that the idea of a single 'life' is a construct, meaning life per se is constructed not biologically essential. He is also taken with the dialectical relation between two different kinds of life: *zoe* or your personal, biological materiality, and *bios*, your public existence. Finally, he is obviously inspired by Arendt's belief that when the Greek state started to make political discourse out of elements pertaining to the *oiko-nomia* or domestic sphere, it altered politics before the concept had even really begun. So much so that, contra-Foucault and for that matter Arendt, Agamben stops thinking of a moment when politics invades biology and begins instead to speak of politics as a matter of biology or, more specifically, that politics, power itself, is defined by the tension, opposition and interchange of two conceptions of life: biological and political (Agamben 1995, p.1). And, like Arendt, for him, this inevitably leads to violence, albeit for very different reasons.

Homo Sacer Redux

When does it lead to violence? There can be no smoking gun but Agamben does identify that Roman legal figure which, for him, marks the emergence, for the first time, of a specific mode of political violence that, tied as it is to the biological existence of a person, is exemplary of our own modern bioviolence. A *homo sacer* is, according to ancient sources, a person who is no longer a Roman citizen, but nor were they a slave, rather they were a kind of legalised and formalised, quasi-religious scapegoat. While alive they were treated as something sacred but, when things went bad, they could be killed sacrificially by the state without this being termed murder. The *homo sacer* occupied an odd suspended spatial relation to the Roman state, in that they were included in it, even enjoying special treatment, but, by the same measure were permanently excluded because, unlike all other citizens, they could be put to death for no reason and yet this will not be considered a criminal act. They were effectively defined by law as being outside the law, if you can grasp such a paradoxical state; they were kept inside the walls of the city as a fragment of the skirmishing animalistic outside that the walls were raised to exclude. This odd legal situation placed their life, in particular, in a state of suspense between life and death as I said. Their vital existence was protected so that they could die outside the protections of the state afforded to all others, when necessary. The *homo sacer* was the original dead man walking. It was they, and not the Haitian slave republicans, that formed the origin of the idea of the zombie. Agamben defines them as occupying an impossible spatial and vital situation which he calls the "included exclusion" or, later on in the book, the camp (Agamben 1995, pp.166–80). As he says: "*Life that cannot be sacrificed and yet may be killed is sacred life*" (Agamben 1995, p.82). He goes on in the book to finally call it bare life.

The *homo sacer* is, for Agamben, an early example of how once the state takes life to be an object of its regard; it can commit an act of violence against a subject that is not determined by simply the biopolitics of letting die, but through actively killing in a manner that is still in keeping with the biopolitical imperative to make live. As in the logic of scapegoating, the *homo sacer* must be killed, so that the rest of the population can live on. It is the first legalised example of how bioviolence pursues an active policy of life destruction as an essential regulatory mechanism of the overall injunction to make live. To make live you must let die, but you must also sacrifice, you must also make die, bringing together the two strands of sovereign and biopower that Foucault mistakenly places in some kind of temporal or historical successive palimpsest. The bioviolence of sacrificeable life, bare life as Agamben goes on to call it (Agamben 1995, p.6), shows us that sovereign right over life and death never goes away, of course, even if Foucault often suggests it is superseded by biopolitical rights to make live and let die. What Agamben adds to Foucault's sketch, which is really all it is in the lectures, is that making live is an active principle of letting die. The state makes *homines sacrii*, it constructs scapegoats, so that it can let them die at opportune moments. There is, in truth, little or no difference between holding a *homo sacer* in reserve to sacrifice to Roman gods when crops fail and regulatory exclusion of the poor, say as a necessary component of food management, who are then neglected to death when, guess what, 2,000 years later, crops still fail.

For the *homo sacer* scapegoat mechanism to be effective, politically and legally—remember this was a result of Roman law, the origin of all our legal systems, not just the wilful act of a cracked emperor with a bloodlust—certain legal and political things had to happen. First the Roman citizen must have their citizenry stripped from them, meaning that the imperative "make live" is clearly tied to something more than simply being human and alive again, contravening Foucault's assertion "life rights replace the rights of citizenship and guild." Second, the death of the *homo sacer* is a propitiatory and inoculatory necessary act to protect real citizens from threats to their life: failed crops, barbarian invasion, the wrath of gods, that sort of thing. Thus it becomes clear that in terms of the demand that a state make live, it was always the case that this would mean, inevitably, that it would have to kill someone, not by letting die, but thanks to a form of state-sanctioned execution that was not, however, an execution or a murder, but a sacrifice. Third, it means we should look again at the term 'make live' focusing on the activity of making more than living, so as to realise here that, yes, life is a mode of construction and that the life of the *homo sacer* had to be reconstructed such that the removal of their biological life, their *zoe*, did not impinge on their political existence, their *bios*.

Obviously, in this matter, the inheritance of two kinds of life, biological and political, is both a help, you can take one and leave the other unmolested, and a hindrance, as the two are taken to be interrelated and yet also out of bounds, in that a state should only concern itself with *bios* and leave *zoe* up to the head of the household, the vagaries of the ancient milieu and, ultimately, the gods. So we need a kind of life that can be described only in terms of its biology, such that when one expunges it, legally speaking no crime is committed, and of a sort that it is impossible to speak of it as in any way politically valuable. What the state needs is a life divested of all meaning, a sacred life in the sense of the term which originally simply meant separate; a life that is not made, that is devoid of significance, denuded of value, a bare life. The scapegoating of Shamima Begum performs precisely this purpose.

10

SHAMIMA BEGUM, OUR *FEMINA SACRA*

When Raqqa finally fell, Begum and thousands of other 'wives' either fled or were forced out of the city by the remaining ISIS fighters. They were deemed to be in the way of the last days of jihad. A disproportionate number of the women were with child, as was Shamima, who ended up in the al-Hawl camp, a displacement facility set-up to collect and massify the wives and children of ISIS fighters. The conditions in this camp remain appalling. As one recent report has it:

> Small children and babies lie unattended on the muddy ground: one boy, no more than two years old, is clearly in a feverish sleep. Children with no shoes walk on the dirty nappies and other rubbish that litters the area. The smell of human waste is overpowering.
>
> *(McKernan 2019)*

It is perhaps no surprise therefore that Begum sought to be repatriated to her home country, which she assumed to be Great Britain. However, once her request was processed, then Home Secretary Sajiv Javid, pursuing Theresa May's populist credo of 'hostile environment' for refugees, asylum seekers and immigrants, instead refused Begum the right to return to these unwelcoming shores. A decision that shocked the liberal left to some degree, but which on the whole appeared to be, if not popular, at least not particularly contested. It transpired that few here in the UK wanted Shamima Begum or her child to come home, their crimes being too great to forgive one can only assume. The vitriol poured down on this misguided young woman was, frankly, disgusting. One commentator in *The Sun* tabloid newspaper demanded that the government gave up trying to get the Bethnal Green girls back to the UK suggesting "we should leave them to get on with epilating their leg hair and pleasuring spawn of Satan."

While a piece in the normally liberal *The Independent* was literally dripping with hate concluding, "I'd go so far as to say you shouldn't be allowed back into the country ever" (Moaveni 2019, pp.204–5).

The lack of perspective in the UK over this issue perhaps explains how successful the bioviolence of coercion and massification has been in demonising the decisions of the Bethnal Green girls. Begum did a bad thing in leaving for Raqqa, committed a crime indeed, albeit one due to the controversial anti-terror legislation that was ushered in after 9/11 and has been a significant drain on our rights ever since, and it is of course speculated that she may have done bad things while she was there, or at least been complicit in them, so that she was particularly vilified in the right-wing popular press is not too difficult to understand. That said, her main crime does not appear to be joining ISIS as a child-bride, but her lack of remorse for doing so. She made it abundantly clear in that first *Times* interview that she only left Raqqa because she was forced to, that she was not sorry about joining ISIS and that she wanted to return to the UK mainly for the sake of her unborn son. When questioned, infamously, about seeing that severed head in a bin she responded: "Were these not journalists and stuff that were caught spying?" (Loyd 2019). This was not interpreted as a child desensitised to violence due to trauma, as it has been for the actual natives of Raqqa, but evidence that she was simply evil. Why is that? Her lack of remorse is important as it seems to be the primary reason for the scapegoating of Shamima Begum who, in reality, has not actually been proven to have committed any atrocities. All the same her decision to join ISIS is presented as wilful and shocking, even though at 15, according to the UN law at least, she qualifies for the status of child-soldier which includes not just young boys in the Congo forced to carry Kalashnikovs, but also women trafficked into sex-work including forcible marriage, as was the case with 15-year-old Shamima from North London. Yet Begum was not treated as a child-soldier by Javid in contravention, by the way, of more of those pesky international laws. Again, why is that Sajiv Javid?

There is, I think, something misogynistic and gynophobic about her treatment if I can for the moment make this distinction. You can see it clearly in the sexualised imagery of that execrable piece in *The Sun* which also, incongruously, makes reference to the ISIS brides as "sporting nothing more than a burka and industrial lubricant" (Moaveni 2019, p.204), which I can only presume is a sexual slur. Young brides, fleeing our shores, to breed terrorists, in an 'industrial' yet also supposedly medieval set-up, biologically creating young radical offspring, bypassing the complex and time-consuming process of 'radicalisation,' speaks to the very heart of our paedophobic treatment of the 'child migrant' interloper as a potential disease in the heart of the body politics that calls for radical immunisation. It is as if Begum has allowed herself to be absorbed by the genetic swarming pattern of ISIS' natal terrorism programme strapline: breeding the terrorists of the future. There is no question that these offspring are innocent children, but at the deeper imaginary level of Esposito's logic of immunisation, there is also an uncanny sense that they have to have become terrorists almost at a genetic, pre-birth level, as if infected in the womb by the distorted words of firebrand clerics echoing through the amniotic gloom. This is what I mean by gynophobia, the fear of the monstrous woman of the womb that French feminist Julia Kristeva often talks of as the basis of all that we find abject, that which we set aside in order that we may live, those we exclude by expelling them from the inside (Kristeva 1982). According to Kristeva, for the man, the womb-woman is monstrous, while for the women, the child itself is an intruder her body strives to eject as some abject, parasitic thing. As for the misogyny inherent on Begum's treatment, that is only too easy to detect. Feminist commentators mentioned at the time that the hatred in our society towards the unrepentant woman who transgresses the laws of correct gender behavioural types is particularly pronounced.

Put all these unspoken prejudices together and you find that the admittedly unsympathetic Begum is the victim of a triple-threat of Islamo-, paedo- and gyno-phobias. Resulting in the fact that even now you would be hard-pressed to find many in the UK with sympathy for her terrible situation. While I don't buy this vilification, one can see where it comes from. Begum is a natural candidate for *homo sacralisation*, and if her life is now made bare, in Agamben's sense, living as surviving in some benighted camp, then I can appreciate that she ought to join the end of the lengthy queue of victims of the Syrian war and the war on terror her life, any other preferential treatment forfeited by her actions. But it is not just about her life is it, what about that of Jarrah, her third child?

The bare lifing of Jarrah, Shamima Begum's third child

Shamima Begum's third child, Jarrah, died on Friday, 8 March 2019, in a Syrian refugee camp located on Jordanian territory called al Roj, although it was born in the notorious al-Hawl camp, before being transferred to al Roj in the third and final week of its illness-blighted life. The boy had been suffering from breathing difficulties and appears to have died from asphyxiation due to pneumonia. This wheezing little child who managed only 21 days on this earth before he went blue and cold and died was, in fact, the third child Begum had lost. He was also one of literally thousands of ISIS children being raised in holding camps all around Syria and the surrounding overspill nations, many born to European nationals. Predictably most European countries have been as unwilling as the UK to take any responsibility for these infants for reasons that are perhaps now becoming a little clearer: paedophobia, gynophobia and the biopolitical need for autoimmunisation against those citizens that turn against the state and become infectious agents that threaten the health of the whole organism if not dealt with rapidly and harshly. Yet one cannot, biopolitically speaking, simply eradicate such threats for, as we know, an essential part of the biopolitical contract is the preservation and enhancement of life, even if it is the lives of tiny proto-terrorists that are visible only when shoved under the biopolitical microscope. To convert these ticking terror-bomb broods into beings that can be policed, deported, excluded, even stripped of their nationhood, a process is habitually pursued, and much of Agamben's *Homo Sacer* tells the story of how this occurs through history.

For the *homo sacer* to be legally sacrificeable, their life has to be converted from one kind of legal currency, to a post-legal, anomic one. What Agamben stipulates very clearly is that bare life, a life that can be taken and it not be called murder, is the end product of a cultural, bioconstructed, bioproduction if you will. In our culture we have, over time, travelled from no specific word for human life but rather two specific types of life existence, *zoe* and *bios* (the Greeks), through the conflation of the two into one sense of human life, Roman law, to a point in Roman law where the animal part of the *zoe–bios* pairing, the *zoe* part in other words, is foregrounded by the *bios*, or public sense of life, citizenry and existence, through being ritualistically stripped away: the *homo sacer*. Bare life, on this reading, is very much animal life, or life as mere animalistic, biological, genetic existence. But it is not the same as *zoe*, our sense of biological, animal existence, because it is constructed as the animalising of *bios*, a construction of divestment or Kristevan abjection, a process mere animals cannot experience because they are never afforded the status of *bios*.

What particularly matters for Agamben in this process is the narrativisation of the idea of life, the step-by-step process of the construction of an idea of an articulated human life, in preparation for the re-animalisation of the victim, by confiscating the better part of their humanity, their *bios*. Agamben concludes that while it is intrinsic to the modern sense of life that we are all part animal, hum-animals as I have called us, just as there is sacred power in the elevating of certain animals to personhood status, #Harambe, there is a special place in hell for those abject humans that have allowed themselves to degenerate from human back towards mere animal existence. Terrorists of all waters, including those who are not terrorists but are deemed to be asymptomatic carriers of the disease such as Begum, her son and all those other ISIS offspring held in refugee camp limbo, naturally fall into this category. One of Agamben's great insights is that it is not bare life that we hate so much as characters placed within the story of laying bare our animal vitalism, or how you had the temerity to renounce your right to *bios*, though your own lamentable actions or even when this renunciation is enforced upon you by outside agencies. To become sacred, which means little more than set apart, you first of all need to be an intrinsic part.

I suppose the final piece of this puzzle, or the twist in the tale, is that there is no such thing as animal or bare life, until humans look back retroactively to historically invent it. Factually speaking, first, there is no clear definition of biological life at the present time, and second, the idea of animal life as being within us, but not the same as human life, is a fairy tale we tell so as to better define human life. So that while the shaggy dog tale says animals came first then human life was animal life+, the order of the narrative is human life first, animal life constructed second, and bare life, the re-animalising of certain baleful humans, coming a very poor third. Which is all a very complicated way of saying bare life, the *homo sacer*, the scapegoat, the terrorist, Donald Trump Jr's poisoned skittle and so on, (all these contemporary abject vitalities not punishable by death or murder, but by a contemporary, secular sacrificial rite of exclusionary quarantine), do not name states of being, but functions and operations of *coming to be*. Bare lifed humans are not hated so much as entered into a nightmarish narrative of life as punishment, through our hatred of what they might become or what they might turn us into. As I said, there is a special place in hell reserved for such nasty individuals, literally beyond the pale, and that special place, in our corrupted century is called the downstream holding camp.

How was Begum's third child inducted into the holding camp's processing of its delicate life into sacrificeable bare life? Agamben's three-part consideration of the making of the juridical exception of *homo sacer* is a helpful model to better explain this arcane set of regulations and procedures. First, we noted, the person in question needs to be stripped of citizenship. Then their death must be determined as possessive of an inoculatory power. And third, their bare life, has to be literally made up, constructed, created through storytelling. Let's go back then to Shamima Begum's rejected request to return home to her country of birth, why was it refused, how could it be legally? Sajiv Javid, in a pigeon-hearted playing to the crowd, rapidly moved to, and was eventually successful in, stripping Begum of her British citizenship because, it was claimed, she possessed joint citizenship with Bangladesh. This stipulation is necessary, it being illegal otherwise to deny a UK national their citizenship. Admittedly, there was a spike in the revocation of UK citizenship in 2017, with just over 100 cases reported, all on the ground that they were deemed "conducive to the public good," but all of these involved dual citizenship, it being considered inhuman by two separate UN laws to leave any peoples stateless regardless of their crimes. Although Theresa May tried in 2014 to pass a law that got around this problem, it was defeated in the lords, and a protection against statelessness clause added in. In any case, the 2014 law primarily concerned 'naturalised' citizens, not born here, whereas Begum was born in London and is as British as any of us.

Bangladeshi heritage may or may not confer Bangladeshi nationality, as Javid argued, but in this case it clearly did not. Begum is not a Bangladeshi citizen according to the authorities in Bangladesh whom, one must assume, would know this better than anyone. All the same, her British citizenship was stolen from her and at present she remains de facto stateless in a holding camp in north-east Syria, the precise outcome the UN wished to avoid with their international lawmaking. Why is being stateless so terrible, well, to use Butler's term, it ramps up the precarity of your existence. Recent individuals who have had their citizenship revoked have been killed by drone strikes, for example, or tried in nations without the same rule of law they might enjoy back at home. Children without papers are easily trafficked, as are women. While overwhelming evidence suggests that statelessness makes one more vulnerable to radicalisation and, perhaps, misguided acts of terrorism (Bisset 2019), nationality, therefore, whatever else it is, is a prophylactic against abuse and threat to life which is another way of stating the biopolitical codicil to the Hobbesian social contract. If a government whose biopolitical role is to make live its citizens, actively revokes their citizenship, then this is one more example of how bare life reveals that there is an active violence inherent to biopolitical states, a calculated manner by which to make live becomes make, not just let, die. This is, in effect, what Begum's being divested of her UK citizenship meant, and while I am sure it was not the intention of the UK government for this to result in the death of her son, it is hardly surprising that it did, statistically speaking which is, may I remind you, the lingua franca of every biopolitical state.

So what of Shamima Begum's third child? Was he a UK citizen when he was born in a holding camp on Jordanian soil? The simple answer to that is, yes, yes he was. Children born to British citizens, whatever the circumstances, are British. By the same gesture, according to international law, even if you wanted to refuse Begum her nationality, as we said she falls under the child-soldier provision which means we, in the UK, are compelled by law to protect her, whatever it is perceived she may have done. Let me now quote the list of rights that lawyers agree are extendable to all children born of Islamic State to European citizens, UK included:

> The UK is under binding, legal obligations to consider the best interests of these children, to ensure their rights to life, survival and development, to be legally registered with a name and nationality. As far as is possible, they have rights to know and be cared for by their parents, and to the highest attainable standards of health and education.
>
> *(Bisset 2019)*

All of these rights are deemed unlikely, to say the least, if the parents of the children are detained in refugee camps, as in the case of Shamima Begum. In short, the first mechanism for the state to actively make death by downgrading human life to bare life is to remove citizenship. Even the Nazis followed this logic when they began to detain the German Jews. When Sajiv Javid took Begum's nationality from her, illegally as far as I am concerned, he by definition transformed her son into a child born into bare life. Even if he had survived, it remains a bone of contention if Javid would have recognised his British status. Evidence suggests this would hardly be likely to occupy the top of his in-tray.

Our second mode of making bare life as an active process of the bioviolence of making die is the fear of contamination. This is not an idle fear in this case. ISIS was explicit that the ISIS brides were in Raqqa to breed as many future soldiers to the cause as possible. Javid's justification for stealing Begum's citizen's rights may have been motivated by base populism rather than internalised racism, but he knew that it was fear of the radical in our midst that would permit him to get away with breaking international law, at least on the home front. As we saw with the whole, is he or isn't he a child migrant spectacle of 2016. There is a fundamental fear of 'racial' and 'ideological' infection in the UK that is typical of Esposito's definition of the biopolitical as *immunitas*.

The final piece of the puzzle, the story of Shamima Begum, the terror-bride of ISIS, need not and indeed should not be recounted. It was hardly my nation's finest hour. All we ought to say is how devastatingly effective it has been. While it remains unclear what Begum's crimes specifically are, it is easy to say that if she gave up her precious *bios*, well, it was her own choice after all. This argument is one I find deeply disturbing indeed, and I don't use this word lightly, fascist. It demands of me that I at the very least pose counter-narratives to the self-bare-lifing story that continues to make the rounds of the popular and right-wing press. Begum did not choose to leave the UK and join a terror organisation. She was manipulated and groomed while she was still a minor. While in Raqqa, as it stands, there is no proof that she was anything other than the victim of an enforced marriage, which initially was statutory rape and, in that she was not free to leave the city until the brides were forcibly ejected by their husbands, was also kidnapping. When she was interviewed in the holding camp, her inability to express remorse, did not by any means suggest she no longer wanted to be a British Citizen. Criticising your own nation is surely one of the most important privileges of being a citizen of a democracy as is hating your country, betraying elements of its culture and so on. Another important element is that if you commit a crime, you are brought home to face UK justice. It seems to me that Begum's perpetual encampment will remain an open wound in our culture, because after all, justice is as much if not more about the community coming to terms with a rupture, and reconvening over its values, as it is base punishment. An untried, unpunished Begum remains a kind of bogeywoman at large, a useful gremlin for the powers that be, but in the end a source of anxiety and maybe guilt for the rest of us. It may be going a tad too far to suggest it, but then again Sajiv Javid started with the excessive overkill in this case so I will take his actions as my permission for what is to follow, but in my eyes, Begum was never a more effective terrorist than she is now. Our petty refusal to allow her to come home seems to be based almost entirely on our national fear of what might happen if she were to do so. A petulant 19-year-old appears to have the world's fifth largest economy running scared. If Begum seemed to have no regret in regards of her actions, why is that not an indication of the brutality she was subjected to? If she finds a head in a bin rather ho-hum, this is only evidence of her evil if she put it there. Otherwise it is simply a powerful symptom of her becoming numbed to atrocity through repeated exposure.

When it comes to her son, things get much more complicated. The narrative of Begum's unrepentant radicalisation is a necessary part of the manner by which the UK government scapegoated Begum, made her into a *homo sacer* by systematically laying bare her *bios* until there was nothing of her right to life left, except survival. The classic definition of the bare life of the *homo sacer* in Agamben being the denizen of the concentration camp. What is missing however from this description is what happens if bare life bears life. We know that a child born of a UK citizen is British, but what is a child born of a *homo sacer*, or of a stateless woman called? We may have carefully composed processes for narrativising the divestiture and active dispossession of life rights through the processes of bare lifing, but we do not appear to have worked through a process of rehabilitation for their offspring. Would Begum's son have had his citizenship revoked along with his mother's? If not, would this not entail his forcible removal from his mother, and if this were the case would this not contravene the UN's interdiction of enforced statelessness and so on and so on? All ancient societies had a workable system of scapegoating, few it seems had an equivalent mechanism for its reversal. So it seems that along with the violence of neglect, and the willed coercive act of bare lifing, we have a third means by which biopolitical states can cause harm to the lives of the very citizens they are sworn to protect, bare life by proxy, *homo sacralisation* as collateral damage. The title of this chapter should perhaps have been, 'The accidental scapegoat.'

Sacrificeable life: theorising the scapegoat

Another name for the bare life of a child deemed of no legal and regulatory value is what anthropologist René Girard calls a sacrificeable life. After the shooting of Harambe, the lowland gorilla in 2016, it was often said that the animal had been 'sacrificed' to save the life of Isiah Gregg. Sometimes we speak of sacrifice to justify the death of members of the military during incursions that are not quite wars, whose final outcomes are both obscure and perhaps ultimately impossible, like the so-called war on terror. As anti-immigrant policies lose their moral footing around the globe, it is not uncommon to consider migrants as sacrificeable bare lives of what Girard prefers to call them, scapegoats. While the regular expunging of civilian life during drone sorties is called collateral damage, modern parlance, surely, for the ancient practices of scapegoating and sacrifice. The vocabulary and machinery of sacrifice, in other words, remains intrinsic to contemporary global and local politics, yet our understanding of the mechanism remains vague, that is unless one reads Girard's great study of sacrifice, *Violence and the Sacred* (Girard 1988). People sometimes call Girard a philosophical anthropologist, but to be brutally frank, he was no philosopher and not much of an anthropologist either. His observations weren't based on first-hand field work, for example, but very often used literary sources as ritualistic evidence, looking for patterns of universal human behaviour across bodies of national literatures. This is an approach that even my fellow literary scholars would find risible and is certainly a method that during these data-obsessed days would be mocked in most academies. Yet, all the same, Girard's suspect methodology resulted in observations on human behaviour with no real science behind them, but which still chime at a deep level with our own intimations about who we are and why we do the things we do to those who are alien to us or who we instinctively fear. Think of Girard as a sort of post-war French Freud with an eye more drawn to the tribe, than the family, and to literature rather than the fiction of personal recollection. And like Freud, Girard's work begins with a consideration of the assumed universality of human desire.

Girard's basic point is that human beings differ from animals in that they are post-evolved. By this he means animals act out of necessity, but humans with advanced cognitive skills, tool-making tools, settled agrarian lives, capable of civilisation, are able to meet their survival needs such that they can start to act out of desire rather than necessity or do what they want rather than what they have to do to ensure their gene pool. It is an idea with sustainable power because it accords with observations of other thinkers, for example, Arendt who defines the human condition as coming together, talking, such that a decision can be made based on what a community wants or desires that is a new act, non-necessary in essence, something she argues animals are simply incapable of experiencing (Arendt 1958).

If it is true that humans don't act out of necessity, Girard asks in his early work (Kirwan 2004, pp.14–37), why do they do the things they do in a communal manner? He concludes that all human desires are effectively mimetic. We see what others around us want, and perhaps what our ancestors wanted and, being mimetic beings, we want the same thing. If we all want the same things, and we are all ostensibly similar, then this leads to rivalry, probably the great theme of Girard's work (Girard 1988, pp.161–8). We want what our neighbours want and, because they also want it, then naturally conflict will ensue. Again it is an idea with strong advocates. For example, it barely differs from Thomas Hobbes' famous example of the war of all against all if no sovereign is in place to adjudicate, one of the main justifications for contemporary Western democracies. Yet the two great thinkers also differ in that Girard sees perpetual war as a result of not being in a state of nature, while Hobbes sees it as a result of our animalistic aspect with his famous description of our bestial lives as "solitary, poor, nasty, brutish and short" (Hobbes 1996, p.84). Rivalrous violence based on indifference of desire, by this I mean there is no differentiation to be drawn between what each of us wants, no difference in our powers to get it and no real reason why we want these things, by definition can have no end. Girard in fact writes often and with great eloquence on the violence that results from indifferentiation in Greek tragedy and Shakespeare alike.

Pre-legal societies, ostensibly ruled by religious and ritualistic precepts rather than legal and politically enshrined laws, need a mechanism to put a stop to the cycles of mimetic violence that result from the indifference of human desire. Otherwise, the very thing that leads to mimetic rivalry, civilisation as the removal of evolutionary necessity, would result in the destruction of all cultures. This mechanism Girard famously calls scapegoating after an ancient Jewish custom, although his sense of the term differs a good deal from that (Girard 1988, pp.1–43; Kirwan 2004, pp.38–62). A scapegoat is a being determined by a community to be sacrificeable. What does that mean precisely? First the term sacrifice comes from the word to separate. So a scapegoat must be separable. What does this mean in practice? They must be similar enough to a community to be seen as not totally other and alien, otherwise you cannot ritualistically separate them from a community, because they were never a part of that community. Yet at the same time their separation must be such that a cycle of mimetic violence is not incurred by their death. For example, while the Jews used scapegoats as propitiatory offerings to appease the gods, the wider use of the scapegoat was a pre-legal method for settling internal tensions and disputes.

If, for example, someone in the tribe kills another member due to mimetic rivalry or steals from them for the same reason, then a member of the wronged person's family will retaliate in kind. This will then lead to an internal rivalry amongst familial groups, all part of the same community, all of equal power, all equally wronged. This is a classic indifferentiation of desire; everyone the same wanting the same thing with the same justification, for which there is no solution, and which can destroy entire tribes, civilisations even. As pre-legal societies do not yet have a judicial Leviathan á la Hobbes to adjudicate on these matters, the law being effectively, according to Girard, the differentiation of justice or finding for one party over the other, from time to time cycles of violence need to be appeased in a way that is differentiated. So to be sacrificeable means to be similar enough to be in a community so that they can be expelled from it. But different enough so that they have no relatives within the tribe asking for revenge, but also so that the mimetic function of rivalry is fulfilled for all parties: they are like me, their death satisfies me that in terms of what I want, I was successful and they were not.

Girard notes numerous examples of the difficulty in finding this balance. It is no coincidence, he says, that brothers and twins are often the basis for folk tales and tragedies of violence, as excess of visible similarity is a real threat for rivalrous indifferentiation (Girard 1988, pp.64–6). If you want to kill someone to appease indetermination of desire in this way, then you need a rival surrogate. If another human, they must be from a different tribe. Ostensibly similar to you in terms of desires, but different enough in terms of kinship, that you can kill them to create a point of difference that will not return to immediately bite you back. Animals also function well because they possess *zoe*, or animal life, as do humans, but they lack *bios*; they have no political status. If an animal is to be killed, then its indifferential inclusion is harder to attain; goats differ greatly from relatives on the whole, so they should be kept in the community for long periods of time as already earmarked for sacrifice yet also able to feel part of the furniture. Thus it was over time that a scapegoat was ostensibly an animal thought of as sacred in the same manner as the *homo sacer*, maintained as separate from, yet included in, a community, say in a special pen, such that they could be sacrificed when internal tensions based on rivalrous indetermination threatened the stability of the tribal culture.

To sum up, to be an effective scapegoat, to be sacrificeable, the victim has to be similar enough to assuage rivalrous desire so that one has the sense that one's rival has been dispatched, but different enough to avoid starting a new spiral of rivalrous violence due to being dispatched. The scapegoat, therefore, tells the story of sacrifice as separation where being separate or being different is a process you have to go through, not a state of being that you simply possess. It is a mode of construction wherein indifferentiation is systematically converted into differentiation, so that it is less accurate to say a scapegoat is someone picked on because they are different, but someone who comes to be said to be different, because they can be picked on.

Scapegoating is not quite bare lifing

One can see I hope the similarities between scapegoating and bare life. *Homo sacer* means the sacrificeable man. What Agamben makes clear is that his sacredness is merely the peculiarity of his being a separable part of a human culture. In addition, because his life has been converted into bare life, this also allows us to say that his *zoe* or animal existence can be stripped from his *bios* or political life. If you remember, the difference between *zoe* and bare life is the mechanism of confiscating a citizen's *bios*, of denuding them of it, hence the efficacy of the idea of bareness, both laying bare your mere animality and stripping you bare of the vestments of citizenship. However, there is a radical and important difference between our two great thinkers of scapegoating. Girard sees scapegoating as a function of pre-legal societies, a bad habit of tribalism, that perhaps still lives on as a negative tendency to victimise the other, that the law has to be ever vigilant to stamp out. Agamben views the *homo sacer* as almost diametrically opposed to Girard's much more optimistic Hobbesian humanism. For Agamben rather the very idea of law, of the state, the judiciary and the sovereign is the necessary selection by the powers that be of an internalised abnormality, a proportion of any population held in reserve, suspended between citizen and animal, life and death, so that in times of crisis, these abject individuals are pre-selected for sacrifice. It is, in fact, brutally Foucauldian in essence.

If you remember, Foucault argued that regulatory norms which facilitate massification into populations that can be managed, by definition, have to have irregular abnormalities which must then be sacrificed when changes in the milieu put the majority at risk. These ir-regulated, to coin a new term, elements are the *homines sacrii* of any modern, democratic, managerial state. Again in contradistinction to Girard, they are not killed to avoid a spiral of retributive violence due to indifference of desires, but they are let die for the good of the many, the regular mass, if you are a gentle-spirited Foucauldian biotheorist, or they are actively selected for exclusion as the *homo sacer*, if you favour Agamben's more interventionist model. From this we can also see that the *homo sacer* is not a return to an active sovereign violence, because the *homo sacer* is not exterminated, rather they are extracted from the body politic, in a kind of bizarre organ transplant, into another animal-like host allowed to live out the rest of its life, internal to the state, in an almost impossibly paradoxical situation Agamben calls included exclusion (Watkin 2014, pp.187–8).

For the past five years, especially in Brexit Britain, Fortress Europe, and MAGA America, the idea that migrants in particular have been scapegoated has been widely discussed. They are often called the other, and I have regularly been asked to explain why 'we always exclude the other.' On the hoof I have struggled to come up with an answer not because I didn't know the reason, but rather due to the fact that it takes thousands of words to explain the reason. Finally, then, I can answer this question once and for all. First it is incorrect to look back at modern times, premodern, ancient Greek and pre-legal tribal societies and see a continuum of scapegoating. Just as it is false of Foucault so assume biopolitics began in the 18th century. Thanks to Agamben, we can both trace scapegoating back to the beginning of modern law and see it as a feature of the nomos, the law, to have embedded in it fear of anomie, the lawless zone outside the city or state boundary (Agamben 1998, pp.17–18). Yet we can also differentiate pre-legal and legal scapegoating and realise they are not the same at all. Pre-legal scapegoating is due to fear of indifferentiation, leading to the development of a mechanism for differentiation among equals, which we call law, and which also defines our impossible-to-maintain human rights. Post-legal scapegoating is the opposite, fear of differentiation, fear of the other as it is often called. Why do we fear the other? Because, as theorist Brad Evans explains in his book *Liberal Terror*, states founded on law require that fear as a safety valve for blame, victimisation, the so-called necessary violence and inequality of treatment that allows them to hold in reserve the right to purloin the rights of any of their subjects, without appearing to be committing an abuse of rights of its actual citizens (Evans 2013, pp.1–41). Foucault sees this in essentialist terms, crops will fail and regulators have to let some starve for the good of the many. Agamben's more mordant gaze rather sees it as the very essence of Western power. Which means not only can we explain scapegoating, in so doing, we can reveal the heart of the mechanism of potency that allows the powers that be to, well, *be* at all. Power, is by definition, the ability to separate off a proportion of any population, and surgically remove their human rights organ, yet appear to not be attacking one's own citizens because you have constructed a narrative of difference for certain groups in preparation for their victimisation. Yet this power of differentiation is, as was the case with pre-legal scapegoating, the result of indifferentiation or rather three elements of indifference.

The first indifference is between all humanimals. They all possess life so they all have the same rights which, biopolitically speaking, is a nightmare to regulate. Foucault argues that race is then the necessary differentiator, but race is just a paradigm of the overall signature of life, one example of how bare life operates. In other words, race is not what allows one to separate some human lives from others and argue they are worth less, rather bare life is the narrative process which allows you to separate off an internalised group of any population as no longer worthy of their rights: race is a paradigm of the signature of bare life (Watkin 2014, pp.183–6). The second indistinction is between the *homo sacer* and the rest of us. Essential it is for the state for the population to appreciate, perhaps at a subconscious level, that the others, the immigrant, the Jew, the Roma, the gay man, the handicapped, the hysterical woman, the child, are no different than the rest of us. This is the implicit threat in the biopolitical active principle of not to make die but to make bare your life. There but for the grace of the powers that be go I. First they came for the Jews, next they may come for me. This is why the *homo sacer* is best kept inside or close by the state, in what Agamben calls camps, because the population at large need to be able to see through their hatred and distrust of Romanians next door, realise they are not that different to your own family who, being Irish perhaps, were once like the Romanians, and see what could happen to you if the boot was on the other foot. Hopping about trying to keep the boot off the other foot is, basically, what most of us do to get by with the hope that this side of the fence doesn't suddenly become inside the fence boundary.

Again fear, fear from those of us whose backgrounds, families, long histories of abject poverty mean we have almost a preternatural sense that today's hate-fuelled Brexit-braying vox pop on the streets of Stoke-on-Trent, could be tomorrow's sacrificeable *homo sacer*, because after all we realise that is our natural role for the powers that be. We are the proles, the chavs, the plebs, the masses, whose sole function within the biopolitical narrative of power is to be an undifferentiated mass, herded against our will into various normativised regulatory bodies, not for our own good so much as to be the correct raw material for victimisation, indifferently differentiated, should it all go pear-shaped, which it will, because in reality the globe is pear-shaped. Which is not only why we fear the other, but also, while you are asking, why we voted for Brexit. Brexit, a mass movement of marginalised peoples to remove themselves from Fortress Europe so that they can be seen to own the process of exclusion, to opt for it and so no longer be victims of it. Brexit, revenge of the scapegoats, revolution of the *homines sacrii*. Brexit, behind the scenes, regulatory milieu-making. Brexit, the powers that be, Prospero-like, calling up a storm to justify extreme measures of separation and neglect by making it seem as if it was the people's will.

The last indifference we need to consider is the blurring that occurs from time to time as the state fiddles about with internal exclusions, different kinds of life and so on. If you squint, or look long enough, or if there is a malfunction in the machine, or if I point out the architecture of power as I am trying to do, you will see that the essential difference, say, between the English and their Polish neighbours, or the terror child and your own kids, or the West African migrant and my own Welsh migrant heritage, can very easily become fuzzy, indistinct, indifferentiated. Where I differ from Agamben is that he thinks of this as a political opportunity, the laying bare of power, the emperor's new clothes, the Wizard of Oz, while I think he is being too naïve, too hopeful. Because, you see, the state wants you to see the indifferentiation of self and other, citizen and migrant, child and terrorist, *zoe* and *bios*, so that you can observe without the powers that be ever having to say it, that in a world turned upside down, where the excluded can be included as the excluded, are you sure that your borders are keeping the scapegoat, the *homines sacrii*, the swarm, the infected, the radicalised, the zombies out or is the vast holding camp of the developing world, in reality not just one huge fence or wall designed to keep most of us in the state, grateful for the scapegoating mechanism as a means of making live the rest of us? Is the biopolitical state making live, as Foucault says it, or making bare life, as Agamben suggests, or simply making distinction indistinct? I think it is the last of the three.

That is how the powers that be make us do what they want. They include the excluded as a barely veiled threat, or better a barely audible question. Are you sure, citizen, that you are on the inside and the migrant hordes on the outside, or is this inside, surrounded by refugee camps and walls and channels and downstream outsourced regulatory data gathering and application processing, the means by which we are all encamped? This is surely the real *Border as Method* to appropriate for a moment the title of Mazzadra and Neilson's masterful study. The border does not separate us from them, it literally makes and maintains the essential us and them distinction, which is at the same time haunted but the suspicion of the potential for an us and them indistinction. And all the while storms rage, the waters rise, the crops will fail giving us scant time to just sit down for a moment, not least because our phones have colonised every inattentive moment, and just, well, see things as they are. Smoke and mirrors chavs, smoke and mirrors swarm–folk;a vast, historical, global, politicised, at times, fatal game of now you see me, now you don't. We, the included excluded, are on the outside looking out and on the inside looking in. We are the sweet Skittles that everyone loves, that is, until an expert study demonstrates sugar is poison and a regulatory body, with deepest regrets, has to root us out, and throw us in the waste bin with all the other discarded abject bio–matter. And we know it. And that is why we voted. Because if we were going to be the homo sacer, at the very least we wanted to choose it, or feel that we did. Which is, as you are asking, the real purpose of our democracies, the fiction of an agency of differentiation, the sacralisation of the active process of an, actually indifferent, choice.

The green bird and the muhajirat

According to Azadeh Moaveni, the female ISIS brides were called muhajirat, which when translated means literally female migrants. However the meaning of the term migrant, for ISIS at least, is very particular, for whom "migration was not such an innocent or neutral transfer of location … It meant signing up to the caliphate's disruptive everyone–punishing project of extreme violence" (Moaveni 2019, p.113). Many thousands of words have been spent trying to characterise this muhajirat, to explain away their awful transgression. Certainly the images of Shamima Begum the muhajirat is a conundrum for a girl described by her sister as "unadventurous and skittish," who didn't like to go on her own to buy milk (Moaveni 2019, p.118). She was also a girl of fearsome intelligence apparently, certainly not on display in her rather ill–advised comments when interviewed by the press. The *hajira* have a significant presence online, of course, and may have been the central recruiters for the Bethnal Green girls. They are ideologically driven and intellectually astute. When quizzed, for example, on Twitter as to justifications for the beheading of Western journalists, they quite rightly point to even greater atrocities committed by the Assad regime, the Russians, the Americans and thus, by association, the Brits (Moaveni 2019, p.114). They might ask whether nonviolence protest was going to work against Assad's chemical weapons and torture factories, for example.

We may never get to the bottom of the real reason for the rise of the muhajirat, but perhaps that is because we have been asking the wrong question. It is not why did the Bethnal Green girls leave that should concern us, but why did the security forces let them go. After the disappearance of the first of the girls, the charismatic and brilliant Sharmeena, it was pretty obvious to her teachers and the security forces that she had been radicalised. Her social media activity had already painted a clear portrait of potential radicalisation that the controversial, and seemingly ineffective, prevent programme should have picked up, especially as it has been criticised for being designed to be overreactive (Moaveni 2019, p.206). Yet when the remaining girls were questioned, they were then sent home with a letter which contained no direct reference to Sharmeena joining ISIS and which none of the girls delivered in any case. It is not a mystery how the girls fooled their parents, they all came from struggling, somewhat haphazard home lives, but it is so surprising that they evaded the authorities that the metropolitan police eventually issued an apology. Moaveni is under no doubt that the Twitter account of Amira Abase alone should have alerted counterterrorism. In fact all the girls were regularly in touch online with known hajira and ISIS bride recruiters. The girls were filmed on CCTV as they left the UK, of course, ours being the most surveilled nation in the world per capita. They got to Turkey easily, and while intelligence forces claim they sent info to the Turkish authorities, the Turks claim the documents were blank. Almost certainly their contact on the border with Syria was a spook. Even after the girls were reported as missing, the authorities seemed more concerned with using the girls and their families as a means of gathering intelligence, than as a method of bringing them home (Moaveni 2019, p.203). The evidence is pretty compelling I think that the security forces were aware of the girls' intentions, did nothing to stop them leaving the country and have since used the girls as both a means of gaining intel and as a new front in the ideological biowar on terror.

It is not the crimes, real or otherwise, of Shamima Begum that concern me, or even the loss of her children. These are, sadly, commonplace occurrences when one is at war, and war, let us be clear, is not bioviolence, it is just violent. Rather, it is the specifics of the topology of terror, the place of terror, perfectly expressed by the concept of the muhajirat. Begum, after all, migrated to Syria and if we are concerned with the effects of her return, shouldn't we also spare a thought for what these women did to the political and social fabric of Syria itself, specifically in the black city of Raqqa? When commentators left and right refused to entertain the idea of Begum coming home, it was with some justification in fact. The muhajirat are basically bio-weapons, called upon to carry out jihad through the expansion of the terror gene pool. Where we have it wrong is that, thanks to the rampant misogyny of ISIS, they are primarily required to carry out this duty within the caliphate itself, as brides of ISIS and widows of their beloved green birds, the symbol of the martyr for jihad. This is the peculiarity of the Begum case; in fact, everything seems to be running backwards. The security forces at the very least allowed these terror-brides to leave the UK to become radicalised, at worst facilitated their journey. And then used their disappearance as an element of their nefarious statecraft. Of course they don't want Begum back, not because they fear her womb, and certainly not her moody inarticulations on jihad and the failures of the West, but because she serves our national interests much more from where she is.

The involvement of intelligence agencies in the bioviolence of Begum's sacralisation is fitting of course. Is there a *dispositif* anywhere in history more apt to the indifferential suspension of national certainties than our own much mythologised MI5? And it is fitting that modern statecraft began in the UK, masters as we are at saying one thing and meaning another, and another, or maybe the thing we actually said in the first place. The suspension of Begum is complete, a masterpiece of contemporary warfare. She is not an ISIS terror-bride or even a muhajirat, rather she is a national hero. Her vilification is an essential component of the continued justification of our odd biowar against a terror organisation that is, frankly, less than laughable as a threat to UK nationals at home. Considerably more British nationals die from lunch than Islamic terrorism, for example. And our national outrage is just another example of the archetypal mode of discursive communicability that has allowed Britain to punch above her weight for over a century: hypocrisy.

Begum, if she were ever to return, poses no national threat, and if she did recruit further terror-brides, it would only be because the security forces let her because they need these brides to keep us all terrified in our beds that their hideous offspring are on their way to murder us all. While the odd suspension of her nationality means her life of suspended animation in the al–Hawl camp is an endless stream of information and data on ISIS and their possible future manifestations. In this way, Begum is the most powerful and conspicuous example of the indifferential complexity of the biowar's digital draft. Recruited online by the enemy, it remains permanently suspended as to which side she is actually fighting for, making her also a new innovation in the idea of the *femina sacra*. Begum shows us that sacrifice does not necessarily mean one death, but that sacrifice can be repurposed, its affordances reapplied according to the ever-changing situations of our nebulous war on terror. Begum has sacrificed her life, and that of her friends and her children, *several* times since she was filmed boarding that plane to Turkey back in 2015, and who knows, she may still have a significant sacrifice to make for our greater good in the months and years to follow. She left the UK a dreaded muhajirat, but each time her name comes up in print, she is magically transformed yet again into a sacred green bird for our collective cause.

11

READING GUANTANAMO OR CAMP AS COERCION

The line is drawn at the AIC.[1]

Although Mohamedou Ould Slahi entered the gates of Guantanamo Bay in August of 2002, in a sense he had been predestined to the camp his whole life, perhaps even before he was born. Once inside the camp he was held, without charge, for 14 years, but his sentence adds up to considerably more than that. That is, if we take Guantanamo to be not just a place, but also a certain state of being, the being of encampment, a placeless place that you carry with you as a potential or asymptomatic infection wherever you go if you happen to be from the wrong country, know the wrong kind of people or worship in the wrong kind of building. I know this might sound contentious, which is where Guantanamo's unique legal situation is particularly educational. Guantanamo Bay holding facility of GTMO is located on Cuban soil, raised on a patch of land leased from Cuba by the US against the will of the Cuban authorities. It is, therefore, neither part of the US nor of Cuba, a location that Cuba insists is unwelcome and illegal (Siems 2015). This locational shortfall, neither Cuban nor American, allows for a certain, shall we say, laxness as regards the observation of norms of jurisprudence that would have to be observed if the camp were, say, in Texas or Connecticut. For a long time after the establishment of the holding camp by the Bush administration in 2002, the identity of the prisoners kept there was a secret. Later they came to be called 'enemy combatants,' seized during the war on terror. The terminology is of course a mode of massification, what is a holding camp but the physical manifestation of massification that also determines a new kind of ab-norm that allows for both regulatory irregularity and the rapid bare lifing of around 800 souls. In that 'enemy combatants' was a new legal term developed by the Americans to replace 'prisoner of war' so that they did not have to extend the Geneva conventions to the inmates of the camp, and that the war on terror was the first world war against an emotion, and hence not a real war at all, the camp itself was beneficiary of a kind of three strikes and you're out ontological negativity. GTMO was located on a non-national location; its inmates were non-people, first secrets and then a new invented legal state, and the justification for its existence was ostensibly inexistent, because of a strategically impossible war against emotional dread. The inside/outside status of the camp, its being hidden in plain sight, the ontological suspension of rights thanks to a statement of terminology, the material concretisation of this bare life situation, the manner by which an abnormality is invented so as to justify an otherwise illegal massification, the strict regulatory measure taken against inmates versus the total, legal and territorial irregularity of GTMO, deniability, humanimality, narratives of infection and inoculation and Islamophobia, the list goes on and on: Guantanamo is, in other words, the archetypal end point and paradigm of bioviolence through encampment and thus of the oft times rather intangible concept of bioviolence itself

That hour by hour the decision is taken, who leaves the language

When Ould Slahi entered GTMO in 2002, he became an unwilling occupant of a land of contradictions. American's Gulag, as it has been called, was a kind of legal Never-Never Land where the detainees, assumed to be terrorists involved in the 9/11 attacks, were never allowed to 'grow up' into innocent or guilty but rather held in a permanent mode of both legal and ontological suspense. Mohamedou, for example, was held in a sort of juridical limbo for well over a decade along with his fellow 800 or so 'lost boys.' During his incarceration and torture by the same gesture, America was held in a kind of suspended state, like the despotic Peter Pan himself, constantly urging their followers to attack their assumed aggressors, making them live in fear of the chimerical Captain Hook, played in the Guantanamo adaptation by Osama Bin Laden of course, disallowed from asking questions: how did we get here? How long have we been here? Isn't it time we went back to our motherlands? Fanciful though this might be, if we take Guantanamo for the moment as a kind of hellish version of Never-Never Land, it becomes a legitimate question to ask: at what point did America scatter its fairy dust on Ould Slahi, making him weightless, allowing him to fly from his home into a world of distant adventure?

Ould Slahi formally entered the camp in 2002, but he was part of what I am going to call a global encampment well before that. By global encampment what I want to suggest is that while geographic holding camps exist, Guantanamo, the Jungle, Dadaab refugee camp (Rawlence 2016) and Brook House Gatwick, the nature of their existence is not tied to where they are, the chain-link, razor wire and CCTV that determine their borders, the exact number of detainees and so on. These are important factors, each possesses a material importance and a symbolic meaning of course, but they do not constitute the camp as a global phenomenon or, perhaps it is better to say they constitute simply the most visible and contentious sites of this phenomenon. In his controversial essay "The Camp as the 'Nomos' of the Modern," Agamben concedes that while the main concern is the Nazi death camps, encampment per se can happen anywhere at any time:

> In all these cases, an apparently innocuous space ... actually delimits a space in which the normal order is de facto suspended and in which whether or not atrocities are committed depends not on law but on the civility and ethical sense of the police who temporarily act as sovereign.

He goes on to define a camp as the "creation of a space in which bare life and the juridical rule enter into a threshold of indistinction" (Agamben 1998, p.174), such that the facts of life that are normally overseen by the rule of law become confused and rule becomes a direct rule of life, not distant regulation of situations to protect and enhance life. When this happens, wherever you are, this becomes a camp in the form of a "dislocating localization" (Agamben 1998, p.175), where being here is tantamount to not being here. So not only does the essential division between power and your life become indistinct, confused, indifferentiated, but also the foundational condition of being here in this state as a subject protected by the rules of this state becomes indistinct and blurred also, because where you find yourself is a place outside of place. This is Vaughan-Williams' point when he suggests that Agamben's bare life is essentially a conception of personal encampment that we carry with us wherever we go, like an infection of which we are either a carrier or a victim waiting for the clock of the incubation period to stop ticking and the alarm of encampment to sound. This is Mezzadra and Neilson's contention that the border is a method, a *dispositif*, ostensibly a process of internalised/externalised coercion (Mezzadra and Neilsen 2013). Guantanamo Bay then is just the most obvious stage set for a global drama of encampment that can happen at any time, in any location, and which is not even determined by the will of a sovereign state, but can be something you carry inside you to such a degree that it becomes all but impossible to remember when it was you first entered your own personal camp. All but impossible, but still we have to try.

This is where the action is, though for the most part the action is waiting

Mohamedou Ould Slahi was born into a large Mauritanian family. If encampment is defined by the state taking direct control and interest in your life, by placing you in a location where the bare details of your biological survival become the basis of their rule, rather than laws or norms of accepted behaviour, one can imagine the West had literally no interest or even inkling of his existence for the longest time, making him all but immune to encampment as a mode of surveillance. What is more, Mohamedou appeared to be favoured by the gods, or specifically Allah, as Mauritania is a Muslim state of around 3.5 million located in

West Africa between the Sahara and the Atlantic. While his father was a nomadic camel trader, he was a brilliant student winning a scholarship to study electrical engineering in Germany, the promised land.

I don't think it is meaningless to reflect on how the renunciation of a nomadic, desert existence to a curtailed, Westernised profession feeds into the slow movement of Ould Slahi from free to encamped. The ancient history of the territory called Mauritania belongs to nomadic tribes such as the Berbers. Such nomadism has often formed the romanticised core of philosophical studies of migration and revolutionary thought such as you find famously in Deleuze and Guattari's *A Thousand Plateaus*, part-refuted by Nail's excellent post-Deleuzian study *The Figure of the Migrant*. Yet it is hard to think of Berber nomadism as exemplary of a certain pre-Leviathan freedom from territorial claims and exploitation, what Deleuze valorises as a kind of revolutionary gesture towards de-territorialisation, when it was intrinsically tied to a deep cultural commitment to owning slaves. Mauritania was the last country in the world to abolish slavery, an abolition that did not take hold as slavery is still widely practised in the country to this day, as indeed it is around the world.

Nor is it meaningless to mention the colonial history of the country, with France taking hold of the national territories in the 19th century and reluctant, as ever, to give them back. Mauritania finally became an independent country in 1960, but as is always the case colonial rule had dramatically altered the tribal and cultural balance of the region which, for better or worse, had functioned for hundreds if not thousands of years as a basis of relative regional stability. A series of coups followed and while the country is rich in natural resources including oil, its people remain desperately poor. This historical combination of nomadism and colonialism combines to tell a story of freedom and encampment of some complexity that feed into Ould Slahi's first act of migration, a moment of leaving home from which it seems he was destined never to return, a biopolitical *periplus* less to do with geographic translocation and more the result of an embedded dual-tempo biohistory, this time not the temporal disjunction of sapiens and the human, than between colonialism and modernity.

It is Deleuze and Guattari I think who first make a philosophical differentiation between nomads and migrants and point out that it is incorrect to define nomadism in terms of movement:

> Whereas the migrant leaves behind a milieu that has become amorphous or hostile, the nomad is one who does not depart, does not want to depart, who clings to the smooth space left by the receding forest, where the steppe or desert advances, and who invents nomadism as a response to this challenge.
>
> (Deleuze and Guattari 1992, p.381)

Migration here is conceived as an abandonment of the milieu which has determined the migrant's settled existence. The migrant forcibly removes themselves not only from this milieu but, as Foucault shows, they also subtract themselves from the forces that manage and regulate this milieu becoming something like a de-massified mass that moves across territory that it never possesses or anymore belongs to.

In contrast, a nomad traverses a territory in an immobile sense, partly in that they come to define that territory in terms of a common, stable cultural set of norms, which means they never leave the territory even when they break camp and move down the valley as winter approaches. And partly because the way they occupy a territory forces us to reconsider what is meant by the term territory or our land. "The nomad has a territory," Deleuze and Guattari insist. "He follows customary paths: he goes from one point to another; he is not ignorant of points (water points, dwelling points, assembly points etc.)" (Deleuze and Guattari 1992, p.381). These points are essentially camps, places where they linger, points along a line which together combine to form a single, stable territory that nomads occupy by movement such that they do not really move but rather expand and distribute themselves over a large, rather than small, geographic area. "Although the points determine paths, they are strictly subordinated to the paths they determine, the reverse of what happens with the sedentary" (Deleuze and Guattari 1992, p.380).

The topology of the biohistory of the migrant is, as ever, an Escheresque, Lewis Carroll kind of place; a Foucauldian invention of a place to create a subjectivity, an Agambenian inside/outside, Esposito's immunisation of the body against itself, Deleuze and Guattari's stable nomad–migrating territory reversal. Similarly, the temporality of migration is simply all wrong. Clocks run backwards, immense epochs are somehow mapped onto compacted periodisations, the before comes after the after and retrogradation rules. Genetic timescales in the billions of years are somehow located within say the creation of modern states in the past three centuries, the incompatible times of the nomad, the migrant and the tribal folk, and colonised and the post-colonial terror threat appear to occur simultaneously, out of sync. The presumed order of causation is a nonsense, biopolitically speaking, which is why I could not write a history of bioviolence, which is why our study appears to begin at the end and end nearer the beginning and which is why I agree with Agamben that for all his genius, the precipitous racehorse of philosophy that Michel Foucault got it wrong, biopower did not begin on the 18th century. Rather it began with the beginning of the *polis* itself, meaning on the downside, it is much more intransigent than we might imagine but, going against Foucault's determinist pessimism, *all* power is biopower, meaning power has a biohistory, meaning it had something approaching a beginning, which implies that we can bring it to an end. There is, on this reading, no such thing therefore as bioviolence as a subcategory of, or innovation in, violence per se. All violence is bioviolent, all political violence anyway, which is also all violence because violence is a construct, not a materially real act of physical or psychological harm, a construct that can only serve one purpose, the perpetuation, justification and indeed construction of the endless yet endable reign of the powers that be.

More like waiting as an administrative weapon

Ould Slahi's talent meant he emerged from a nomadic culture that however depended on slavery. His was a free country still in the thrall of post-colonial fascism. Mauritania owned a territory that culturally, however, demanded a different concept of the territory, as a series of points determined by paths, rather than a series of paths to join up points. He became a migrant due to the poverty and political instability of his home nation, demanding that he give up his milieu and begin a journey that is not nomadic or sedentary, but something entirely other. This journey, of the de-massified mass that we call migrants, of which there is believed to be 272 million international migrants and a billion displaced people in the world today, took him out of the regulatory controls of his home nation. In truth these, as in most African states, cannot really be described as biopolitical because precarity is bound to their statecraft thanks to the post-colonial situation they are forced to occupy. Which mean Ould Slahi exited a deregulated state of precarity and entered into the regulatory controls of a biopolitical state par excellence: Germany. All of these factors were combining to create his state of encampment well before the Americans got to hear of him. Indeed Mohamedou may be said to have become encamped generations before he was born, somewhere between the point of nomadism and colonialism that came to define the peculiar territorial milieu of his home nation.

While studying in Germany, Ould Slahi took a couple of sabbaticals to fight jihad with Al Qaeda in Afghanistan. Incriminating though that sounds now, at the time it was a pretty common thing to do, encouraged by the Americans, for example, who, back then, counted Al Qaeda as allies. Nothing untoward about that, friends can become enemies after all. After his trips to Afghanistan, Ould Slahi stayed in touch with many of the young men he fought with, only natural, some of whom remained in Al Qaeda when they swapped from being allies to being enemies of the American state. During this time he also became related by marriage to a man who was to become a key Al Qaeda operative, once speaking to him by phone. Again a natural or normal thing to do on the whole, to talk to a relative you are accidentally linked to by birth and marriage. Although later, Ould Slahi was described by one American military man as a kind of Forest Gump character, always turning up in the background of the next atrocity, this was not so much due to Ould Slahi's choices than the shifting geopolitical landscape over which he had no control or knowledge. Meaning it wasn't so much that he popped up in the background of 9/11, say, than the background of international affairs made him pop up from background to foreground. In keeping with the bio-topology we keep encountered, it was as if Ould Slahi stayed still, while the frames of incrimination filtered past, each leaving a speck of pathogen which, over time, agglomerated, another means by which massification works this time at the somatic level, until they became a life-threatening yet operable terror-tumour.

In 1999 Ould Slahi and his new wife moved to Canada where they attended a mosque that was under surveillance because one of its attendees was behind a failed attempt to blow up LAX, the so-called Millennium Plot. Due to his previous links with Al Qaeda, Ould Slahi was placed under regular surveillance. Why not? He was questioned at one point by the Canadian police who concluded he had nothing to do with the plot, a position that has since been upheld. The young couple were cleared of any wrongdoing but they were still kept under surveillance. Thanks to this Mohamedou and his wife felt uncomfortable in Canada. They had an uncanny sense that they were being watched because, actually, they were. It is an unease, a suspicion, a prickling sensation on the back of your neck the sense of surveillance, which is surely a new kind of sixth sense that we will all have to nurture in the years to come as our lives are increasingly surveilled for our own good.

Families like the Ould Slahi's are innovators, coerced early adopters. Their stories read like messages from a potential dystopian future that may have already arrived, without fanfare, somewhere up there in the lofty, silent heights of the meta-data. After all, the circumstances of their being under suspicion were all, well, circumstantial. They went about their lives in a normal way as we all do. They were as normal as any Canadian, as normal as you or I; it was just that the developing war on terror was creating a new normal or, in fact, a new abnormal. Mohamedou was being de-regulated and re-regulated, de-massified and re-massified in a complex, systematic but also aleatory sense thanks to events thousands of miles away and many decades before. Ould Slahi, ever the nomad, was immobile. He did not take a wrong step, and so end up on the bad side of history or the wrong side of a Syrian fence. Even when he crossed the globe he stayed true to his points, not occupying a territory but allowing his milieu, his territory to occupy him. He didn't change; it was the world that changed, so that the entire globe came to form a camp around him without his ever even realising it. If it happened to him, read about it in his *Guantanamo Diary*, it could happen to any of you.

What somebody once dreamed was an indefinitely enduring holding pen

Thomas Nail in his study *The Figure of the Migrant* speaks of nomadism in terms of movement, disagreeing with Deleuze, Guattari and others such as Toynbee, but it is not the movement from one place to another so much as an oscillation between two 'places' which become displaced thanks to the movement of the nomad. When the seasons change, the nomad leaves winter pasture, down in the valley, and moves 'outside' to summer pastures high up. Then, as the nights draw in and become cooler, they make their way back down the slopes, heading outside the summer pastures to the winter ones which become their new inside, if you will. "From the perspective of the motion itself," he writes,

> neither side is ontologically distinguishable as inside or outside. The concepts of inside and outside make sense only from a fixed referent or

perspective … Oscillating movement is like the movement "across" a Möbius strip, where the movement between inside and outside is absolutely continuous.

(Nail 2015, p.131)

If the nomad and the migrant are clearly definable as different kinds of figures, differing ontological constructs, all the same there is something in common between them. The key I think is the construction of the idea or political imaginary of being inside and outside a territory. Where you are located has nothing to do with a set of geographic co-ordinates and everything to do with the fixed point of reference that determines that territory of where you belong or what you own, and where you do not belong or what may be a threat to what you own. What typifies contemporary geopolitics is the erosion of nationality and statehood as a fixed point of reference. Issues such as the debilitation of nationhood, globalisation, transnational digital communities, non-national power bases as diverse as Google and G8, mass-migration, rogue and failing states and a war on an emotion and terror rather than a nation, Afghanistan, mean that the fixity of territory is becoming blurred at best, unhinged at worst. Mohamedou Ould Slahi, therefore, in his movement from nomad, through post-colonial citizen, to migrant, to suspect was constantly experiencing an indetermination of inside and outside that is beyond his control and which Agamben defines as the very essence of encampment. As soon as he left his home nation, he abandoned the norms of his milieu that allowed his being, his life, to clearly occupy the inside of its existence. To the point where the dialectic between inside and out, or inclusion and exclusion, becomes indifferentiated and Ould Slahi enters a zone of indistinction, a term invented by Deleuze but made famous by Agamben, as a kind of biopolitical state of suspension the most significant of which is that of bare life or the humanimal. This zone of indistinction becomes a camp when states forget that law is there to protect the lives of subjects and instead begin to use law as a means of downgrading sacred life rights to bare life status. This is what the Americans began to do, on the day Ould Slahi left Canada to return to his home country.

This may sound a tad abstract but *Guantanamo Diary* is exceptional in the way it embodies theories of nomadism, migration and geopolitical indistinction in Ould Slahi's choices, their consequences and those consequences that were beyond his volition. On the day he left Canada, for example, he ruminates at one point that he was but a few feet away from American national territory. If he had stepped across *that* border his life would have been different. Yes he would have been watched wherever he went, subject to constant suspicion, but at least he would have avoided his fate worse than death because he would have been protected by the laws of the territory owned and run by the very authorities that despised him. Instead, he and his wife took a plane back to Mauritania like the good migrants they were and in doing the right thing, in going home, ironically it was there that the nightmare began. On setting foot in his own continent when he left the plane to change in Senegal, he was suddenly, bizarrely, no longer protected by the regulatory laws of the very nation that immediately captured him and removed him from his homeland through a process that came to be called extraordinary rendition.

Extraordinary rendition is the forcible abduction of a suspect by one country from another due to their agreement and the relocation of the suspect in a third nation not bound by the rule of international law. The first rendition took place in 1987 during the Regan years. What it allows is a subject to be extradited to a country that routinely uses torture. The suspect can then be tortured to get information which the US, for example, can then use as intelligence because while they cannot legally practice torture to get information, they can of course benefit from said information once it has been acquired.

Since its invention in the 1980s, rendition has become a central driver in a new kind of global bioviolence that we might term the bioviolence of the dislocation of rights. Although life rights are supposed to be located in living human beings, irrespective of their status as citizens, for example, that after all is the meaning of universal human rights, in reality this appears untrue. Or perhaps better rights are a value-potential that all humans possess which is actualised, augmented or eradicated due to our sliding scale of responsibility, in the sense of both a state taking responsibility for your rights and also how the world responds when they are abused or when your life is lost. Rights as potential exist in us all, but the actualisation of those rights is very much still tied to territory, meaning if you want to weaken or remove rights of subjects, you need to displace them from the land of their rights as protected, to a territory where they are not. This process of displacement is what we mean by encampment, and rendition has become a key weapon, not in the chimerical war on terror, but in the actual war we have become enmeshed in since the wall fell in Berlin in 1989, the global Rights War, a scramble for the rights enrichment of the lucky few, at the cost of rights impoverishment for the global many.

Because biopolitics is defined by the elimination of violence, the exportation of rights-removal, through rendition, droning, migration laws, ecological exploitation, poverty and post-colonial dispensations, is a central method in committing acts of coercion, aggression and execution offstage or better off-territory. Extraordinary rendition, then, is the literalisation and actualisation of the zone of indistinction, where a displaced person is neither inside nor outside of their national territory, because the fixed point of reference has been permanently displaced by their being moved to a location where no one can hear them scream.

There, in abeyance, where the administration dreamed them

Ould Slahi was first arrested on his way back home at the airport in Senegal. He was subject to rendition to Mauritania itself, where he was arrested. In Mauritania he was arrested and released before handing himself in for questioning after

9/11. Although he was cleared of any involvement, he was then taken from Mauritania by US authorities to Jordan where he was tortured by the Jordanian authorities. Then he was relocated to Afghanistan before finally being incarcerated in Guantanamo in the August of 2002. What is interesting in Mohammed's description of his rendition is how geographical translocation is not merely destabilising for the subject themselves, who no longer know whether they are inside or outside of a state, their home, their country of residence, but also to the basic life rights of that subject. Having being tortured in Jordan, he is then subject to rendition to Bagram. During the rendition no one speaks to him. His clothes are cut from him while he is chained to the floor. He was then dressed in a diaper for the journey. When his plane arrived he was too exhausted to move "which compelled the escort to pull me up the steps like a dead body" (Ould Slahi 2015, p.5). For the journey he was chained to the floor and not allowed to use the bathroom. While in Bagram under US jurisdiction but, crucially, not on US soil, he was chained up for 24 hours a day. If you were designated a 'bad' detainee this would be in a corridor where people would walk on you as they went past. Force-feeding was not uncommon. Detainees were not allowed to talk to each other. If they did their punishment consisted of "hanging the detainee by the hands with his feet barely touching the ground" (Ould Slahi 2015, p.16). One detainee suffering from mental illness could not stop talking, and he was constantly hung up for this. Much of this was overseen by someone called "William the Torturer." For example, a teenage boy was made to stand for three days without being allowed to sleep. One interesting exchange between Ould Slahi and an interrogator ends with Ould Slahi protesting his innocence:

"But I've done no crimes against your country."
"I'm sorry if you haven't. Just think of it as if you had cancer!"
(Ould Slahi 2015, p.21)

Often Ould Slahi was placed in blindfolding glasses, for up to 40 hours, which were intensely painful. Cavity searches appear to have been one or the more humiliating practices for most inmates. The effect these constant low and mid-level tortures had was to leave Mohammed feeling like he was a "living dead." At one point, he was asphyxiated. At another, so much blood was taken from him that he almost passed out. Sleep deprivation was common, as was being kept immobilised in positions that over time resulted in intense pain. The descriptions of torture go on and on, and that is before he is even interred in Guantanamo.

While this narrative is disturbing, what it shows is a roll call of different techniques of bioviolence. In theory, at least, bioviolence does not dirty its hands with the penetration, pummelling and policing of flesh. The eradication of torture for state punishment was a crucial step towards governmental rule by law and punitive incarceration which, in time, gave way to peaceable biopolitical regulation of norms rather than laws, allowing a state to participate in every aspect of your life in a benevolent manner so that it will not need to threaten you to get you to comply, let alone carry out such threats against your body. This is all well and good if you are a subject placed in a regulatory mass where you are in accordance with positive norms deserving of life rights. But what it also means is that if you are instead found to be in a de-massified mass where you do not adhere to said norms, for example, if you are a terrorist, then the state's ability to terrorise your life is dramatically enhanced. Many of the tortures practised by "William the Torturer" and his flunkies almost appear to be designed to debase the very essentials of living: going to the toilet, eating, drinking, breathing, talking, standing, sleeping, and so on. These are pointedly bio-tortures. They are not just designed to cause pain to bring about confessions, they are located in the cusp of acceptable behaviour, giving them a degree of deniability, but also seem construed so that their victims are forced to question basic biorights, such as sleeping, talking and breathing, and realise the extension of these rights is precisely that, a reaching out, an offer, a gift. One that can be refused or forcibly removed at any time.

As Mohammed Ould Slahi was shunted between Senegal, Mauritania, Jordan, Afghanistan, probably Turkey and finally Cuba, he experienced an old Islamic saying "Travel is a piece of torture" (Ould Slahi 2015, p.32). Just the constant relocation meant he was permanently between agreed legal protections of his life rights. And as he was moved, the centre of gravity of his being collapsed, facilitated by the disorientation of petty, even ingenious pieces of localised torture. What we see is the complex detail of the narratology of bare life that Agamben spoke of. You don't just become an animal again, rather you enter into a story of your dehumanisation, a process of denuding that is literal and symbolic. As each of your life rights is stripped from you by its being debased and made torturous, for example, being force-fed water when your bladder is fit to bursting, once it becomes added into the depressing roster of what these rights are, how basic they are and how mistaken we ever were to give the state access to them. And as Ould Slahi was deconstructed then suspended as a human, through territorial indefiniteness and biological profanation, he was simultaneously reconstructed as a new kind of subject, the detainee, the enemy combatant, the terrorist, the 'rag head.' There are, it would seem, two kinds of encampment. That of the nomad where the very exclusionary categories of inside and outside dissolve due to the stability of one's own ontological sense of belonging. In this state you are not subject to the vagaries of the milieu because you are that milieu. In the second, however, the indistinction of inside and outside are designed rather to negate your sense of subjective stability. By finding yourself, as Ould Slahi did, systematically denied geographic, legal and even biological access to where you are, included as excluded, excluded because included in a new mass called [terrorist], your very being is suspended, stripped and then thrown in a cell. This is how bare life is brought about in the new millennium.

What the tribunal judges is the language

Giorgio Agamben's bible of biopolitical theory, *Homo Sacer*, makes two sweeping, chilling statements that have reverberated through the halls of the academy since he made them in the mid-1990s. The first is that we are all *homines sacrii* now, we are all Shamima Begums, the second that the camp is the political *nomos* of our age, and we are all inhabitants of a kind of global Guantanamo. Agamben is regularly called out for his political pessimism and so to justify his traumatic portrait of our modern age we need to make one last effort to understand the precise nature of bioviolent modes of coercion, by considering in particular this term *nomos*. *Nomos* is the Greek word for law or lawmaking, but as Thanos Zartaloudis' excavation of the term *The Birth of Nomos* shows, its meanings extend far beyond law itself including a sense of *nomos* as the interior space of a state and of *nomos* as the origin of our biopolitical conceptualisation of the norm (Zartaloudis 2019). For Agamben, therefore, the camp as *nomos* is both the law of our age, the interior space of our age and the political normative zone of our age. As Zartaloudis' study shows quite clearly, *nomos* is a space that is continually evacuating itself. *Nomos* as lawmaking, wishes to inscribe a set of social behaviours and interdictions within a location, with law often being associated with a kind of conceptual space. Think of the door into the kingdom, for example, in Kafka's much-interpreted "Form of Law," or the dramaturgy of the courtroom skirmish in Hollywood films. We are speaking here of the synecdochic overlay of the law as state, of the internalised punitive states for those who break the law and, perhaps most importantly, of those anomic hinterlands that exist outside and pre-exist in every case the Leviathanised legal states that come to define the modern political state as *nomos*, as ruled by law. *Nomos* then is the topology of power as the very definition of power, and bioviolence the means of coercion appropriate to this mode of rule where inside and outside can readily change location without the overall coherence of the state being affected, the way a torus ring in topology can be both a coffee-cup and a doughnut, or a young woman be both an agent and enemy of the state as she moves through literal and conceptual space, without ever tearing the form of the state itself.

If *nomos* is to be taken variously as meaning law, space and norm in a powerful overlay of palimpsestic interconnections, typical of the Möbius-strip convolutions of topology, then by the same gesture *nomos* cannot be thought without reference to the threat of anomie. Anomic spaces, the lawless zones outside the city-state that have, since at least Hobbes with their roots in ancient Greece, justified the so-called necessary and foundational state violence, function as a regulatory threat to anyone who might question the efficacy or indeed ethics of nomos or normativised states. Anomic states are by definition located outside our ordered societies because *nomos* is the space of law and anomie is the state of lawlessness. Anomic states are often used as exemplars of all that is evil in the world, although we tend to call them lawless, Afghanistan, failed, Syria, or terror states, any territory still occupied by ISIS.

Yet we already saw through such mechanisms as scapegoating and the *homo sacer* that every *nomos* appears to reserve a space inside its borders for a controlled, legally sanctioned anomic space, a location occupied by those humanimalistic non-citizens who Agamben calls the *homines sacrii*. One reason for this paradoxical situation is that to become a *homo sacer* you need to be a human citizen denuded of your rights to the point of becoming a mere animal, a transformation that requires that you were once in a state and a narrative that only makes sense within a state in that *homines sacrii* are not animals out there but humanimals in here. Perhaps the point is made with most simplicity by Agamben: the *nomos* as an inside space, only functional in contrast to the anomic outside that we, paradoxically, retain inside the state because the purpose of the anomic location is to be a visual justification for the enforced foundation, perpetuation and eventual 'exceptional' suspense of the *nomos*. Which is surely why the Bethnal Green girls were allowed to leave the UK unchallenged. Examples of contemporary anomic spaces include Guantanamo Bay, the Jungle, immigration processing units, those caged kids of Texas and American inner cities. Agamben uses a single word to define all these different anomic spaces, they are called camps, and their occupants all versions of that original Roman *homo sacer* figure.

The AIC's function is as a portal to a 'hostile environment'

The archetype of the camp as location for bare life is of course the concentration camp. Concentration camps were invented at the end of 19th and the beginning of 20th century either by the Spanish or British. The term concentration refers to gathering together large numbers of people who are problematic to a state. Often they are colonially displaced tribes people who do not sit easily in the newly defined colonial states, perhaps because their peoples ranged freely over territory not cut through by borders. Coherent groups of people, tribes let's say, that cannot be accounted for by new, legalistic state definitions, of a Westphalian or colonial order, are often the cause of state disintegration. Think of Yugoslavia, of Iraq, of Pakistan, of Syria. All of these are countries whose instabilities were created in this manner. A concentration camp is, basically, a geographical or topographical zone for large numbers of scapegoated *homines sacrii*, separated off simply because they are in the *nomos*, yet their status deemed anomic. In a camp your citizenship is revoked as is your national identity. All you are left with is that which is sacred to all human beings, your life.

The movement from concentration camp to death camps in Nazi Germany was systematic and took place over several years. To set up a concentration camp, special legal permission was required, for example, a *nomos* of anomic designations. This established the camps as legal states of exception where legally law was suspended. Before entering a camp Jews, and others, had to be first legally stripped of their citizenship. Thus they existed in a legal exception, what Agamben calls anomie. At the same time they were reduced from citizens to mere bodies, to what he calls bare life. This history is illustrative because it helps us reconsider the prevalence of camps in our own democracies. It is reckoned that 42,500 camps or ghettos were set up during the Nazi regime from 1933–1945. Around 15–20 million died or were imprisoned within. Of these around 6 million Jews were murdered systematically in death camps like Auschwitz using gas chambers. But political prisoners, Roma gypsies, homosexuals, the handicapped and other 'nonhuman' citizens were also killed. Although in all camps people died from maltreatment and neglect, death camps like Auschwitz and Buchenwald were specifically designed for the efficient mass eradication of people. Most concentration camps were not then active death camps of this sort but more profoundly biopolitical processes for letting die by refusal to make live.

Their function being to so diminish the appellant that the judge can comfortably expel them

We saw that central to the political imaginary, in particular social contract theories as justification for a judicially supported Leviathan figure, is a moment of founding or constituting violence, as Walter Benjamin puts it. According the Benjamin, mythic violence or the narrative of justificatory and necessary violence on the part of states is made up of a founding violence as justification for subsequent acts of constituent, localised aggression on the part of the state against its citizens. In the case of concentration camps this myth of founding violence is basically re-enacted and in a sense reversed. Jews are forcibly extracted from the social body and returned back to the animalistic state of nature from whence they came by being placed in holding camps. In these camps inmates were treated as if they were animals, were sent forward into a story of origins so to speak, typical as we saw of the reversed narratological impetus of the bare life mechanism. In this way Jews were located in the camps outside the law but they were also placed before the law. Living at the mercy of law but also existing before law is imposed and after it has been revoked in an impossible zone of temporal, spatial, legal and ontological indistinction. While in the camp they are held in a permanent state of founding violence where the state can do anything because, as yet, it does not legally exist for these people.

The process of removal, refounding, re-animalisation and so on are all necessary stages in a removal of biorights from citizens such that they can be located in the impossible topological torus of the inside/outside of the camp. In truth, all that the camp does is convert the right to life into the right to death when there is a state of emergency. If your right is to do with being born, and you are born a Jew, then the *homo sacer* is distributed amongst every citizen. Which means they all can be killed when law is suspended, because law is there to protect your life rights such that its removal is, by definition, the removal of your right to live. This switch in logic, so simple in its way, but technically and legally difficult to bring about as Ould Slahi's complex rendition process shows, is perhaps the single most frightening conclusion in modern thought. Agamben points out, quite simply, that if biopower is tasked with protecting your life rights, then it needs access to your life, to how you live. His brilliant definition of a totalitarian state is one where the separation between public and personal is removed, which in a sense means all modern biostates are totalitarian in essence. Once it has access, if it is necessary to revoke your rights because your existence as a mass comes to be defined as abnormal in such a way that it threatens the health of the body politic, because you are a Jew, because you are a terrorist, then it already has the data and power to take necessary steps. Finally, in revoking your right to life, by definition it is revoking your life, converting your right to life into bare life which exists without legal rights. Not only can a state legitimately let you die, it can actively go after your life, placing you in a camp where you are more likely to die, and finally turning the camp into a death camp where you go to die. Right to life when things go well, becomes right to death when all goes awry. This scapegoating mechanism at the centre of all democratic states explains why biopolitics, which is tasked with avoiding violence, naturally led to genocide in the last century; biopolitics becomes thanatopolitics.

This is the purpose of the camp. The aim of biopolitics? To encamp us all. This brings about something akin to a global camp. The fundamental mechanism of bioviolence? Aggregation as separation. The entire history of power in the West is encapsulated by the tragic story of the attempt to define rule through differentiation, only to end up having to rule thanks to the biological indifferentiation of those you wish to chide and herd, thanks to their right to life. The camp's attraction, of course, is that you convert the right to life, to the actuality of the right not to die, gifting the state with a powerful tool for differentiation at the very heart of the indifference of life itself. Ultimately the rules of the camp do not differ from those of our states, power oversees our self-regulation, only stepping in as and when they are needed. Power is not a custodian but a manager. The only difference being, according to Agamben, according to the philosophers, according to the writers, is that the inmates of the camp know they are inside the outside, while we, foolish as we are, think we are truly inside and that we can erect a fence, build a wall, stock a database to keep the terrorist out, not realising that such actions are what transform the abstraction of terror into material, and thus potentially fatal, form. Which is, I guess, the ultimate *dispositif* of the biopolitical state; it is an ode, not to universal human rights in the form of the average citizen, but to the terrorist in the form of innocent men like Ould Slahi and disaffected girls like Shamima Begum.

Codicil: people spirited away barely rendered present in the first place

The revelatory message of Primo Levi's *If This Is a Man* (Levi 2013) is not the murder of the prisoners in Auschwitz, but rather the experiment on those still living, in terms of how much one needs to strip from a human being, and their still being able to exist or live. It is, in other words, the archetypal work on the logical relation between the process of encampment and the productivity of bare life. A productivity pushed to its logical end point by the Nazis as quasi-scientific investigation as to what point a 'man' ceases to be a 'human' and is not at the same time an 'animal.' The name of this new ontological minimality is the *Muselmann*.

In the figure of the *Muselmann*, Levi provides us with an ontological halting point, a lowest level of existence as pure survival, below which there is only death:

This word "*Muselmann*," I don't know why, was used by the old ones of the camp to describe the weak, the inept, those doomed to selection … Their life is short, but their number is endless; they the *Muselmänner*, the drowned, form the backbone of the camp, the anonymous mass.

(Levi 2013, pp.94–6; Agamben 2002)

It is the narrator's suspension between humanity and muselmannity and his efforts to avoid the swamp of the camp's drowned, so as to be counted in the final ten days of the camp's liberation as one of the saved, that gives the novel its forward intensity.

The novel's title itself begs the question *If This Is a Man …?* such that you might assume it pitched towards the guards of the camp. If you have read the novel and assumed that to be the case I think perhaps you were mistaken. In truth, Levi is asking of his fellow *homines sacrii*, if this is a man, what does it mean to be a man, and if this is a man, and if this…? It is a novel of radical, dislocating, biomassification wherein even the indifferent mass of the *homines sacrii* are actively regulating themselves into the norm of the abnormal and the abnormal of the abnormal, the *Muselmänner-mass*. What do you need to do to the human, such that they will self-regulate through petty acts of microaggression, microfascism, leaving the guards in many instances as observers of, and tinkerers with, an almost homeostatic machine of life rights divestiture, the camp through the novel seems to ask. And if you are able to reduce human existence to pure or bare life as such, what mechanisms are in place to stratify this mass, such that bare life can be determined as being both what Alain Badiou calls indifferent (Badiou 2005, p.67), impossible to differ from because humanity and bare lifers literally have nothing in common, and yet differentiable should the need to choose some over others occur? As it always does. As is, in fact, dictated by the basic rule of the camp: "Man is bound to pursue his own ends by all possible means, while he who errs but once pays dearly" (Levi 2013, p.19). A rule posed as a syllogistic conclusion to the fundamental question of the novel, Nazism, and, indeed, bioviolence itself: "How can one hit a man without anger" (Levi 2013, p.22).

In a sense, what the novel extrapolates is the Gouldian selfish organism from out of the conditions of Dawkin's selfish gene: competitive, mathematised, calibrated pure survival. The novel could have been subtitled *The Bureaucracy of Cruelty*, or perhaps *Hostile Environments*. It fully explains Arendt's conception of evil as banal for, given an opportunity in the *laager* to totally reinvent the holding camp, to revel in the moral autonomy of total anomie, those mindless guards made all of their 42,500 estimated concentration camps simply the mirror image of the German state, itself the spitting image of our own selective democracies. When totalitarian regimes declare states of exception, as the Nazis did, as the French recently did, the first thing that strikes one is that there is nothing exceptional about them, aside from the fact that the immense and luxurious drapery we call democracy has momentarily been raised. And what we see is not a secret state, but ourselves, not "as we truly behave" as John Ashbery once put it, launching his great career (Ashbery 1997), for as the greatest writer of the second half of the last century came to realise in his work, there is no true behaviour apt to the human animal. Instead, if you raise the valences of exception and emergency, declare a war on terror, for example, all that you see is a mirror that reflects the image through which the state secretly sees us, inmates of a large holding facility somewhere on the edge of the territory, a place or better topos called, for the sake of argument, the UK—a large and complicated, forcible regulatory undertaking. And occupying that topos, littering about the place, the tedious mass, that population of bastards whose regulation requires special measures, global kettling, the erection of hostile environments, a line drawn very firmly in the sand of our beaches, a wall that does not need building because in saying it, the barriers are already in place.

Or perhaps I go too far or show you things you do not wish to see? I would love to stay and discuss these matters with you further, break the walls of our echo chambers, puncture the delicate viscosity of our filter bubbles, but time is now short, I hear their footsteps at the door. I think it is time to drop the curtain again, melt once more into the mass, become peak-regulation intellectual, before I get a friendly visit from those kindly powers that be, bearing a muzzle for the beast inside of me, that insists on having its voice heard, that can never be silenced. Before I am asked, in reality told, to leave the language, before I am "driven through" the regulatory separation of a global, conceptual and discursive AIC.

The language formed in the act of separation not acknowledging the absence of those it compels to leave, established by the breach, the act of shipping people out

That ourselves know

Driven through

The AIC.

Note

1 All subchapter headings are taken from David Herd's poem "Who Leaves the Language" from his collection *Through* (Herd, 2016, pp.11–13). The poems in the collection investigate the impact of the official UK policy of "hostile environment" on the lives of migrants and asylum seekers in Great Britain. The AIC is the court where the immigrant and asylum court sits. I have not cited Herd's work in the accepted manner for specific effect, but they are taken in chronological order. If you wish to know where in the poem they occur, you will need to drive through the language of that work.

PART FIVE

2020, I can't breathe

12
GEORGE FLOYD AND #BLACKLIVESMATTER: THOUGHTS

Take a knee and wait, wait with me, for 8 minutes and 46 seconds.

As we kneel together, we can share a prayer, whatever your beliefs, a secular prayer if you will, more like an incantation.

The origins of poetry, and so our culture, reside in such incantations at the gravesides of the deceased. In ancient times the names of the dead would be repeated over and over as part of funerary rituals, and while their names were still on the mourners' minds, suspended in their breath, literally absorbed into their bodies and expelled as one body through the tiny aerosols that no mask can catch, they were thought to live on a little. We allowed them, in a sense, to infect us, then we breathed out their molecules together, and willingly caught the virus of their stay of death as a community. The rituals vaccinated us as a group, a pack, a herd, against the deleterious effects of our inconceivable loss so that, over time, we became immune to it, we could release our hearts from their lockdown, and our lives go back to normal.

This is not mere superstition; it goes far deeper than that. Peter Sloterdijk's magnificent tome *Bubbles* traces the entire cultural/philosophical/biopolitical significance of breath from ancient times to our present age, in particular how our need for communality, our bubbles, is performed physically through the "pneumatic pact between the giver and taker of breath … where the communicative or communal alliance builds up." This "pneumatic reciprocity" results in a situation where "the one breathed on is by necessity the ontological twin of the breather" (Sloterdijk 2011, pp.41–44). Breath then determines physically and biologically the ontological conceptions that we still live according to today and these conceptions are always communal. Ours is a herding, breathing, bespittled, bubbling being, he argues. How we breathe on each other, well that is also how we are able to live together, or at least that is what I have learnt this year. Sloterdijk captures it perfectly when he says: "Breath science can only get underway as a theory of pairs" (Sloterdijk 2011, p.41). Has a breath science ever been more needful than it is right now? Has breath ever been so political as it is today?

I won't ask you to repeat the name George Floyd as part of our intimate ritual. He is only one of many, one of up to a thousand young black males who die at the hands of the US police force every year. Instead, let's repeat his last words together and breathe them all over each over, for nearly nine minutes, in an enclosed space, face to face, unmasked, with all the windows shut, because they speak to the problems of racism in America, in the UK and beyond. But also because, in the midst of the COVID pandemic, they form a bubble with those who are not black, not of the margins, not obviously oppressed but who, suddenly, find themselves consulting the breath sciences, asking if their deep need to pair has been permanently stymied by this incredible, historically indelible, year of breathlessness. In so doing, perhaps, over time, they will allow us to find common ground and recuperate something from the dead corpse of this doleful year.

> breathe I can't breathe I can't breathe I can't breathe I can't breathe I can't
> breathe I can't breathe I can't breathe I can't breathe I can't breathe I can't
> breathe I can't breathe I can't breathe I can't breathe I can't breathe I can't
> breathe I can't breathe I can't breathe I can't breathe I can't breathe I can't
> breathe I can't

Fuck your breath!

In April 2015 Eric Harris was running once more from the Tulsa police. The incident was filmed, as you might imagine, on a smartphone. In the clip, which is fuzzy, you can still easily see Harris being brought heavily to the ground. A shot goes off. Sounding in its undeniable reality, not at all what you might expect it to sound like. Harris also seems initially unimpressed by the handgun's clipped reverberation when he says, in disbelief, "He shot me! Oh my God, I can't breathe."

"Fuck your breath!" replies one of the cops, a phrase as initially meaningless and vile as it has proven over the years to be culturally significant.

Harris later died in custody. But he was killed on the street.

This baleful incident took place right in the middle of the go-slow on death row in US penitentiaries due to the limited availability of drugs needed for lethal injections (Watkin 2016). Writing about both events in parallel at the time, it struck me that Harris' death was capital punishment of a novel kind, the next logical step after the spate of multiple deaths by botching that has caused global outrage, where untested drug combinations had led to the phenomenon called 'air hunger.' Then there was this parity around the issue of breath, the right to it, and how permitted capital punishment in penitentiaries and sanctioned executions on American's streets seemed to come together in some kind of terrible dance of themes and attitudes, around Harris' simple phrase, "I can't breathe." For him a literal statement, for African Americans all over his country, a metaphor that could be brutally realised at any moment.

Harris' death on a Tulsa street is an example of how the normally tentative and indirect machinations of biopolitical coercion can actively pursue the death of its own citizens while still purporting to be making live the wider populace. It is an execution in all but name, a stipulation of central importance, of course. In Eric Harris' case the accused is spared the living torture of the American penal system, by being gunned down there and then on the spot. His innocence need not be debated as he is a young black male involved in petty crime who is already a convicted felon. It is statistically probable that, had he been given enough breath to do so, Harris would have spent much of his adult life incarcerated. He may eventually have become the perpetrator of the kind of violent crime that means he would have to be executed anyway. If this were the case, then it is probable that the combination of drugs used in his lethal injection will be experimental and untested, being likely these days he may have ended up "flopping around like a landed fish"—as 'executee' John Albert Taylor memorably described death by asphyxiation through the lethal injection, justifying his choice of an Ohio firing squad, a victim of that euphemistic 'air hunger.' Whichever of the two eventualities, Harris seemed destined to spend the short term of his adult life in a process of slow, racially motivated asphyxiation. To be young, black and male in the ghetto-plantations of America is to be in a state of constant hyperventilation, pulling at one's collar, asking for windows and doors to be opened, constantly complaining to the impervious powers that be, "I can't breathe!" Complaining and being, not so much ignored, a biopolitical tactic par excellence, as mocked and derided as the air in their lungs is exhausted and not replenished.

The statistical justification for the infringement of rights of black Americans, along the lines that he's black, he has a record, he looks suspicious, he is running, he's likely to be a criminal, is so pervasive in American culture that it has captured the hearts of leading public liberals like Malcolm Gladwell. Gladwell, for a good long time, supported the Broken Windows policing policy, first proposed by academics Kelling and Wilson (Wilson and Kelling 1982) and now widely discredited as a form of racial profiling (Maloney, September 29, 2015), although he has since recanted. Broken Windows, if you have not heard of it, is blamed by many for the rise in the killing of young black males such as Trayvon Martin in Sanford in 2013, Michael Brown in Ferguson in 2014, Eric Harris in Tulsa in 2015, Philando Castille in St. Minnesota in 2016 and, most pressingly, George Floyd in Minneapolis in 2020. These deaths, it is suggested, were the result of a certain implied and actual sanction authorised by Broken Windows, legitimating ad hoc executions of young black males by an over-zealous police force supposedly stopping these young men for minor crimes to avoid escalation into a recidivism, which usually proves impossible, in our prisons, to pull back from. The idea of Broken Windows was to crack down on minor misdemeanours such as vandalism, breaking windows, traffic offences and such like so as to reduce the escalation of anti-social behaviours into more serious crimes later. Statistically, in some communities, this policy was successful. One cannot deny the statistics that certain thinkers so love to roll out, that overall in the US crime has dropped since the inception of the policy in the 1980s.

A statistical good news story it may be, sadly over longer periods of time and with a deeper and wider conception of the causes of crime, one is able to say that the system is rife for exploitation and racial profiling. It is regularly blamed by black activists for the disproportionate number of black inmates in US prisons, and it has a disturbing historical precedent in the so-called black laws in place after the civil war, which effectively criminalised and perpetuated black poverty. The biopolitical nature of such policies is perhaps best illustrated by the blinkered perspective of Stephen Pinker's observation in his popular book on violence, *The Better Angels of Ourselves*, that as the large majority of crimes are committed by the same minority of people, if you were to lock these people up indefinitely, crime would be almost completely eradicated (Pinker 2011, p.111). Pinker is not advocating this, but his comments imply that if the state were to inoculate itself against the recidivist parts of its own citizenry, then it would much more effec-tively 'make live' the majority, through the 'letting die,' in jail, of this trouble-some minority. It goes without saying that this minority is disproportionately black, a fact that is far from accidental, although you might think so if you read Gladwell and Pinker. Pinker's comments are a typical example of what Evans and Giroux call the 'neoliberal tendency' towards privatised racism in their recent book *Disposable Futures*. Privatising racism means you blame the individuals rather than the system for attitudes towards race, as Pinker appears to blame certain young black repeat offenders for disappointing crime figures. When Pinker ima-gines you could lock up the bad apples and reduce crime to almost zero, he mis-takes the agents of crime, disproportionately young black males, for the structures that drive them to crime, racism, poverty, alienation and the like.

Harris' death tells us so much about the despised other at the heart of the American judicial system, that enemy with whom they will never be at peace. He is not just a waste of space—he is a waste of breath. When the police called out, "Fuck your breath!" to Harris on an innocuous-looking Tulsa street, they revealed a subtle understanding of the still-nascent field of biorights. When they knelt on the neck of George Floyd for 8 minutes and 46 seconds, a full three minutes after he had died from 'air hunger' as his asphyxiation would have been termed if he had been suffocated by an ill-administered, not-reliably-lethal injec-tion in an Oklahoma penitentiary, for example, they announced to the world that the policy of choking to death had become a centralised part of their war on the African-American community. In the space of just five years then, Fuck Your Breath! had been transformed from a taunt to an axiom enshrined in a *dispositif* sanctioned by experts, embedded in regulatory norms and made materially pre-sent on the streets. It had, I would argue, moved from being an idea, a passing notion, to an axiomatic component of American policing. Fuck Your Breath! had, in other words, gone through a systematic process of dispositification, if I can coin such a term.

The Fuck Your Breath! axiom takes us all back to school to rethink entirely the nature of punishment in all its forms. The bioright to air, or not in the case of American black males, has indeed been under furious debate for some time amongst the leading community of philosophers in the world today, the US police force. At a police rally in 2014 some officers wore T-shirts that read "I can breathe," taunting Eric Garner's last words, another victim of Broken Windows, who died from asphyxiation after a choke-hold was placed on him. Garner repeatedly claimed he was suffocating (Capelouto 12 April 2014). It turns out he was right. That Garner was arrested on suspicion of selling single cigarettes to avoid tax duty, and George Floyd for buying cigarettes with fake dollars, results in a bizarre combination of America's poisonous respiratory addiction, the Fuck Your Breath! axiom and the most regulatory of all techniques, money/taxation.

Taking a dialectical counter-position to the police force's Fuck Your Breath! axiom, the African-American community started to sport T-shirts echoing Garner's last words, most notably during the protest riots in Ferguson and Baltimore and then all across American cities in the wake of the Floyd murder. A searing piece by Stephen W. Thrasher, in particular, explains the metaphoric sense of claustrophobia and choking urban black communities feel under the yoke of the Broken Windows regime and the constant threat of judge and jury, 'accidental' or 'defensive' executions (Thrasher 13 April 2015). Fuck Your Breath! has also shone a dark light on the peculiarity of the American penal system in which both incarceration and execution are weapons of America's ongoing race war, revealing American black males in particular as permanently housed in a penal colony from which, it appears, they can never escape. Choked on the streets; choked in the pen; if sentenced to death, choked on a gurney—what's the difference? To listen to Foucault we would say that America's race war is a prime example of one of the few legitimised forms of bioviolence. Turning to Agamben, we might note the animalisation of the African-American community and the dual encampment of the American male, in particular, in prisons and on the streets. Indeed we might go so far as to say that prison and street have become indifferentiated. Finally, if we were to let Esposito join in, it would be obvious that the ongoing de facto executions of young black males in their hundreds annually is a kind of auto-immunity of the body politic against the 'infection' of racial purity that is the oxygen of the false science behind much racism. Yet none of these fascinating conversations would quite possess the historical specificity needed to fully explain the Fuck Your Breath! versus #Blacklivesmatter dialectic now reverberating around the globe. For that we need a new voice, a different discourse, a particular sensibility. For that we need activist and author Angela Y. Davis.

Prisons as plantations

Davis argues, in her remarkably prescient *Are Prisons Obsolete?*, that there is a direct causal link between slavery, the complexities of its abolition and the modern American penal system. Her point is not just that there is inherent racism in American prisons, but these houses of correction are themselves a means of regulating and massifying populations due to race, that is nothing other than a continuation of slavery in another form, such that being black has basically been criminalised with the aim of using said criminalisation as a means of the perpetuation of the exploitation of African Americans that began with the cotton plantations.

Due to the distressing history of slavery in the US, there was always going to be an awful fit between slavery and incarceration. There are just so many elements of the prison system that resemble slavery, such as the subordination of subjects to the will of others, the strict daily routine overseen by third parties, the dependency of inmates on others for basic needs such as food and shelter, the isolation of subjects from the general population and, most notably, forced labour. After the abolition of slavery the Slave Code, which oversaw the abnegation of all basic rights to slaves, was replaced by the Black Codes, which, in some states, regulated, this is Davis' word, "the behaviour of free blacks in ways similar to those that had existed during slavery" (Davis 2003, p.29). Things such as vagrancy, absence from work or rude gestures were criminal acts only if the perpetrator was black. What these laws basically allowed for was an orderly, regulatory, transition from a life of servitude as a slave to that of hard labour as a convicted vagrant, often on the very same plantations that the slaves had been released from. This had the effect of criminalising blackness such that certain crimes were only crimes if they were committed by black people, while poverty imposed upon the recently freed black population meant that misdemeanours such as vagrancy, only punishable if you were black, became unavoidable. To be black was to be poor; to be poor was to be precarious; this precarity would lead to vagrancy and vagrancy to imprisonment. Or, to be black was to be a criminal—a lethal, inevitable syllogism. The combination of social deprivation and the Black Codes meant that being poor and black replaced being a slave such that, ultimately, the results were the same: a lifetime of incarceration and hard labour.

Davis says the result of the southern Black Codes was to "impute crime with color," an imputation that has, she argues, never been lifted in the US (Davis 2003, p.30). It also began to mark a significant demographic shift as regards the population of prisons, which had been 95% white during slavery, but which suddenly became predominantly populated by black people. Not only did the prison system operate as an alternative means of perpetuating slavery in terms of it being an inescapable incarceration due to 'race,' but the punishments inside the prisons began to resemble those of the old plantations. Whipping was not uncommon, and the use of the chain, specifically the chain gang, meant from a distance it might be hard to differentiate a chain gang from the old-fashioned practice of chaining slaves together and marching them to market to be sold. Indeed the chain gang itself resembled very closely the exploitation of black populations for cheap labour, while the convict lease system, as it was called, also had the subtle effect of determining black labour in specific ways: working in gangs, under supervision, disciplined by the lash. One could argue that the effect of this was to redefine slavery not as a one-off period or extended event but as just one in a series of regulatory measures designed to massify people into groups due to norms pertaining to skin colour and origin of birth or ancestry, which continues to the present day. Some have even speculated that the convict lease system was in some ways worse than slavery; for example individual slaves had some value, while convicts were leased as already-composed masses, gangs, who, if worked to death, caused no financial loss to anyone. This carried on right through to the living conditions of chain gangs, which are generally thought of, now, as potentially worse than that of plantation slaves. None of this intended to diminish the eternal repugnance of American slavery or cleanse its indelible stains from US history.

Davis ends her devastating analysis of this regulatory transition from slavery to the convict lease system with a brief overview of how much the American economy has benefitted in modern times by the cheap labour of black inmates, and I am sure this isn't negligible, but what is perhaps more interesting economically is how much the penal system as a whole is currently worth. There are, at present, close to 3 million people in prison in the US. The majority of those sentenced are black, with around a third of all young black men on parole, on probation or in prison. The annual turn-over of the private prison conglomerates is in the trillions, their annual profits in the billions. What this shows us is that it is good business to imprison folk and that because the modern penal system is literally a *dispositif* to regulate the African-American population post-slavery, incarcerating black folks is economically inevitable.

Inevitable though it may be, states still like to double-down on the process to make sure black people are disproportionally and in large numbers held in prisons. In a recent BBC documentary journalist Simon Reeve visited the prison city of Canon, Colorado (Reeve 13 October 2019). There he spoke with a local activist who explained how being imprisoned in that state was close to unavoidable through the simple regulatory procedure of accreting criminalisation of minor offences. Tiny infringements such as a broken tail light lead to hefty fines, which, if not paid, would be sold out to private debt collectors, which then would lead, eventually, to a prison sentence. Basically this is the legacy of the Broken Windows program, here upcycled to broken tail light and gifting the malingering legacy of the black laws with new, legal and at times lethal affordances. Taken in isolation, poverty, the history of black criminalisation, a broken tail light, a fine and the criminalisation of non-payment seem minor rights infringements. But in reality they form another brutal, regulatory syllogism, which basically says if you are born black in certain towns you most likely will be poor, meaning your car will need work, such that you will be fined, because the local police force are watching you, because you are black. These authorities are benefitting locally from all these fines, fines you will eventually be unable to pay, because you are poor, such that failure to pay debt can then permit the state to incarcerate you, which they will, because the entire local economy is based on the prisons, as well as the national economic wellbeing, irrespective of the fact that local law enforcement agencies may also be institutionally racist and happy to see you in prison under any pretext. Fascinating though this concatenation of real-world premises may be, if anything, this racist syllogism should be a prophylaxis against street executions, because imprisoning young black males is good business, while killing them should impact your profit margin. There are, in other words, more questions to ask by the modern, black Socrates of his white police officers, as they pin him to the ground and ask him to give his life in service of his beliefs.

Prisons: the concrete plantations

Why did the black laws, which replaced the Slave Codes, seek to criminalise blackness, by making sure the black population was impoverished? And why did they design the new penal system to resemble so much the old one of slavery? Finally, how is it that this racialisation of punishment continues apace in the 21st century? If your answer is racism you are right, but you barely scratch the surface of what racism actually means in practice, which is why we need, in support of #Blacklivesmatter, to turn to Foucault again so that we can add in a theoretical machinery that will rest atop Davis' historical advocacy approach, such that we can see the modern US penal system as the archetypal example of bioviolent punishment. What we are arguing is that racism is not a word describing attitudes towards race but is a process, a machinery, a function, an economy, an architecture, a mode of procurement, a legal process, a type of poverty, a massification, a set of regulatory procedures, a diversification of the idea of incarceration, a materiality of concretisation of the old plantations, a topology, a tax system, a set of knowledge power, the testimony of experts and so on. Racism, people on the streets, is not a word, a behaviour or an attitude of individuals. It is rather a *dispositif* that has been constructed, consolidated, innovated and diversified since the very first slave had set a free foot on American soil back in 1865.

With the abolition of slavery the US had a population of around 4 million traumatised black citizens. Suddenly, within the body politic, the biopoliticised state had an internal race 'infection' that threatened to overwhelm the state as a whole, as the autoimmune system of slavery struggled to reconstitute itself within the new legal situation. To achieve this of course the American body politic went to war with itself, civil war being the archetypal auto-immunising gesture. In many ways the prevalence of slavery in the US had already made it a prototype modern biopower, in that the owners of slaves had absolute control over the private and bodily lives of their slaves. In some senses this echoed in reverse the great conundrum of modern biopower and how it flipped from regulatory modes of care to totalitarian concentration camps. America found itself in the post-abolition period with the opposite problem, how to switch overnight from totalitarian concentration camps to a managerial, semi-democratic state of care. This sudden reversal has taken a couple of centuries to be achieved and, indeed, arguably, has never been very successful.

To protect the lives of its white citizens, financially, culturally and also literally, after all fear of vengeance must have been a concern, albeit a false one, the state used its imperative to 'make live' as a means of regulating freed slaves into servitude. As a crucial first step in this procedure black people were massified by defining them as exceptions due to local race laws, thanks to poverty, and then the criminalisation of poverty. Prisons were repurposed from being houses of correction for dangerous white folk to factories for the control and economic exploitation of the black population. The criminalisation of the black population was of small scale, nit-picking, jobsworthy. Back in the day it busied itself around charges of vagrancy, drunkenness and those intriguing rude gestures. These days the biostate is more concerned with broken tail lights, minor traffic infringements and, in one county, mismatching curtains. The regulations established the norms of behaviour whose prime objective was to identify an abnormal mass. While the southern states are not overly squeamish as regards massifying African Americans due to race, modern governmentality in general much prefers modes of coercion and violence that come from the necessary neglect of the ir-regulated ab-norms, so that they can deny any direct racism in their processes. These regulatory norms, then, produce a new kind of conceptual plantation, one where forcible removal from your African home by slave ships and being worked to death on a planation are modified to a period of time in prison due to your committing a crime and being worked to death on a chain gang until you have served your sentence.

What Davis' argument proposes is that the punitive *dispositif* in America, which we call jail, also works in parallel as a regulatory massification machine. Jails in America are not simply institutions that reflect the racism inherent in the country; nor is it so simple as to say the preponderance of black people in those jails is because of poverty and urban alienation. These are the easy observations of any impassioned feature writer, the meat and potatoes of the advocacy journalist. Rather, Davis asks us to go further and say that American jails, in particular, are not just versions of the generic governmentality of the post-torture age with a bit of racism thrown in, but are a historically and culturally specific process of post-enslavement regulation and construction of 'race' masquerading as mode of enforced rehabilitation and retribution. In truth, American penitentiaries are concretised plantations. Slavery, when faced with an actual threat to its existence, experienced a kind of punitive metempsychosis. It transitioned from the plantation and the cotton fields to the prison and the chain gangs, with poverty and black-only crimes, replacing dependency and lawless chattel status.

Even terms like 'poverty,' 'law' and 'crime' are effectively meaningless when applied to the white versus the black population. Black poverty is not a lack of money but a prelude to vagrancy. The freed slaves were kept poor so they could be regulated. The idea of the law again is radically dissimilar for whites and blacks. Black people are not put in prison because they break a law; rather the law is created so that freed slaves can be legally returned to enslavement. Crimes, on this reading, are not things individuals commit by breaking laws, but, if you are black, at least, crimes are an ontological determination. To be a black means to be a criminalised being, at least in America. Being black allows the judiciary to judge you according to your soul, and your life, so as to be able to design its laws so that they perfectly encapsulate Kafka's dictum of totalitarian, colonial racism in "In the Penal Colony": "Guilt is never to be doubted," because guilt, let us be clear, is written on the body of every black citizen simply due to the colour of their skin, which means the skin of black people is not skin at all, but judgement. The breath of black people is not their breath but the theft of our air. The lives of black people are not their life but the get-out clause of the black laws, should they feel that their new slaves are getting overly uppity.

People talk fast and loose right now about institutionalised racism. Ok, well, this is what is meant by the institutionalisation of racism. First it is a series of laws and words. Then it is enshrined in a set of regulatory procedures. At some point it will establish itself in buildings, literally making concrete the plantation. But the final act of true institutionalisation, the ultimate *dispositif*, is the one missing from Foucault to be revealed later by Italian philosophy, Agamben and Esposito, in particular. To truly institutionalise racism, the *dispositif* has to insert the apparatus of the powers into the very body of its citizens. The institutionalisation of racism is not the treatment of black people by the institutions of the state but the indifferentiation of black people from the institutions of the state. It is not that institutions behave differently for black Americans but rather that the very essence of being black in American is an institution, a *dispositif*, a legal system, an economy, an urban plan. As the late, great Toni Morrison once explained as regards America's oft-touted commitment to freedom, America, as a set or massification of all its institutions, exists as a power because of its imputing not just crime with color but everything with color.

To abolish racism in America would mean to abolish slavery from the pages of American history. To abolish racism would mean to turn back time. Not to rewrite history, that is already a *dispositif* the state owns, but to change it. To abolish racism in America would mean to abolish time and not just time but space also. Not just space but the physical, extended bodies that Descartes explains occupy that space, our bodies. To abolish racism in America would not just ask of the abolitionists the Sisyphean task of rewriting history but the scientifically impossible importunity to rewrite our very genes themselves.

This is what is meant by American institutionalised racism. Such racism is written on and in the body—a tattoo of betrayal, a lethal implant. More than that, it is the very definition of the composition of the body—the body of the state, the bodies the state massifies and the actual physical bodies of all of its citizens. Perhaps this chapter should have been called "From your tail light to your genome" for this is indeed the incredible, I would say perpetually terrifying, ingenuity of the American *dispositif* of race, and of course our own European *dispositif* of the empire. Or maybe better "From the plantation to the implantation of race", for it is the very bodily assumption of the racist *dispositif* that we are surely battling when we casually, but with good intentions, share or tweet a #BlackLivesMatter meme.

The legalisation of slavery was a biopolitical means of converting sovereign violence to managerial bioviolence through regulatory coercion. These Black Codes of the post-abolition period have remained implicit in American society ever since, demonstrating a secret that biopowers would like to keep under wraps, yet in plain view if they can. This recondite activity is an active means of creating the violence of neglect. Biopolitical institutions don't accidentally, or regretfully, neglect certain abnormal groups within a mass when times get tough; rather they are constructed in advance to facilitate the exclusion and victimisation of the poor, women, the insane, gay men and women and, of course, the racially determined other. Prisons therefore are not a means of punishment, prophylaxis, warning or rehabilitation. Rather, the methods they employ to massify the urban black poor into secure encampments called ghettos are an active mechanism for the continued enslavement, impoverishment, alienation, torture and, through capital punishment—legal or merely tolerated—murder of a post-slavery population seen as so abnormal to the deep-seated American sense of national self that no amount of internal regulation could make them "one of us."

Or, in answer to Davis' question, *Are Prisons Obsolete?* the answer is yes. America no longer needs prisons to execute its anti-bodies against the anti-gen of race in the form of those constitutional Black Codes, a kind of secret or implied 28th Amendment, because it has the streets themselves—the streets where young black males are not free, cannot breathe, can be executed at any time without concerns in relation to the 8th Amendment, the opinions of lawyers and medical professionals or access to lethal drug combinations manufactured in Europe. It is true that shooting a black man in the back as he runs from you over a minor taxation issue costs the state money in the short term, but the right to do is more valuable because this right, this 28th Amendment right, is the right of all rights, I believe. I say this because, at the present time at least, and for all time up to this time, the Fuck Your Breath! axiom is the very right to be America at all. This has to change.

13

HERD IMMUNITY
COVID and coercion

A week is a long time in politics

On 13 March 2020, three middle-aged, white men stepped up to old-fashioned podia in a wood-panelled chamber reminiscent of their august boarding schools and delivered a message somewhat akin to the end of the world. Those three horsemen of the apocalypse were Chief Medical Officer Chris Whitty and Chief Science Officer Patrick Vallance, flanking a struggling-for-sombre-setting Boris Johnson who, for some reason, had ended up as our prime minister. Over the next few minutes the three harbingers of doom calmly outlined the government's strategy of tackling the imminent threat of the COVID-19 pandemic by adopting what is called, by epidemiologists, herd immunity. Like doctors surrounding a brave, yet fatal, case, their tone was measured, clipped by Eton and softened by the emollient demands of Whitehall machinations. The whole performance with graphs and whatnot was boffinish, typical of a British understatement—I say chaps I am sorry, but you are all going to cop it. I briefly bought the performance and allowed myself to be lulled into a false state of security as I listened to the calm explanation of my impending doom. "Following the science" felt a bit like following the yellow brick road in the company of scarecrow Whitty, Tin Man Vallance and the tousled, leonine Johnson goofing betwixt them. I should have known, of course, it wouldn't be long before the curtain was raised and the wizard's diminution exposed, and so it proved to be. But before we get to that rude awakening, let's slumber awhile in the poppy-field of dreams that was herd immunity, a policy that suggested just as we had invented computers, deciphered DNA and cracked the enigma code, the same British ingenuity had realised that every other country in the world had got it wrong, except Sweden. All you had to do was *not* lock down, have fun, go to the races and then to the pub and wait for around 70% of

British people to become infected so that there would be enough of the population with antibodies that the spread of the disease would be halted. Vallance,
I recall, pointed at a graph. A big red line sliced across it. But this was a good
thing. Infection, after all, was a necessary precursor to immunity, although this
was no reason for us to rush the infection buffet all at the same time. We are,
after all, British, and this means a cultural sense of herding kicks in, in our case
herding as a form of fatalistic queuing. Don't worry! There is enough COVID
to go around; we just need to distribute it with caution, you know, to "flatten
the sombrero"?

   In my household we chose to pause, scepticism's silence being a regular visitor
therein. The population of the UK is around 65 million, we brilliantly noted.
The death rate at the time was estimated to be, I looked it up using my incredible IT skills, 1–2%, 1–2% of 65 million was, I needed my wife's advanced maths
to model this one, more than a half a million people! More than half a million,
possibly a million as, let's face it, we are an obese nation with diseased hearts,
diabetic tendencies and a love of gathering in drunken packs to hug and spit out
anthems. At that time the largest mortality rate from COVID-19 was in Italy,
approaching 20,000, a number that was seen as a national disaster. Vallance and
Whitty were suggesting instead that half a million would be more like it here. It
was as if we had followed the science into a post-apocalyptic moment captured
by Bowie's plangent "Five Years":

> Pushing through the market square, so many mothers sighing / News had
> just come over, we had five years left to cry in / News guy wept and told
> us, earth was really dying / Cried so much his face was wet, then I knew
> he was not lying.

(Bowie, 1972)

Except Vallance wasn't crying. Is that why I doubted him?

What do you call a policy that is not a policy?

It is now widely accepted that the 'policy' of herd immunity was first publically expressed on 11 March by Dr. David Halpern, a behavioural psychologist
and head of the famous Behavioural Insights Team or Nudge Unit, as it has
come to called. Halpern was a key element of SPI-B or the Scientific Pandemic
Influenza Group on Behavior, the main committee behind predictions of how
we as a nation would respond to lock down and what policies and messages could
facilitate this difficult transition. Halpern explained on that otherwise ordinary
Wednesday:

> There's going to be a point, assuming the epidemic flows and grows, as
> we think it probably will do, where you'll want to cocoon, you'll want to
> protect those at-risk groups so that they basically don't catch the disease

and by the time they come out of their cocooning, herd immunity's been achieved in the rest of the population.

(Boseley, 1 April 2020)

By the following Wednesday, this policy of herd immunity had been dismissed by the government as an ontological conundrum, my words, not theirs. It was never policy, they explained, and yet, for a few essential days, we, the population of the UK thought that it must be, because at that early point in the pandemic, we were still minded to believe the messaging of our leaders, Brexit or no Brexit, because, well, this was different, wasn't it! This was our Churchillian moment? If, as the record states, herd immunity was not a policy, and yet, as the same record also, begrudgingly, admits, it was something the government said they were pursuing, what was this strange breed of 'not-policy'? I went away that second Wednesday in March and looked up what a policy actually was in the OED: "A course of action or principle adopted or proposed by a government ..." Hmm.

Looking again at Halpern's words now I am struck by the potential veracity of the later claims that this herd immunity did not in fact meet the requirements mapped out by the OED's definition, not just because Halpern is not exactly part of the government but also because his explanation resembles more a missing segment of Kafka's "Metamorphosis," than a boring policy briefing. As the pandemic grew exponentially, Halpern appeared to be aware of the need of certain individuals to hide away, to become-as-insect as Deleuze might say, to cocoon until the plague had passed, to indulge in some duvet months, Gregor Samsa style. As Samsa tragically discovered that fateful first morning when he did finally rise from his nest-bed, not everyone, however, can cocoon. To enter that bronze carapace you needed to be old, a diabetic, missing an essential organ. You needed, primarily, to be defined and massified by experts on pandemics as vulnerable.

While our elders are metamorphosed into suspended state insects, the rest of us are transmogrified, by Halpern's words, into herding beasts of the arctic tundra, taking hits from the rampage of predators, while, I imagine, David Attenborough whispers his concern for our safety as moving music wells up. Our job was to do nothing, and in not acting, not taking precautions, we would be standing firm against the virus like shielding heroes until it is safe for our caterpillar-codgers to emerge from their homes, shrug off their beige fleece and take to the skies on myriad-coloured wings. In many ways, therefore, government denials of herd immunity were not the first pings of rubble on the road through the pandemic, presaging the avalanche of policy U-turns to follow. Halpern's dream is clearly not dressed in the language of a policy, more akin as it is to a kind of poetry, leaving me wondering what do you call a policy that is not a policy that encourages you to do the right thing, but never insists that you do?

On that cursed 12 March, journalist Robert Peston had blogged that the government's strategy to minimise the impact of COVID-19 is to allow the virus to pass through the entire population so that we acquire herd immunity, but at a much delayed speed so that those who suffer the most acute symptoms are able to receive the medical support they need, and such that the health service is not overwhelmed and crushed by the sheer number of cases it has to treat at any one time.

(Peston 2020)

Now *that* sounds like a policy, even when modulated through the odd hesitancies and anapaests of Pestonese. Yet, by the following day, Health Secretary Matt Hancock, in an article for the *Telegraph*, clarified the government's position: "We have a plan, based on the expertise of world-leading scientists. Herd immunity is not a part of it. That is a scientific concept, not a goal or a strategy" (Titheradge and Kirkland 2020). When pressed about the herd immunity concept on Andrew Marr the next day, Hancock further clarified: "Herd immunity is not our policy, it's not our goal" (Staunton 2020), an odd thing to say because, scientifically, herd immunity is the aim of all vaccinations against infectious diseases.

Semantics aside, on the morning of 23 March 2020, after an Imperial College study predicted a possible 250,000 deaths if herd immunity is pursued in favour of more traditional epidemiological strategies, the UK's unprecedented and yet totally predictable lockdown began, lasting a full 12 weeks before measures began to be eased. At the end of the first lockdown, unofficial figures put the death rate at over 60,000, with perhaps half of those being elderly people who failed to emerge out of the protective shield of their care-home cocoons. At one point our death rate was the third-worst in the world and by far the worst in Europe. The same Imperial scientist, Dr. Neill Ferguson, who modelled the predicted quarter of a million deaths that put paid to herd immunity practically overnight, has subsequently gone on record to say the prevarication of just a week during which we discussed the non-policy cost the UK more than 10,000 unnecessary deaths. Yet, for all of this, Hancock was right in his denial; herd immunity was never a policy; I see that now—it is rather what is called a nudge, but it was hard to know that at the time.

Nudge!

Nudges are non-coercive techniques applied to prompt people to alter their behaviour based on predictions of their already-existing tendencies provided by work done in evolutionary behavioural science and economics (Thaler and Sunstein 2009). These tendencies, we all possess, to behave in certain ways, especially when making choices without the time or inclination to work out the best option, like a scientist or philosopher would, but what just feels right in your gut, are called heuristics (Kahneman 2011). Heuristics show that people do not decide rationally based on the overall chance of success, but locally at the moment using irrational assumptions that are part of our psychological evolution. There is a pretty long list of heuristics behavioural scientists have composed over the years, all of which shed fascinating illumination on lockdown behaviour and policies, but most notable amongst them for COVID-19 compliance culture are following the herd (Thaler and Sunsetein 2009, p.x) and fear of contagion (Nemeroff and Rozin 1994). The herding heuristic adds reliable data to the well-known fact that people will tend to flock together, because according to the science we are all basically birds of a feather, suggesting to lawmakers to find prompts that initiate this innate behaviour when it came to lockdown policy to make them safe. Clap for Carers is one example of this nurturing of the inherent sociality of human animals when, for several Thursdays, we were encouraged to stand outside our houses and applaud as a socially distanced mass.

People also, as you might expect, fear contagion, although specifically the law of similarity as it is also called (Kahneman 2011, p.147) suggests that if someone has touched something bad, they will be infected with this bad thing, even if the science says otherwise. Anthropologists have, for decades, called this 'magical thinking.' This irrational fear of appearances that do not actually tally with reality means another idea would be to find nudges that capitalise on this apprehension to instigate healthy, but perhaps unpopular, behaviour: social distancing and self-isolation. Distance = protection basically. Yet humans also crave contagion conditions due to their communal instincts. the paradox of *communitas/immunitas* we will consider later in Esposito. In fact to arrive at immunity, the herd has to become infected by the contagious to a large part. So one must find ways that capitalise on things in common as a mode of massifying behaviour while playing on anxieties of contagion to simultaneously encourage social distancing—a tricky paradox I have to concede.

This paradox is encapsulated in the conflicting phraseology of lockdown, herd immunity, social distancing—a seeming disaster surely for nurturing a lockdown culture? Perhaps, to a degree, but as these are irrational responses, the contradiction inherent in avoiding contagion by following the herd, wonderfully, doesn't matter to nudge theory when you are thinking quickly on your feet in an ever-changing environment of risk. It is only when you take a step back that it does seem literally impossible that one could pursue simultaneously a herding heuristic and a distancing prompt at the same time. Herd immunity was asking of the British people to isolate as a herd, to come together to keep their distance. A kind of mirror reversal of the "alone together" sensation of our digitally mediated lives according to Sherry Turkle (Turkle 2017), herd immunity made the almost impossible demand on us that we come together alone. The question was not so much which nudges to use to promote the paradox of herd attraction and contagion anxiety, as how long you could dissuade the populace from taking a collective step back and start to reflect on social distancing rationally, because once we did that, all nudges are off.

One thing that is clear from the herding-contagion heuristic contradiction is that nudge theory is a kind of meta-example of both. Nudges assume that, given the same options and little time to think, all humans are likely to respond in preprogramed ways that are the result of evolved cultural behaviours. There are very good motivations when trying to survive the ice age 11,000 years ago to herd together. It is now widely accepted that the reason sapiens survived this winter and Neanderthals did not was not so much our physical or even cognitive superiority, as our sociability. Our love of getting together around fires to sing, adorn, narrate, dance and indulge in rhythmicality meant that we were the better herd at the point where herding was all. We also practised a kind of self-isolation, I suppose, cocooned in caves, laying low until the weather improved and the coast was clear. When we did emerge to become agrarian, sedentary beings and build civilisations, our proximity to our domesticated animals, and each other, meant that infection, both literal and metaphorical, began to become another of our inbuilt cultural and behavioural prompts. Indeed, following the complex logic of Esposito's *immunitas* I mentioned earlier, the very quality that allowed humans to become all conquering humanimals, herding, was the same one that began our endless anxiety about *immunitas*, or the exception to the *munus*, the one who has faced infection and is now immune. As soon as the body politic was formed as a political imaginary, the body as a potential subject of infection developed as a narrative of risk and justification for all kinds of coercion cultures.

There is, embedded in this discussion, a possible reason that herd immunity was favoured over the term 'community immunity,' which some scientists use instead. According to Esposito at least, the *munus* we find in im*munity* and com*munity* relates to a sense of duty or office (Esposito 2011, p.X). Community is the collective responsibility to take up duty, while being immune means the one who has no duty or office. On this reading, community immunity is simply a policy impossible for us in the West to think. Community immunity is politically extremely dangerous in a pandemic, for example, for what it says is that there are those who are immune to their duty to keep others safe, whether that be individuals like Dominic Cummings who believe their duty is such that it makes them immune to ordinary lockdown rules, or the growing sense of invulnerability that developed during the summer of 2020 as those of us who showed no symptoms, in particular it is argued the 18–25 age group, reneged upon their isolation duties and gathered in isolated fields to party.

Inside the nudge unit

The fact that herding and infection are names of heuristics is interesting, no doubt, but it still does not prove that herd immunity was a nudge. The evidence of this contention resides instead in the very manual of the BIT nudge strategies used by David Halpern's team to influence government policy, laid out in meticulous detail in his fascinating and frightening book *Inside the Nudge Unit*. Halpern defines a nudge as "not what people shouldn't do but what they should" (Halpern 2019, p.35), locating nudge, for better or worse, not only in the centre of our democracy—the book tells the rags to riches story of how this came about—but also at the centre of millennial, post-digital biopower, for what better definition of biopolitical regulatory norms is there than a set of procedures to encourage or nudge you to do what is best for your life?

Reading Halpern's book in the middle of the first lockdown I was struck by the incredible similarities between the findings of the nudge unit during their time, influencing government over the last decade or so, and what I have come to realise is the herd immunity nudge. If we cast our minds back to the evening of 12 March, it is as if the government had opened Halpern's book and concluded, "Yes, we will just copy everything he says." Halpern's unit developed an acronym early on to convey the four main heuristic principles of nudging to policy makers—they called it EAST or Easy, Attractive, Social and Timely. Easy is the headline here and has influenced lockdown profoundly, I think (at the time the position paper on EAST was the most downloaded in the history of Whitehall). For example the "Stay Home, Stay Safe, Protect the NHS" slogan is composed of three easy pieces of advice, also conforming to Cummings' much-beloved rule of three words: Take Back Control, Get Brexit Done. This easy communication also makes use of the Attract heuristic or attentional spotlight, "something has to stand out"—it has to be "salient" (Halpern 2019, p.103), basically making the message appear to be directed specifically at YOU! Philosophers call this 'subjectification,' and of course it is a well-worn technique of biopolitics, the way in which the state interpolates and thus subjectivates you through massification or humanimalisation. Clearly a decision was made that the deictic subjectivation would be implied rather than expressed here, with references to home, presumably the seat of your sense of social/domestic self, and the NHS, the central regulatory agency of our biological well-being in this country.

Salience and Attraction are simple technical aspects of all nudge messaging. The more the message stands out, the more salient it is, hence those garish green and yellow chevrons on the podia, surrounded by an otherwise entirely brown, panelled room. This is Halpern's writing several years before the pandemic on the "Messenger effect," for example:

> Seeing a politician on the news suggesting your kids should get vaccinated may have little impact, but seeing the Chief Medical Officer or senior doctor, white coat and stethoscope around their neck, suggesting the same thing is much more likely to be acted on.
>
> *(Halpern, p.103)*

With the exception of the white coat, this is word for word the set up for the delivery of the herd immunity message and countless others.

A fascinating component of nudge theory is the almost paradoxical relation between clarity of message and indirection of purpose. Yes, it is revealed to no one's particular surprise that people respond well to simple, consistent suggestions repeated without variation. Yet the actual efficacy of the nudge is only *supported* by the content of the communication, the real meaning of a nudge residing always elsewhere in your 'gut' reaction. This overlap between expressed content and intended outcome is the essence of Foucault's idea of intelligibility and Agamben's concept of language as pure communicability, two founding stones of biopolitical theory. Our hardly conscious responses to certain stimuli, colour, simple language, social pressure and so on are the essence of all identified heuristics. What a heuristic does is inform the nudger what message to use to get the person in question to act in their own best interests, without even thinking about it. What this means in practice is, if the nudge unit is involved in COVID messaging wherein the communicability of the message is not so much in the words as the context of their production and transmission (SPI-B leading to the "three white men at a podium" setup), there will always be what we literary theorists used to call, after Freud, the manifest content, stay home and protect the NHS, and the latent content, we don't have the capacity in the system to treat you, so we need to keep a lid on rates of infections, accepting that, in truth, we cannot stop them and tens of thousands of you will simply have to die. In other words, what nudges say might be Easy and Salient, but what they want you to do is often complex and occluded.

Herd immunity in terms of manifest content is something of a disaster. Transparently treating the British people as if they are bovine creatures is taking our famous love of conformity a bit too far, don't you think? Immunity is also, as we are currently realising, a glorious promise that cannot be kept. Why would the government send out such a message, knowing as we now do how damaging the message was, and how short-lived? Also why would they break their own heuristic schema? By no stretch of the imagination was herd immunity easy to understand; the idea of it is far from attractive, although it did attract attention, albeit the wrong kind. Certainly it was Social but also anti-social, asking us to herd together in isolation, which leaves us with the only heuristic we haven't yet considered from the EAST schema, its Timeliness, which is significant as it was time that was the real force behind the nudge as we shall come to see.

Freedman investigates

I think the first person to work out that herd immunity was a nudge was Lawrence Freedman in an article in *The New Statesman*. Freedman had the vision and application to go back over the papers of SPI-B to ascertain what conversations were had that led up the adoption and then abandonment of herd immunity. Armed with this data, the ever-inquisitive Freedman argues that from 12 to 16 March it was clear herd immunity was going to be a key government message, for all their tetchy refutations, until the release of that data from Imperial College. Freedman also comes to realise that the actual aim of herd immunity, to 'flatten the curve' of infection, was not to avoid loss of life but, as stated, to protect the NHS. On this point, the simple heuristic of the podia-placed garish messaging, stay home, stay safe, protect the NHS, could not be clearer and yet more confounding. Why did it not say stay home, stay safe, save lives, for example, and leave the NHS to the grandees who run the NHS? The reason for this is that herd immunity does not save lives, and it is hardwired into nudge theory, to its credit, not to lie, because a nudge theory that lies is simply the bastard love-child of a Cambridge Analytica and Brexit Bus love-affair.

On the surface there is something powerfully biopolitical in Freedman's conclusions. What is of utmost importance for the biopolitical state in regulating risk are the dispositifs of health management over the medium to long term. Just as, Foucault explains, during periods of poor harvest, millions will be left to die so that the overall agrarian economy might survive, so too, Whitty, Vallance and Johnson argued, the robust among us must risk infection, not to protect the weak, which is what herd immunity is supposed to do, but to protect an institution, the NHS. Just as in times of famine certain parts of the population should be let die, so too here.

Keeping our eyes on the time, an important behavioural belief back in February and March was "behavioural fatigue" (Mills 2020). It was assumed that if we entered lockdown too early, we would get bored of it, a problem when it came to flattening the curve, which is a durational policy. Durational policies, by the by, do not sit that well with impulsive nudge behaviour. Although this heuristic has since been questioned, what it indicates is to what degree SPI-B thought they could manipulate us, down to the week or even the day, nudging us in one direction and then another, to maximise their intended outcomes. The hubris of this approach is rather shocking, but back in March the nudge unit seemed to have the government totally convinced of their preternatural powers of persuasive control. So we had to wait, where other countries had not. Timeliness, therefore, was all.

Here then, in full, is the actual thought processes behind the herd immunity nudge as laid out in the SPI-B papers from the period. First of all, treat the infected and then protect the vulnerable to flatten the curve. At the same time avoid large-scale lockdowns such as schools, because while this would flatten the curve of infections, it would also farm out contagion to those caring for their children, which would include key workers and care workers. At that time it was known that infections tended to spread in small groups spending lots of time together. If large-scale events were cancelled, then it was assumed the same people would gather in living rooms and pubs to watch the sporting event. This reasoning led to the now-infamous decision to go ahead with the Cheltenham Cup and a champions league fixture between Liverpool and Madrid, both resulting in very significant super-spreader events.

Here is SPI-B admirably planning ahead as early as February, nobly battling against the double-headed snake of the herd mentality:

> On the one hand, stopping some public gatherings could mean people replace this with other activities (i.e. playing football behind closed doors could mean fans watch the match in the pub), potentially slightly accelerating epidemic spread. On the other hand, the message sent by stopping them would be expected to change people's behaviour in other ways,

potentially slowing epidemic spread. It is not possible to quantify either of these effects.

(Cited in Freedman 2020)

It is a carefully considered, nuanced approach. Think of it as honing your spearhead to perfection, not realising that the sabre-tooth is already upon you, and all it needs is a whack over the head with a blunt instrument located right to hand but ignored. A spanner in the works of this game of COVID chess was a certain group that came to be called the 'vulnerable,' initially the over-70s and people with co-morbidities. The question that faced SPI-B was if it would be possible to delay a total lockdown culture, while at the same time insisting on a policy of cocooning for this [vulnerable] mass. As Freedman's piece shows, the conversations around this contradiction of libertarian coercion must have been highly involved and perhaps verging on the interminable:

> The point of contention was still the potential divisiveness of isolating only the most vulnerable. This is where the concept of herd immunity was raised. … It was a justification for letting mass gatherings continue, while isolating the elderly and the vulnerable at the same time. "One view," noted an SPI-B paper for Sage, "is that explaining that members of the community are building some immunity will make this [approach] acceptable. Another view is that recommending isolation to only one section of society risks causing discontent." Although opinion at Sage was divided, the argument for this herd immunity approach won out.
>
> *(Freedman 2020)*

Won out and then within the week lucked out, a week during which maybe tens of thousands died. If the art of nudge is, as Halpern's books say, how small changes can make a big difference, then the herd immunity nudge, which perhaps can be faulted for over-estimating the intelligence of its choice architects and underestimating the perspicacity of the British people, let die a lot of people.

The death of nudge?

I believe this week of prevarication and risk will go down in history as the moment that nudge theory lost sight of its limitations and overstepped the line of libertarian paternalism rather dramatically. It had too many balls in the air, and when it dropped them, thousands died needlessly. Trying to walk a tightrope between permitting mass gathering events to put off compliance fatigue and the mass restriction of the freedoms and liberties of others, the 'vulnerable,' nudged SPI-B to advise the government to adopt herd immunity. 'Herd immunity' as a term was designed to nudge us into behaving in our own best interests amid the almost contradictory ideas of protection, immunity and precarity, herding. It would be too complex, it was assumed, to explain to the population the balancing act experts were pursuing here; you would need a thousand podia or more to achieve that, so best just to nudge the herd in one direction and then the other, without lying certainly, but also without telling the whole truth. Herd immunity, to its credit, had our best interests as regards health in mind, but to its discredit, it was also motivated by a deep mistrust in our ability as a people to act well for a long time. This is the reason that the British people were, unconsciously perhaps, converted into the British herd. Herd immunity was expressive of the contradiction of treating one mass of people as an indifferentiated beast-assemblage, whose hard-earned immunity will release another mass of humanimals, the cocooned vulnerable, from incarceration before they got sick of watching Midsomer Murders re-runs and started flooding back into the garden centres and M&S cafes. But that didn't matter because the herd don't think; they just feel and act.

And they might have got away with it if it wasn't for the fact that, faced with data, such as the prediction of a quarter to half a million deaths, we were able as a people to make the rational choice to self-isolate and socially distance as a thinking mass, days before our government told us to. Parents removed their kids from school, sports fixtures were cancelled by the fixtures themselves, businesses sent their workers home and the British people created their own paradox by inventing a non-compliant, compliance culture, in advance of the decision to lock down, which precipitated government policy. In perhaps our finest hour as an otherwise rather risible nation in the eyes of our neighbours, we home-schooled, zoomed and click-shopped the powers that be into following our example. In other words: we nudged them, they did not nudge us! Perhaps this will become the abiding headline of these times. When faced with certain death; the British herd acted as one, against the advice of their nudge-masters, to indulge in a suicidal herd immunity, and instead literally self-isolated, literally took the rational decision to distance as a society, not of unthinking, instinctual humanimals, but as intelligent, well-informed and, yes, rational humans, to draw a little distance from each other, for as long as it took, so our parents and nurses wouldn't all die, alone, gasping for breath on a ventilator.

Coda: nudge and coercion

There is no doubt that herd immunity was a biopolitical policy. As the term suggests, herding implicitly acknowledges massifying finding a scientific justification, no less, for the tendency of biopower to collect us into groups of assumed similarity. The herding instinct actually implies that we prefer more to be massified when it comes to making choices than we do to being free to choose how we see fit. The policy is also archetypally a mode of regulatory norms backed up by the testimony of experts. Being led by the science is a fundamental biopolitical means by which to coerce us without appearing to do anything other than listening to knowledge systems about what is best for us all. Yet to what degree nudge is a kind of new bioviolence is a question that is too new and complex for me to answer, not least because when the dust has settled and aerosols have dissipated, it may be that the BIT team have irrevocably lost the ear of the government who might come to realise that nudge is good for reducing traffic offences and encouraging the early submission of tax forms, but does not cut the mustard when it comes to saving the world. What I do know is that once this pandemic has passed over us, very little, if anything, of our old world will survive, and that has to include 'old' philosophical systems like biopolitics. Perhaps this then is the last word in bioviolence, the violence done to thought by the resurgence of the body, not as a discursive construct, but as a very real seat of threat, debility and mortality.

Put simply, if biopower is a means of regulation of the two areas of power that the powers that be acknowledge they cannot control, population and milieu, then after COVID, which affected the *entire* population and literally destroyed and remade the entire *milieu*, it may be that biopolitical states conclude that the regulation of life rights to protect the body politic is, well, a bit wishy-washy. It is possible that the combination of COVID, digitisation and the capture of our bodies as genetic information will be the watershed moment when we move away from biopolitical control into new forms of rule—new forms of rule possessive of novel, as yet un-thought of means of coercion, control and violence.

It began with a dead pangolin, mild fever and a dry, persistent cough. This was the way the world ended. Not from within our states but from the very insides of our bodies, which is perhaps the most biopolitical statement of all.

CONCLUSION

Apologia for a theory of political Acéphalism

What the fuck is bioviolence anyway? Do we need any more of these crappy terms? Shitty snowflakes, global elite bastards! Just get a life and stop bloody whingeing. What's done is done; now let's get it done. And by the way, we do not tolerate people speaking other languages than English in the flats. It's a simple choice, obey the rules of the majority or leave. Happy Brexit Day! (BBC, February 2020).

Or ... when Michel Foucault identified a new kind of power structure in his famous lectures of the 1970s, he spent little time on the problem of violence, but he did leave us those two tantalising clues. The first that the basic injunction of biopolitical states, make live and let die, could not be violent in the way that sovereign states used to be. The overwhelming statistical evidence is in accord with Foucault's intuition. Advanced, democratic states do not need to menace, threat, kill or excessively punish their citizens. The modern biostate makes you do what the powers that be want you to do, not by the threat of removal, the taking away of your life or rights to a good life, but by the promise of enhancement, the extension and improvement of your basic life rights. These pacifist, generous, managerial, prophylactic, value-added states have less need to kill than any state we are aware of in history. Even the great paradox of Giorgio Agamben's work, how did the biopolitical state of life-protection capsize into totalitarian death camps, is explained away statistically. We now know, thanks to Pinker and his statistician friends, that the two world wars may have killed more people than any war in history, but because there are more people than ever before in history, as regards per capita impact, those wars were bad, but far from exceptional.

The second clue is Foucault's idea of a race war. The rise of biopower presented itself with a political paradox. All power is determined by a dynamic narrative interchange between equality and difference. In that power is the imposition of the will of one over that of another, Nietzsche's basic definition of existence as will to power thanks to Hegel's great essay on power as determined by the master/slave dialectic and backed up by modern evolutionary theory, then if two subjects find themselves in a glorious state of equality, there can be no power. Equality negates power. And without power, there can be no powers that be of course. The greatest lie ever told to humanity, I believe, can be found in that short 13th chapter of Hobbes' *Leviathan* where he argues that indifference of potency is the basis of all wars, an idea at the heart of modern evolutionary theory and Girard's influential study of scapegoating of course. What indifference of potency argues is that because we are equal in strength, but the world is limited in resource, indifference or equality will be the basis of perpetual war, meaning you need agents of difference, mechanisms of inequity, to keep Jasper from turning on John over his desire for Felicity or her five-bed Hertfordshire executive show home, and returning them to that fake state of nature represented by the sink estates of neighbouring Essex.

In this sense biopower is the greatest disaster ever to befall the powers that be, and when Giorgio Agamben argues with his great forebear Foucault over the periodisation of biopolitics, arguing life has been the purview of power since the Greeks developed the conceptual and actual architecture of democratic states over two millennia ago, what Agamben was trying to show was that since its inception, power, the state and the *nomos* have been at odds with themselves, are founded on paradox, are ostensibly their own self-infecting political anomie. As soon as a state is based on life rather than citizenship or nationality, then said state admits that there is no reason for power to actually exist, because the only reason you needed a Leviathan was to introduce difference into the rabid indifferentiation of life itself, which is the real terrifying truth of the animalistic state of nature, not perpetual war, but interminable, indifferential peace.

Thinking of Esposito, perhaps the one fact the great man fails to notice is that there is but one virus or infection the body politic needs to inoculate itself against, and that is the pathogen of bio-founded, political indifferentiation. Once you start saying the purpose of the state is to preserve and perpetuate indifference of life, and that this statistically shows that state violence against its citizens, and indeed interpersonal violence between those citizens, is decreasing, then you don't need a Leviathan because, in fact, when left to their own devices, Jasper and John and Felicity just sort of muddle along actually. Biopower then did not seize on life rights as a new mode of rule, but was more forced into it by those external agencies the powers that be as-yet cannot control, in particular population and milieu. Large numbers with limited resources demand that the state intervene with regulatory norms of massification.

Race war then is a rather clumsy phrase that Foucault proposes to explain the necessity for a second strand of biopolitical theory which asks: if all humans are equal as a species, and yet power continues to exist and wars to be fought, is it possible to differentiate within the indifference of the human race so that power continues to be the law of all human existence, such that war and punishment and exclusion and neglect persist in being the four horsemen of the biopolitical, indefinitely postponed, apocalypse? The thread of this unravelling thought is picked up and woven into the second strand of biopolitical theory by Italian thinkers, in particular Agamben and Esposito. Race, according to the Italians, becomes an agency of the wider myth of human specie-fication that allows us to biologically and genetically differentiate the indifferent mass of the 7+ billion humans on this planet, all of whom must be extended the same life rights. The human and the animal now becomes the key differentiation and disparity of all political power, not as a basic opposition or dialectic, such as you find in Foucault's un-reconstructed Nietzschean Hegelianism, but rather as steps within a syllogistic narrative. Subjects are no longer pitched against each other in a Hobbesian war of all against all, but are located along a spectrum of humanimal status from animal, through human, to humanimal indistinction resulting in bare life, *homines sacrii* and human scapegoats, with gorillas in possession of personhood heading across the same spectrum in the opposite direction.

This much more sophisticated consideration of the humanimal and the auto-immunising body political replaces Foucault's dubious race war concept as well as radicalising those rather problematic moments where he abandons his archaeology of knowledge in favour of the genealogical late work with its tendency to essentialise certain historical materialities such as the fading of our fear of death, the perpetual threat of the milieu and the impact of the impossible to determine shift from citizens to population. Indeed, Foucault increasingly sounds like the spokesperson for the powers that be, an apologist for the rise of biopolitical managerial neglect, when he takes it as read that there is such a thing as the milieu, and that large numbers called populations are impossible to rule by direct means. In contrast, Agamben, ever the gentle disrupter, reminds the great French thinker that it was ever thus; how did the Romans manage their empire, for example, and what does large mean vis-à-vis a population, is there an absolute magnitude, isn't the concept of size culturally determined when it comes to politics? And what of the limitations and vagaries of milieu if, even 2,000 years ago, empires were transforming the landscape and natural rhythms to suit their own social needs?

So Agamben stops for a moment and thinks again. Why do states use means of coercion to make life and let die, if the double chimera of population and milieu sound more like justificatory fictions, rather than actual, material limitations on statecraft? How can it be that at the very heart of the biopolitical project, there is nothing more biopotent after all than totalitarianism as an Italian of a certain age knows only too well, defined by Agamben via Kafka as the abolition of the difference between the public and domestic spheres, the famous zone of indistinction between *bios* and *zoe*, we get concentration camps, holocaust, genocide, world war and nuclear weapons? The answer is rather simple, it transpires. In that democracies have always been about power over life taken in its constructed double aspect, public and private, political and biological; all power is, by definition, biopower. The very point of access that permits a state a degree of efficacy when it comes to the making of life is also the mode by which making life becomes making death. Just like the toroid coffee-cup become doughnut that we spoke of in relation to the topology of the camp, biopolitics can easily become thanatopolitics without, and this is pretty crucial, ever 'tearing' the form of the nation, the state, the sovereign, the empire, the territory or indeed the very idea of power itself. Biopower then is not the power to make life or let die from the 18th century onwards, that's just Foucault succumbing in haste to the bewitchment of the apparent certainties of historical data. Rather biopower is the very anamorphic dynamism of topology where a hole can be on the edge of the state, separating the handle from the mug, and at the same time become the very centre of the state, hollowing out the doughnut hole that all leaders know is the very negative basis of their power. The *nomos*, to put it succinctly, our norm, is when the hole is able to separate off the handle from the main body, which becomes anomic when that hole is able to creep back into the body politic proper.

Which is what Roberto Esposito means by the impossible logic of *immunitas*, the auto-inoculating, autoimmune concept of the body politic that, in treating a state as if it were a biological body, allows it to succumb to all the problems of infection inherent to the metaphor. Only now, in thinking of power as the body, rather than a means of regulating bodies, the brutal topological logic of Agamben's work becomes intimate and wet, the mucoid overspilling the mobioid. And now we have our answer to how wars can happen, of course. Violence is not, as I said, a dialectic of conflict between two subjects. Rather it is a self-imposed wound or political ouroboros. All homicide is suicide, all wars are civil; there is no war of all against all, only the never-ending skirmish of self against itself. This then is the final indifferentiation of biopolitical theory, the suspension of difference between two opposed beings, the powers that be and the subjects it makes, which allows for the greatest ontological crime of all, the permanent differentiation of any being from itself. Which, when removed from the pages of philosophical ontology, Agamben's natural habitat and my own, and placed between the sticky organs, extended along the tacky veins and located in that syllogistic history of beast, human, *homo sacer*, bare life and humanimal, results in Esposito's *uomo-bestia*. As the dash of the compound Italian term indicates, it is a mode of separation that is also a function of composition, a separation that is a relation, a non-relation that forms a synthesis.

And here we have the basic driver of bioviolence, not how the powers that be differ from and force into shape their subjects, but how we, as the body politic, we as the powers that be, have allowed our political being to differ from itself. It was we the subjects who sanctioned the political theorists, philosophers, evolutionary thinkers, bogus race scientism-ists, part-time anthropo-apologists and liberal populists to suggest that we are all the same, and so that we will perpetually differ, such that we invented a head for the body politics, a wise, vengeful, managerial Leviathan to step in with the differential *ür-dispositif* itself, the institutions of difference, whose ability to parse the *uomo* from *uomo* with the interjection of that devilish *bestia*, had the miraculous effect of creating the modern idea of the politics of the CEO, the demagogue, the dictator and MAGA-lomaniac.

And so the Führer was born, the *Duce*, the glorious leader when fascism rules the corpus, ravaging its cells almost to the point of extinction. And so it is that now we have Trump, Johnson and Salvini, a kind of self-imposed corporeal malaise, born not of autoimmune existential threat, Hitler's logical biopolitical conclusion that the only way to heal the body politic was to kill it in its entirety, but more of political, democratic and consumerist overindulgence. A body suffering from the excesses of its gorging on its own success.

Ours is a politics of gout, sclerosis, liver failure, fact-obesity. We live in the age of political diabetics. There have been too many doughnuts taken with an inundation of tall sugary lattes. The Leviathan has both shrunk and grown physically, swollen on the rich soup of populism he has allowed himself to imbibe without cessation. He is on the verge of cardiac arrest. And when he goes, it will be our choice to go with him, or cut him from us, exchanging centuries of Leviathanism for a new political Acéphalism. A movement whose motto has already been written, by the great yet also insane Georges Bataille, almost a century ago: beyond what I am, I encounter a being who makes me laugh because he is headless.

BIBLIOGRAPHY

Agamben, Giorgio, 1998. *Homo Sacer: Sovereign Power and Bare Life*, trans. Daniel Heller-Roazen. Stanford, CA: Stanford University Press.

Agamben, Giorgio, 2013b. *Opus Dei: The Archaeology of Duty*, trans. Adam Kotsko. Stanford, CA: Stanford University Press.

Agamben, Giorgio, 2002. *Remnants of Auschwitz: The Witness and the Archive*, trans. Daniel Heller-Roazen. New York: Zone Books.

Agamben, Giorgio, 1993. *Stanzas: Word and Phantasm in Western Culture*, trans. Ronald L. Martinez. Minneapolis: University of Minnesota Press.

Agamben, Giorgio, 2005. *State of Exception*, trans. Kevin Attell. Chicago: University of Chicago Press.

Agamben, Giorgio, 2013a. *The Highest Poverty: Monastic Rules and Form-of-Life*, trans. Adam Kotsko. Stanford, CA: Stanford University Press.

Agamben, Giorgio, 2011. *The Kingdom and the Glory: For a Theological Genealogy of Economy and Government*, trans. Lorenzo Chiesa and Matteo Mandarini. Stanford, CA: Stanford University Press.

Agamben, Giorgio, 2004. *The Open: Man and Animal*, trans. Kevin Attell. Stanford, CA: Stanford University Press.

Agamben, Giorgio, 2010. *The Sacrament of Language: An Archaeology of the Oath*, trans. Adam Kotsko. Stanford, CA: Stanford University Press.

Agamben, Giorgio, 2009. *The Signature of All Things: On Method*, trans. Luca D'Isanto and Kevin Attell. New York: Zone Books.

Agamben, Giorgio, 2005. *The Time That Remains*, trans. Patricia Dailey. Stanford, CA: Stanford University Press.

Agamben, Giorgio, 2016. *The Use of Bodies*, trans. Adam Kotsko. Stanford, CA: Stanford University Press.

Agamben, Giorgio, 2009. *What Is an Apparatus? And Other Essays*, trans. David Kishik and Stefan Pedatella. Stanford, CA: Stanford University Press.

al-Raqqawi, Abu Ibrahim, 2015. "Inside the Islamic State 'capital': no end in sight to its grim rule", *The Guardian*, 2015 [Online]. Available at: https://www.theguardian.com/world/2015/feb/21/islamic-state-capital-raqqa-syria-isis [Accessed 31/01/20].

Arendt, Hannah, 1970. *On Violence*. New York: Harcourt Publishers.

Arendt, Hannah, 1958. *The Human Condition*. Chicago: University of Chicago Press.

Arendt, Hannah, 2017. *The Origins of Totalitarianism*. London: Penguin.

Arthur, Charles, 2015. "Naked celebrity pics and the James Foley video: how many have clicked?", *The Guardian*, 2015 [Online]. Available at: https://www.theguardian.com /technology/2014/sep/03/naked-celebrity-pictures-james-foley-jennifer-lawrence -how-many-viewed [Accessed 31/01/20].

Ashbery, John, 1997. *The Mooring of Starting Out*. Hopewell, NJ: The Ecco Press.

Atwan, Abdel–Bari, 2015. *Islamic State: The Digital Caliphate*. London: Saqi Books.

Atwood, Margaret, 2017. *The Handmaid's Tale*. London: Vintage.

Badiou, Alain. 2005. *Being and Event*, trans. Oliver Feltham. London: Continuum.

Badiou, Alain. 2003. *St. Paul: The Foundation of Universalism*, trans. Ray Brassier. Stanford, CA: Stanford University Press.

Bartlett, Jamie, 2015. *The Dark Net*. London: Windmill Books.

Bateson, Gregory, 1972. *Steps to an Ecology of Mind*. San Francisco: Chandler Books.

Baudelaire, Charles, 1972. *Selected Writings on Art and Literature*. London: Penguin.

Baudrillard, Jean, 1994. *Simulacra and Simulation*. Ann Arbor: University of Michigan Press.

BBC News 2016. "Cincinnati gorilla shooting: police to investigate parents", *BBC News*, 2016 [Online]. Available at https://www.bbc.co.uk/news/world-us-canada-3642043 7 [Accessed 24 June 2016].

BBC News 2020. "'Happy Brexit Day' signs at Norwich flats are 'racially aggravating', say police", *BBC News*, 2020 [Online]. Available at: https://www.bbc.co.uk/news/ uk-england-norfolk-51348812 [Accessed 13/02/20].

Beard, Mary, 2018. *Women and Power*. London: Profile Books.

Benjamin, Andrew, 2010. *Of Jews and Animals*. Edinburgh: Edinburgh University Press.

Benjamin, Walter, 2008. *One-Way Street*. London: Penguin.

Bernard, Jay, 2019. *Surge*. London: Chatto & Windus.

Bisset, Alison, 2019. "What rights do the children of Islamic State have under international law?", *The Conversation*, 2019 [Online]. Available at: https://theconv ersation.com/what-rights-do-the-children-of-islamic-state-have-under-internation al-law-112322 [Accessed 31/01/20].

Blanchot, Maurice, 1992. *The Step Not Beyond*, trans. Lycette Nelson. Albany, NY: SUNY Press.

Booth, Robert, 2019. "Grenfell Cladding Firm spends £30 m defending its role in disaster", *The Guardian*, 2019 [Online]. Available at: https://www.theguardian.com/ uk-news/2019/nov/27/grenfell-cladding-firm-spends-30m-defending-its-role-in-d isaster [Accessed 31/01/20].

Boseley, Sarah, 2020. "'Absolutely wrong': how UK's coronavirus test strategy unravelled", *The Guardian*, 2019 [Online]. Available at: https://www.theguardian .com/world/2020/apr/01/absolutely-wrong-how-uk-coronavirus-test-strategy unravelled? CMP=Share_ ndroidApp_Add_to_Pocket [Accessed 02/10/20].

Bourke, Joanna, 2007. *Rape*. London: Virago.

Bourke, Joanna, 2011. *What is Means to be Human*. London: Virago.

Bowie, David, 1972. *The Rise and Fall of Ziggey Stardust*. London: RCA.

Browning, Robert, 1962. "Caliban on Setebos", in Abrams, M.H. ed., *Norton Anthology of English Literature Volume 2*. New York: WW Norton, pp. 1402–9.

Burchell, Graham, Gordon, Colin and Miller, Peter eds., 1991. *The Foucault Effect: Studies in Governmentality*. Chicago: University of Chicago Press.

Butler, Judith, 2010. *Frames of War: When is Life Grievable?*. London: Verso.

Butler, Judith, 2004. *Precarious Life: The Powers of Mourning and Violence.* London: Verso.

Campbell, Timothy and Adam Sirte eds., 2013. *Biopolitics: A Reader.* Durham: Duke University Press.

Capelouto, Susanna, 2014. "Eric Garner: the haunting last words of a dying man", *CNN*, 2014 [Online]. Available at: https://edition.cnn.com/2014/12/04/us/garner-last-words/index.html [Accessed 02/10/20].

Chulov, Martin, 2017. "The fall of Raqqa: hunting the last jihadists in Isis's capital of cruelty", *The Guardian*, 2017 [Online]. Available at: https://www.theguardian.com/world/2017/oct/06/the-fall-of-raqqa-hunting-the-last-jihadists-in-isiss-capital-o f-cruelty [Accessed 31/01/20].

Cixous, Hélène, 1981."Castration or decapitation?", *Signs*, vol. 7, no. 1: pp. 41–55.

Cresci, Elena, 2016. "Harambe: the meme that refused to die", *The Guardian*, 2016 [Online]. Available at: https://www.theguardian.com/technology/ 2016/aug/12/harambe-the-meme-that-refused-to-die [Accessed 31/01/20].

Cupp, Richarrd L., 2016. "Gorilla's death calls for human responsibility, not animal personhood", *The Conversation*, 2016 [Online]. Available at: https://theconv ersation.com/gorillas-death-calls-for-human-responsibility-not-animal-personhood -60360 [Accessed 31/01/20].

Curtis, Adam, 2016. *Hypernormalisation* [Film].

Darwin, Charles, 2004. *The Descent of Man.* London: Penguin.

Dave, 2019. *Question Time* [Track].

Davis, Angela, 2003. *Are Prisons Obsolete?* New York: Seven Stories Press.

Dawkins, Richard, 1989. *The Selfish Gene.* Oxford: Oxford University Press.

Debord, Guy, 1994. *Society of the Spectacle.* St Petersburg, FL: Red and Black.

De Londras, Fiona, 2015. "'Jihadi John' strike: the legal and moral questions around targeted drone killings", *The Conversation*, 2015 [Online]. Available at: https://th econversation.com/jihadi-john-strike-the-legal-and-moral-questions-around-target ed-drone-killings-50683 [Accessed 31/01/20].

Deleuze, Gilles and Guattari, Felix. 1992. *A Thousand Plateaus: Capitalism and Schizophrenia*, trans. Brian Massumi. London: Athlone Press.

Derrida, Jacques, 1992. *Acts of Literature.* London: Routledge.

Derrida, Jacques, 1993. *Aporias*, trans. Thomas Dutoit. Stanford, CA: Stanford University Press.

Derrida, Jacques, 1997. *Politics of Friendship.* London: Verso.

Downing, Lisa, 2013. *The Subject of Murder: Gender, Exceptionality and the Modern Killer.* Chicago: Chicago University Press.

Esposito, Roberto, 2008. *Bios: Biopolitics and Philosophy*, trans. Timothy Campbell. Minneapolis: University of Minnesota Press.

Esposito, Roberto, 2011. *Immunitas: The Protection and Negation of Life*, trans. Zakiya Hanafi. London: Polity.

Evans, Brad, 2013. *Liberal Terror.* London: Polity.

Ewald, François and Fontana, Alessandro, 2008. "Preface", in Foucault, Michel ed., trans.Graham Burchell, *The Birth of Biopolitics.* London: Palgrave Macmillan, pp. xiii–xvii.

Foucault, Michel, 1977. *Discipline and Punish: The Birth of the Prison*, trans. Alan Sheridan. London: Penguin.

Foucault, Michel, 2003. *Society Must be Defended*, trans. David Macey. London: Penguin.

Foucault, Michel, 2007. *Security, Territory, Population*, trans. Graham Burchell. London: Palgrave Macmillan.

Foucault, Michel, 1972. *The Archaeology of Knowledge*, trans. A.M. Sheridan Smith. London: Routledge.

Foucault, Michel, 2008. *The Birth of Biopolitics*, trans. Graham Burchell. London: Palgrave Macmillan.

Foucault, Michel, 1978. The History of Sexuality, trans. Robert Hurley. London: Penguin.

Foucault, Michel, 1970. *The Order of Things: An Archaeology of the Human Sciences*, trans. From the French. London: Routledge.

Freedman, Lawrence, 2020. "The real reason the UK government pursued "herd immunity"—and why it was abandoned", *New Statesman*, 2020 [Online]. Available at: https://www.newstatesman.com/politics/uk/2020/04/real-reason-uk-govern ment-pursued-herd-immunity-and-why-it-was-abandoned [Accessed 02/10/20].

Girard, René, 1988. *Violence and the Sacred*. London: Bloomsbury.

Guiffrida, Angela, 2018. "French police cut soles off migrant children's shoes, claims Oxfam", *The Guardian*, 2018 [Online]. Available at: https://www.theguardian.com/ world/2018/jun/14/french-border-police-accused-of-cutting-soles-off-migrant -childrens-shoes [Accessed 31/01/20].

Halliday, Josh, 2017. "'Stay put' safety advice to come under scrutiny after Grenfell Tower fire", *The Guardian*, 2017 [Online]. Available at: https://www.theguardian .com/uk-news/2017/jun/14/stay-put-safety-advice-under-scrutiny-grenfell-tower -fire [Accessed 31/01/20].

Halpern, David, 2019. *Inside the Nudge Unit: How Small Changes Can Make a Big Difference*. London: Penguin.

Harari, Yuval Noah, 2015. *Homo Deus: A Brief History of Tomorrow*. London: Harvill & Seeker.

Harari, Yuval Noah, 2011. *Sapiens: A Brief History of Humankind*. London: Vintage.

Harraway, Donna, 1989. "The biopolitics of postmodern bodies: constitutions of self in immune system discourse", in Campbell, Timothy and Sitze, Adam eds., *Biopolitics: A Reader*. Durham: Duke University Press.

Hawramy, Favel, Mohammed, Shalaw and Shaheen, Kareem, 2015. "Life under Isis in Raqqa and Mosul: 'We're living in a giant prison'", *The Guardian*, 2015 [Online]. Available at: https://www.theguardian.com/world/2015/dec/09/life-under-isis-raq qa-mosul-giant-prison-syria-iraq [Accessed 31/01/20].

Heggedus, Chris and Pennebaker, D.A., 2016. *Unlocking the Cage* [Film].

Heidegger, Martin, 1996. *Being and Time*, trans. Joan Stambaugh. Albany: SUNY.

Heidegger, Martin, 1971. *Poetry Language Thought*, trans. Albert Hofstadter. New York: Harper Colophon Books.

Herd, David, 2016. *Through*. Manchester: Carcanet.

Hobbes, Thomas, 1996. *Leviathan*. Oxford: Oxford University Press.

Holmén, Tom, 2001. *Jesus and Jewish Covenant Thinking*. Leiden: Brill.

Holpuch, Amanda, 2018. "Families divided at the border: 'The most horrific immigration policy I've ever seen'", *The Guardian*, 2018 [Online]. Available at: https://www.the guardian.com/us-news/2018/jun/19/families-border-separations-trump-immigrat ion-policy [Accessed 31/01/20].

Jasper, Alison, 2014. "Taking sides on *Severed Heads*: Kristeva at the Louvre", *Text Matters*, vol. 4, no. 4: pp. 173–83.

Kahneman, Daniel, 2011. *Thinking Fast and Slow*. London: Penguin.

Kandinsky, Wassily, 1977. *Concerning the Spiritual in Art*, trans. Med.T.H. Sadler. New York: Dover.

Keats, John, 2012. "Ode to autumn", in Wu, Ducan ed., *Romanticism: An Anthology*. Oxford: Wiley-Blackwell, p. 1489.

Kipling, Rudyard, 2016. *The Jungle Book*. London: Harper.

Kirwan, Michael, 2004. *Discovering Girard*. London: Darton, Longman & Todd.

Ko, Kwang Hyun, 2016. "Origins of human intelligence: The chain of tool-making and brain evolution", *Anthropological Notebooks*, vol. 22, no. 1: pp. 5–22.

Kottasova, Ivana, 2015. "Is ISIS running out of money?", *CNN*, 2015 [Online]. Available at: https://money.cnn.com/2015/05/20/news/isis-funding-squeeze/index.html [Accessed 31/01/20].

Kraft, Colleen, 2018. "AAP statement opposing separation of children and parents at the border", Available at: https://www.aap.org/en-us/about-the-aap/aap-press-room/Pages/StatementOpposingSeparationofChildrenandParents.aspx [Accessed 31/01/20].

Kristeva, Julia, 1982. *Powers of Horror: An Essay on Abjection*, trans, Leon S. Roudiez. New York: Columbia University Press.

Kristeva, Julia, 2012. *The Severed Head*, trans. Jody Gladding. New York: Columbia University Press.

Kurzweil, Ray, 2005. *The Singularity is Near*. London: Duckworth.

Lagnado, Lisette, 2008. "Documenta 12 at Kassel", *Afterall*, 2008. https://www.afterall.org/online/documenta.12.at.kassel#.XkPYN_Z2taQ. [Accessed 31/01/20].

Lambert, Susan and Moore, Stefan, 2015. *Circus Elephant Rampage* [Film].

Levi, Primo, 2013. *If This is a Man / The Truce*, trans. Stuart Woolf. London: Abacus.

Lewis, Paul, 2006. "Fear of teenagers is growing in Britain, study warns". *The Guardian* 2006 [Online]. Available at: https://www.theguardian.com/society/2006/oct/23/youthjustice.familyandrelationships [Accessed 30/03/21].

Litchfield, Carla, 2016. "Gorillas in zoos – the unpalatable truth". *The Conversation* 2016 [Online]. Available at: https://theconversation.com/gorillas-in-zoos-the-unpalatable-truth-60249 [Accessed 30/03/21].

Loyd, Anthony, 2019. "Shamima Begum: Bring me home, says Bethnal Green girl who left to join Isis", *The Times*, 2019 [Online]. Available at: https://www.thetimes.co.uk/article/shamima-begum-bring-me-home-says-bethnal-green-girl-who-fled-to-join-isis-hgvqw765d [Accessed 31/01/20].

Malkin, Bonnie, 2016. "Donald Trump Jr compares Syrian refugees to poisoned Skittles", *The Guardian*, 2016 [Online]. Available at: https://www.theguardian.com/us-news/2016/sep/20/donald-trump-jnr-compares-refugees-poisoned-skittles-twitter-reacted [Accessed 31/01/20].

Maloney, Alli, 2015 "When police turn violent, activists Brittany Packnett and Johnetta Elzie push back", *NYTimes*, 2015 [Online]. Available at: https://web.archive.org/web/20161219043331/http://nytlive.nytimes.com/womenintheworld/2015/09/29/when-police-turn-violent-activists-brittany-packnett-and-johnetta-elzie-push-back/ [Accessed 02/10/20].

Marsh, James, 2011. *Project Nim* [Film].

McKernan, Bethan, 2019. "Defiant women and dying children: Isis' desert legacy", *The Guardian*, 2019 [Online]. Available at: https://www.theguardian.com/ world/2019/mar/01/defiant-women-and-dying-children-isis-desert-legacy-al-hawl-refugee-camp [Accessed 31/01/20].

Mezzadra, Sandro and Neilson, Brett, 2013. *Border as Method: Or the Multiplication of Labor*. Durham: Duke University Press.

Miller, James. 1993. *The Passion of Michel Foucault*. New York: Anchor Books.

Mills, Stuart, 2020. "Coronavirus: how the UK government is using behavioural science", https://theconversation.com/coronavirus-how-the-uk-government-is-using-behavioural-science-134097 [Accessed 02/10/20].

Moaveni, Azadeh, 2019. *Guest House for Young Widows: Among the Women of Isis*. London: Scribe.

Moltmann, Andreas, 2015. *The Crucified God*, trans. Rev.A. Wilson & John Bowden, London: SCM Press.

More-Bick, Martin, 2019. *Grenfell Tower Inquiry*. https://www.grenfelltowerinquiry.org .uk/ phase-1-report [Accessed 31/01/20].

Morozov, Evgeny, 2011. *The Net Delusion: How Not to Liberate the World*. London: Penguin.

Nail, Thomas, 2015. *The Figure of the Migrant*. Stanford, CA: Stanford University Press.

Nancy, Jean-Luc, 2000. *Being Singular Plural*, trans. Robert D. Richardson and Anne E. O'Byrne. Stanford, CA: Stanford University Press.

Nemeroff, C. and Rozin, P., 1994. "The contagion concept in adult thinking in the United States: Transmission of germs and of interpersonal influence", *Ethos*, vol. 22, no. 2, pp. 158–86.

O'Hagan, Andrew. *The Tower* [Online]. Available at https://www.lrb.co.uk/the-paper/ v40/n11/andrew-o-hagan/the-tower?src=longreads [Accessed 31/01/30].

O'Hara, Dan, 2012. "Skeuomorphology and quotation", *Morphomata*, vol. 2: pp. 281–94.

Ohlheiser, Abby, 2016. "The Internet won't let Harambe rest in peace", *The Washington Post*, 2016 [Online]. Available at: https://www.washingtonpost.com/gdpr-consent/? destination=%2fnews%2fthe-intersect%2fwp%2f2016%2f07%2f27%2fthe-internet -wont-let-harambe-rest-in-peace%2f%3f [Accessed 31/01/20].

Ould Slahi, Mohamedou, 2015. *Guantanamo Diary*. Edinburgh: Canongate.

Parker, Richard. "American internment camps", *New York Times*, 2018 [Online]. Available at: https://www.nytimes.com/2018/06/20/opinion/american-internment -camps.html [Accessed 31/01/20].

Peston, Robert, 2020. "British government wants UK to acquire coronavirus 'herd immunity'", Writes Robert Peston. Available at: https://www.itv.com/news/2020- 03-12/british-government-wants-uk-to-acquire-coronavirus-herd-immunity-writ es-robert-peston [Accessed 02/10/20].

Phillips, Whitney, 2015. *This is Why We Can't Have Nice Things: Mapping the Relationship between Online Trolling and Mainstream Culture*. Cambridge, MA: MIT Press.

Pinker, Steven, 2011. *The Better Angels of Our Nature: A History of Violence and Humanity*. London: Penguin.

Public Enemy 1990. *Fear of a Black Planet* [Album].

Rawlence, Ben, 2016. *City of Thorns: Nine Lives in the World's Largest Refugee Camp*. London: Portobello Books.

Reeve, Simon, 2019. The Americas, Series 1, Episode 2. *BBC* [Online]. Available at: https://www.bbc.co.uk/iplayer/episode/m0009dj7/the-americas-with-simon-reeve -series-1-episode-2 [Accessed 02/10/20].

Ridley, Louise, 2016. "Ai Weiwei recreates drowned alan kurdi beach scene in 'iconic' and 'haunting' art stunt", *Huffington Post*, Feburary 2016. Available at: https://ww w.huffingtonpost.co.uk/2016/02/01/ai-weiwei-alan-kurdi-picture_n_9129512.ht ml?guccounter=1&guce_referrer=aHR0cHM6Ly93d3cuYmluZy5jb20vc2VhcmNo P3E9YWkrd2VppK3dlaStheWxhbitrdXJkaStwaWVjZXMmMzm9ybT1FREdFQVIm cXM9UEYmY3ZpZD00NWYwYzFkZWJjZDI0ZDkwODQwYTI1Y2ZlNT YzNWI3YSZjYz1HQiZzZXRsYW5nPWVuLVVVTJkRBRjA9MQ&guce_referrer _sig=AQAAAKHPkowq-BqW51pqr1mJS2pxwwapuN1jpu5V-l1HLatzwVaT9IajE ygGKRMXepd50w:-asXTMCClvBtez95wX4w4gGKDOTTn-Bgt1RhQzpfM Sr2PockHPlHiSjWJs8PdUkqP5FolWVxlGfDTRQWAFB-AN3wX3OfNy3l iPWBCM3XJ [Accessed 31/01/20].

Robespierre, Maximilien [Online]. Available at https://www.bartleby.com/268/7/23 .html. [Accessed 31/01/30].

Ronson, Jon, 2015. *So You've Been Publicly Shamed*. London: Picador.

Salmon, Natasha, 2017. "Donald Trump takes credit for inventing the word 'fake'", *The Independent*, 2017 [Online]. Available at: https://www.independent.co.uk/news/world/americas/donald-trump-takes-credit-for-inventing-the-word-fake-a7989221.html [Accessed 31/01/20].

Siems, Larry, 2015, "Preface", in Ould Slahi, Mohamedou ed., *Guantanamo Diary*. Edinburgh: Canongate, pp. xvii–li.

Sloterdijk, Peter, 2011. *Bubbles: Spheres 1*. Cambridge, MA: MIT Press.

Staunton, Denis, 2020. 'Herd immunity' is not our policy, says UK's health secretary https://www.irishtimes.com/news/world/uk/herd-immunity-is-not-our-policy-says-uk-s-health-secretary-1.4203637 [Accessed 02/10/20]

Sterelny, Kim, 2001. *Dawkins vs Gould: Survival of the Fittest*. Duxford, Cambridge: Icon Books.

Stiegler, Bernard, 1998. *Technics and Time, 1*, trans. Richard Beardsworth and George Collins. Stanford, CA: Stanford University Press.

Stormzy, 2018. Brits 2018 performance.

Tallis, Raymond, 2003. *The Hand: A Philosophical Inquiry into Human Being*. Edinburgh: Edinburgh University Press.

Thaler, Richard and Sunstein, Cass R., 2009. *Nudge: Improving Decisions About Health, Wealth and Happiness*. London: Penguin.

Thrasher, Steven W., 2015. "The inhumanity of 'Fuck your breath' should stop all of us cold". *The Guardian*, 2015 [Online]. Available at: https://www.theguardian.com/commentisfree/ 2015/apr/13/white-supremacy-takes-the-breath-away-from-black-americans [Accessed 02/10/20].

Timofeeva, Oxana, 2018. *The History of Animals: A Philosophy*. London: Bloomsbury.

Titheradge, Noel and Kirkland, Dr Faye, 2020. "Coronavirus: Did 'herd immunity' change the course of the outbreak?". BBC News, 2020 [Online]. Available at: https://www.bbc.co.uk/news/uk-53433824?intlink_from_url=&link_location=live-reporting-story [Accessed 02/10/20].

Turkle, Sherry, 2017. *Alone Together: Why We Expect More from Technology and Less from Each Other*. New York: Basic Books.

Ullman, Harlan K. and Wade, James P.,1996. *Shock and Awe: Achieving Rapid Dominance*. National Defence University.

UNITED [Online]. Available at https://uploads.guim.co.uk/2018/06/19/TheList.pdf. [Accessed 31/01/20].

Vaughan-Williams, Nick, 2009. *Border Politics: The Limits of Sovereign Power*. Edinburgh: Edinburgh University Press.

Virillio, Paul, 2006. *Speed and Politics*, trans, Sylvère Lotringer. Los Angeles: Semiotext(e).

Vonnegut, Kurt, 1969. *Slaughterhouse Five*. London: Triad Paladin.

Wankhade, Paresh, 2019. "Grenfell Tower inquiry: expert explains four main findings—and how emergency services must improve", The Conversation, October 2019. Available at: https://theconversation.com/grenfell-tower-inquiry-expert-explains-four-main-findings-and-how-emergency-services-must-improve-126163 [Accessed 31/01/20].

Watkin, William, 2014. *Agamben and Indifference*. London: Rowman&Littlefield International.

Watkin, William, 2015. "Agamben, Benjamin and the indifference of violence", in Moran, Brendan and Salzani, Carlo eds., *Towards a Critique of Violence: Walter Benjamin and Giorgio Agamben*. London: Bloomsbury, pp. 139–52.

Watkin, William, 2017. *Badiou and Indifferent Being*. London: Bloomsbury.

Watkin, William, 2000. " 'I want you to give me on a dish the head...': symbolism, decollation and femininity in Mallarmé's 'Hérodiade'", *Psychoanalytic Studies*, vol. 2, no. 2: pp. 141–52.

Watkin, William, 2016. "Lethal injections and the tragedy of America's execution addiction", *The Conversation*, 2016 [Online]. Available at: https://theconversation .com/lethal-injections-and-the-tragedy-of-americas-execution-addiction-59937 [Accessed 02/10/20].

Watkin, William, 2004. *On Mourning: Theories of Loss in Modern Literature*. Edinburgh: Edinburgh University Press.

Watkin, William, 2010. *The Literary Agamben: Adventures in Logopoiesis*. London: Continuum.

Watkin, William, 2019. "The obsolete human being", *The New Philosopher* [Online]. Available at https://www.newphilosopher.com/articles/the-obsolete-human-being/. [Accessed 31/01/20].

Watkin, William, 2015a. "Uneasy lies the head", *The White Review* [Online]. Available at www.thewhitereview.org/feature/uneasy-lies-the-head/. [Accessed 31/01/20].

Watkin, William. [Online]. Available at https://www.youtube.com/watch?v=fzW Ld5AtFLk.

Wilson, James Q. and Kelling, George L, 1982. "Broken windows", *Atlantic* [Online]. Available at: https://www.theatlantic.com/ideastour/archive/windows.html [Accessed 02/10/20].

Wordsworth, William, 2012. "Ode: Intimations on Immortality" in Wu, Duncan, ed., *Romanticism: An Anthology*. Oxford: Wiley Blackwell, pp. 549–54.

Worth, Robert F., 2016. "The Reluctant Jihadi: how one recruit lost faith in isis", *The Guardian*, 2016 [Online]. Available at: https://www.theguardian.com/ news/2016/ apr/12/reluctant-jihadi-recruit-lost-faith-in-isis [Accessed 31/01/20].

Yassin-Kassab, Robin. "The Raqqa Diaries by Samer review—brutal and powerful", *The Guardian*, 2017 [Online]. Available at: https://www.theguardian.com/ /2017/ feb/23/the-raqqa-diaries-escape-from-islamic-state-samer [Accessed 31/01/20].

Yeats, W.B., 2005. "Byzantium", in Rainey ed., *Modernism: An Anthology*. Oxford: Blackwell, pp. 344–5.

Zartaloudis, Thanos, 2010. *Giorgio Agamben: Power. Law and the Uses of Criticism*. London: Routledge.

Zartaloudis, Thanos, 2019. *The Birth of Nomos*. Edinburgh: Edinburgh University Press.

Zelizer, V., 1994. *Pricing the Priceless Child: The Changing Social Value of Children*. Princeton: Princeton University Press.

Zizek, Slavoj, 2009. *Violence*. London: Polity.

Zubov, Shoshana, 2019. *The Age of Surveillance Capitalism*. New York: Profile Books.

INDEX